THE ENCYCLOPAEDIA OF
REPTILES AND
AMPHIBIANS

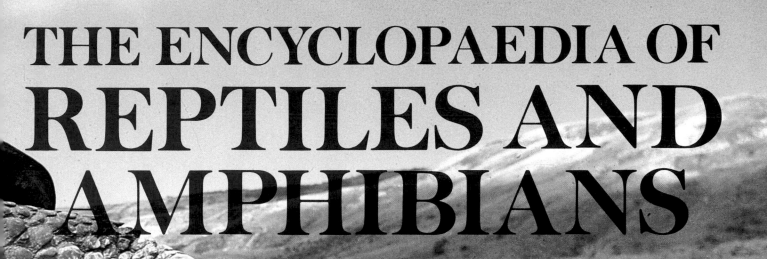

THE ENCYCLOPAEDIA OF
REPTILES AND
AMPHIBIANS

Edited by
Dr Tim R. Halliday and Dr Kraig Adler

Facts On File
New York • Oxford

Project Editor: Graham Bateman
Editor: Stuart McCready
Art Editors: Jerry Burman, Chris Munday
Art Assistants: Wayne Ford, Carol Wells
Picture Research: Alison Renney
Production: Clive Sparling
Design: Andrew Lawson
Index: Stuart McCready

AN EQUINOX BOOK

Published in North America by:
Facts on File Inc
460 Park Avenue South
New York, NY 10016

Planned and produced by:
Andromeda Oxford Ltd
11–15 The Vineyard
Abingdon
Oxfordshire OX14 3PX

Library of Congress Cataloging-in-Publication Data

Halliday, Tim, 1945—
    The encyclopedia of reptiles and amphibians.

    1. Reptiles.   2. Amphibians.   I. Adler, Kraig.
II. Title
QL641.H35   1986   597.6   85-29249
ISBN 0-8160-1359-4

Origination by Fotographics, Hong Kong; Scantrans,
Singapore; Alpha Reprographics Ltd, Harefield, Middx,
England.

Filmset by BAS Printers Limited,
Over Wallop, Stockbridge, Hants, England.

Printed in Spain by Heraclio Fournier S.A. Vitoria.

Contributors

KA   Kraig Adler
Cornell University
New York, USA

AA   Anthony Arak
University of Stockholm
Stockholm
Sweden

AAB   Angus d'A. Bellairs
St Mary's Hospital Medical School
University of London
England

EDB   Edmund D. Brodie
The University of Texas
Arlington, Texas
USA

HRB   H. Robert Bustard
Alyth, Perthshire
Scotland

AJC   Alan J. Charig
British Museum (Natural History)
London
England

HGD   Herndon G. Dowling
New York University
New York
USA

CG   Carl Gans
The University of Michigan
Ann Arbor, Michigan
USA

HCG   H. Carl Gerhardt
University of Missouri
Columbia, Missouri
USA

TRH   Tim R. Halliday
The Open University
Milton Keynes
England

RBH   Raymond B. Huey
University of Washington
Seattle, Washington
USA

AGK   Arnold G. Kluge
The University of Michigan
Ann Arbor, Michigan
USA

SAM   Sherman A. Minton
Indiana University
Indianapolis, Indiana
USA

EOM   Edward O. Moll
Eastern Illinois University
Charleston, Illinois
USA

JRb   Joan Robb
The University of Auckland
Auckland
New Zealand

GSc   Gordon Schuett
The University of Michigan
Ann Arbor, Michigan
USA

PV   Paul Verrell
The Open University
Milton Keynes
England

MHW   Marvalee H. Wake
University of California, Berkeley
California
USA

GZ   George Zug
National Museum of Natural History
Smithsonian Institute
Washington D.C.
USA

Artwork Panels

David M. Dennis

Michael R. Long

Left: male Golden toads (Bufo periglenes) at mating pond (Michael Fogden); half-title: White's tree frog (Litoria caerulea) (Bruce Coleman); title page: Galapagos giant tortoises (Geochelone elephantopus) courting (Oxford Scientific Films).

PREFACE

"These foul and loathsome animals" . . . "their Creator has not exerted his powers (to make) many of them." These remarks about amphibians and reptiles are attributed to the famous Swedish scientist Carolus Linnaeus who, in the mid 1700s, established the system for naming species that is still in use today. Even before this time these "lower forms" of life were regarded as less worthy of study and interest than the "higher" mammals and birds. Such is the historical burden which amphibians and reptiles have borne for many centuries. Today their joint study continues under the name of a single discipline (herpetology: from the Greek *herpeton*, meaning "crawling things"). This also owes more to tradition and to the fact that methods of collecting and keeping amphibians and reptiles have always been very similar, than it does to any great degree of similarity between them. Herpetologists have found that in many ways the differences between the two groups are more marked than their similarities. They have also found that there is much in particular about these animals to arouse fascination, and much to learn from them about animal life in general. An upsurge of interest in these animals has been one of the results.

Apart from the way in which they maintain body temperature and some other similarities, such as having a single ventricle in the heart (birds and mammals have two), amphibians and reptiles differ markedly. Amphibians have a soft, smooth skin that is permeable to water; reptiles are covered in coarse, dry scales that are impervious to water. The eggs of amphibians lack a waterproof outer covering and are always laid in water or in damp places, whereas the reptilian egg has a thick parchment-like or hard shell that holds moisture in, enabling the young to develop within it even on dry land.

These differences reflect the significant position that each group occupies in the evolutionary history of the vertebrates. The amphibians made the transition from the totally aquatic life of fishes and evolved the ability to move about freely on the land. This involved a radical reorganization of the skeleton, particularly of the bones in the limb, in comparison to that in the fins of fishes. It also involved an elaboration of the ability to breathe air, rather than dissolved oxygen, that had already evolved in their lungfish ancestors. The reptiles took the conquest of the land a stage further and, by acquiring an impermeable skin and an impermeable covering for the egg, became completely emancipated from standing water. In different ages, nature has, in fact, exerted its powers to make a great many of these creatures, for early in their history, both groups were a much more prominent feature of the Earth's fauna than they are today. The reptiles were, for many millions of years, the dominant form of life. Each, however, has become much less important in terms of numbers of species so that today the amphibians, with about 3,000 species, are the smallest vertebrate group, while the reptiles, at around 6,000 species, are less numerous than either fishes or birds.

In the present upsurge of interest in amphibians and reptiles among professional biologists, the science of herpetology is making significant contributions to zoological knowledge that compare favorably with those made in ornithology and mammalogy. Partly this is due to the realization that the traditional distinction between "higher" and "lower" vertebrates is no longer valid. Amphibians and reptiles have been thought inferior on account of being "cold-blooded" in contrast to the "warm-blooded" birds and mammals. These terms are now thought misleading and are no longer used by biologists (see p70–71).

Amphibians and reptiles are not degenerate or inferior in comparison to birds and mammals; they simply go about things in different ways and are, in many respects, just as successful. They are, for example, much more efficient in their use of energy and, because of various special features that they possess, are able to live in environments that are inaccessible to other groups. Most notably, reptiles are able to thrive in the driest deserts where birds and mammals cannot.

Another factor in the enhanced status of amphibians and reptiles has been the recognition that they are much more diverse than was previously realized. Modern biology has its foundations in Europe, a continent that is relatively impoverished in terms of numbers of amphibian and reptile species compared with the Americas and, especially, the tropics, where new species are still being discovered. Finally, biologists have discovered that amphibians and reptiles are ideal subjects for study within a variety of different zoological disciplines.

The science of zoology is like a tapestry, with numerous interwoven threads. In one direction run several distinct disciplines, such as anatomy, physiology, ecology and behavior, which consider similar processes in a variety of animal types. In the other direction are those branches of zoology that each consider just one kind of animal, such as insects, fishes or birds. This book reflects the complex, integrated nature of zoology inasmuch as, while it is concerned with only two classes of animals, it also considers phenomena, in physiology and behavior for example, that are found in a wide variety of animals.

The formal plan of the book follows the tapestry's threads in the direction of classification. A major article introduces class Amphibia and another introduces class Reptilia, detailing their evolutionary history and outstanding aspects of physiology, life history and behavior.

A separate main entry is devoted to each of the three orders of amphibians and to each of the six orders and suborders of reptiles. Each entry is introduced by an opening panel giving the number of its species, genera and families, its distribution and a summary of habitat, size, color, reproduction and longevity. The scale drawings indicate the ranges of sizes to be found in the group compared to a whole or part 6-foot (1.8m) man. The main text deals in general with the order's characteristic physiological forms and the varieties of the niches which it has occupied. A major portion at the end of the main text gives a separate description of each of the group's families, highlighting important genera and species.

The pages following the articles on five of these main entries collect fact-box summaries of the families within the groups in question. Each fact box gives the numbers of species and genera in the family, their general distribution, the range of sizes, colors and body forms and, where applicable, the distinctive points of life history. The fact box lists species or genera referred to in the text, together with their scientific names.

At several points, we follow threads running in the other direction, highlighting aspects of the study of amphibians and reptiles which have made it an increasingly important discipline

African chameleon (*Chamaeleo chamaeleon*) (NHPA).

within zoology as a whole. Articles of this kind appear as double-page special features following the two introductions and certain of the main entries, and they also appear within the main entries as shorter boxed features. Here we have allowed authors to report in greater depth on the most up-to-date understanding of fascinating aspects of amphibian and reptile life.

The authors often emphasise the need to conserve species threatened with extinction and by mismanagement. Many species and subspecies described in these pages are listed in the Appendices I to III of the Convention on International Trade in Endangered Species of Wild Flora and Fauna (CITES). The Red Data Book of the International Union for the Conservation of Nature and Natural Resources (IUCN) also lists numerous species as at risk. In this book the following symbols are used to show the status accorded to species by the IUCN at the time of going to press: Ⓔ = Endangered—in danger of extinction unless causal factors are modified (these may include habitat destruction and direct exploitation by man). Ⓥ = Vulnerable—likely to become endangered in the near future. Ⓡ = Rare, but neither endangered nor vulnerable at present. Ⓘ = Threatened but status indeterminate. Ⓚ = Threat suspected but status unknown. We are indebted to the IUCN Monitoring Centre, Cambridge,

England, for giving us the very latest information on status. The symbol ⊡ indicates entire species, genera or families, in addition to those listed in the Red Data Book, that are listed in CITES.

This book is the fruit of labors by an international team of expert authors, all actively engaged in disciplined research into the lives of amphibians and reptiles, some reporting directly from far corners of the globe where their work has taken them. To their efforts have been added those of the photographers and illustrators (particularly David Dennis) whose work has so skillfully brought these pages to life. Acknowledgements are due to all of them and especially my coeditor Dr Kraig Adler, for his painstaking and tireless attention to the accuracy and consistency of all of the information that we have included, and to Dr Graham Bateman and his team of editors, designers and researchers at Equinox (Oxford) Limited who made this information into a book. Finally it is for the reader to decide whether Linnaeus' "foul and loathsome" creatures are in fact some of the most exciting and interesting animals alive today.

Tim R. Halliday
DEPARTMENT OF BIOLOGY
THE OPEN UNIVERSITY, MILTON KEYNES

CONTENTS

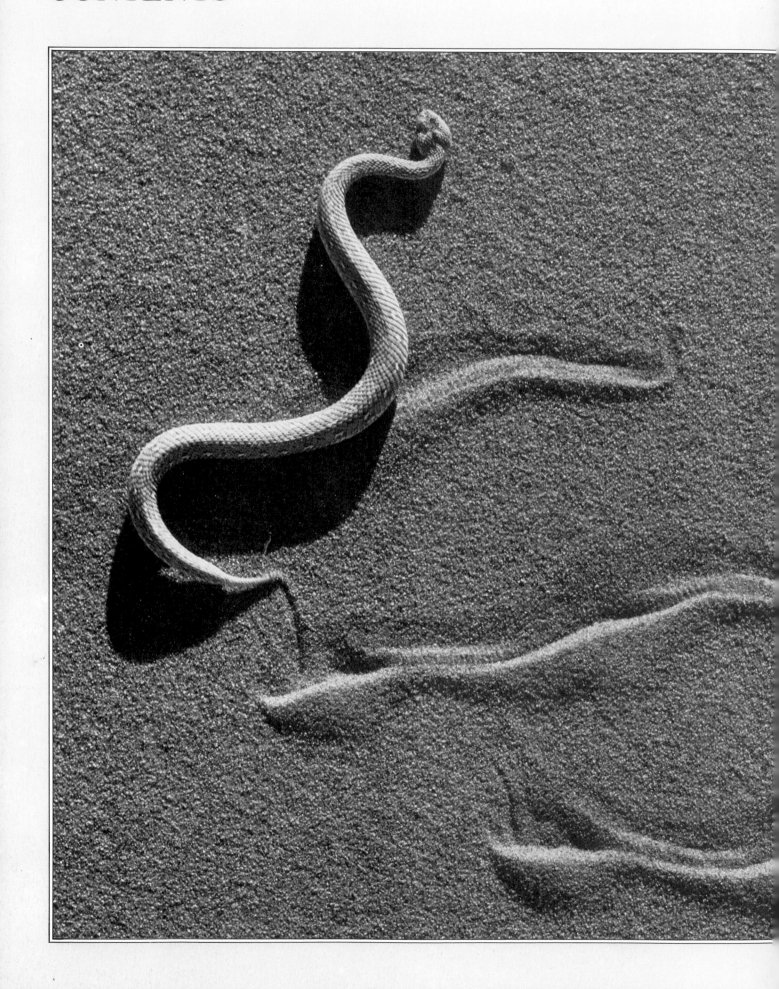

Sidewinding adder (Bitis peringueyi) in desert (Anthony Bannister).

AMPHIBIANS

CLASS: AMPHIBIA
Three orders: 34 families; 398 genera; 4,015 species.

Caecilians
Order: Gymnophiona (Apoda)
One hundred and sixty-three species in 34 genera and 5 families.

Salamanders and Newts
Order: Urodela (Caudata)
Three hundred and fifty-eight species in 60 genera and 9 families.
Includes: **Alpine newt** (*Triturus alpestris*), **American mole salamanders** (genus *Ambystoma*), **amphiumas** (family Amphiumidae), **Asiatic salamanders** (family Hynobiidae), **axolotl** (*Ambystoma mexicanum*), **Fire salamander** (*Salamandra salamandra*), **giant salamanders** (family Cryptobranchidae), **lungless salamanders** (family Plethodontidae), **mudpuppy** (*Necturus maculosus*), **olm** (*Proteus anguinus*), **Red salamander** (*Pseudotriton ruber*), **Red-spotted newt** (*Notophthalmus viridescens*), **sirens** (family Sirenidae).

Frogs and Toads
Order: Anura (Salientia)
Three thousand four hundred and ninety-four species in 303 genera and 20 families.
Includes: **fire-bellied toads** (genus *Bombina*), **Gastric-brooding frog** (*Rheobatrachus silus*), **Hamilton's frog** (*Leiopelma hamiltoni*), **Pouched frog** (*Assa darlingtoni*), **midwife toads** (*Alytes cisternasii, A. obstetricans*), **poison-arrow frogs** (family Dendrobatidae), **Seychelles frog** (*Sooglossus sechellensis*), **Surinam toad** (*Pipa pipa*), **Tailed frog** (*Ascaphus trueii*), **true tree frogs** (family Hylidae).

THE amphibians—frogs, salamanders and caecilians—display a stunning variety: some animals with tails and others without, some looking like snakes or lizards, others hopping on long hind legs, and with colors ranging from drab browns to iridescent blues, greens and reds.

Yet of 40,000 known species of vertebrates (animals with backbones), only about 4,000 are amphibians. They are the smallest class of living vertebrates, all that remain of a once dominant class of animals, some the length of a moderate-sized crocodile, that flourished several hundred million years ago.

Amphibians are an important group for study because they were the first vertebrates to conquer land and also the group which later gave rise to reptiles (and they, in turn, to mammals and birds). Living amphibians are divided into three orders: Urodela (the salamanders, including newts and sirens), Anura (the frogs, including toads) and Gymnophiona (the legless caecilians).

The word "amphibian," from the Greek *amphibios*, means a being with a double life; specifically, one that lives alternately on land and in water. Such a double life is the rule for Amphibia, but there are exceptions; some species are permanently aquatic and others completely terrestrial. All are ectotherms, using environmental temperature to regulate body temperature.

No structure uniquely defines all amphibians—as feathers do birds—so one must resort to a combination of characteristics. Further complicating any definition is the fact that living forms have diverged significantly from the primitive fossil ones and there is no information at all on certain key features in the fossil forms.

Evolution and Fossil History
Some of the oldest known amphibians are *Metaxygnathus*, found in the freshwater beds of late Devonian deposits in Australia, and *Ichthyostega* and *Acanthostega*, found in similar beds in Greenland. All date from about 360 million years ago. Greenland may seem an unlikely place for any amphibian to have lived but its location and climate were very different during the Devonian period (410–345 million years ago), when it straddled the equator and lay within a moist and warm tropical region extending from present-day Australia through Asia to northeastern North America. Very recently, a single amphibian footprint was reported from still older, mid-Devonian deposits in southern Brazil, which was nontropical at the time.

Until the early Jurassic (about 190 million years ago), all of the earth's land mass was united into a single supercontinent called Pangaea. Thus, it is not surprising to find evidence that the earliest amphibians rapidly spread to now distant lands including Europe and eastern North America and, by the early Triassic (about 230 million years ago), even to Antarctica.

The most likely ancestors of these early Amphibia were lobe-finned fishes of the order Crossopterygii. Unlike other members of the class Osteichthyes, which had fins supported by cartilaginous rays, the fins of crossopterygians had bony elements comparable to those of the limbs of land vertebrates (tetrapods).

Furthermore, the crossopterygians had lungs and some had internal nostril openings (nares), so air could be taken into the lungs when the mouth was closed or when only the external nares were above water. Internal nares are characteristic of land vertebrates. In most fish the external nares serve only a sensory function; they lead to blind pockets not connected to the mouth cavity.

Ichthyostega was similar to the extinct crossopterygian fish *Eusthenopteron*, found in Devonian deposits in Europe and North America. Both had lungs and internal nares

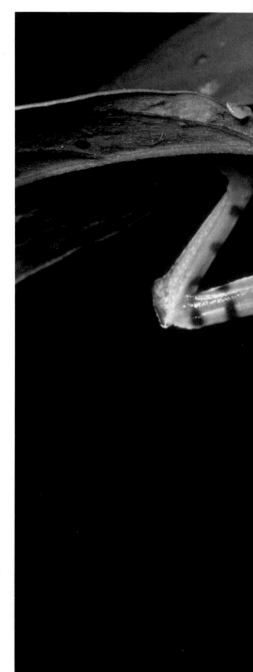

▶ **Slender amphibian.** The Many-ribbed salamander (*Eurycea multiplicata*), a North American lungless salamander, displays the elongated body, long tail, small limbs and smooth, moist skin typical of salamanders. This is one of many species with vertical rib grooves along its body.

▼ **Agile climber.** Like all frogs, the Barred leaf frog (*Phyllomedusa tomopterna*), a tree frog of the Amazon rain forest, has hind limbs much longer than its forelimbs. The very large eyes of frogs reflect the importance of vision, in particular for locating prey.

and shared two traits found only in some other crossopterygians and in the earliest amphibians: a brain case divided transversely into anterior and posterior portions and, secondly, an infolding of the enameled surface of the teeth that creates, in cross section, a complex labyrinthine pattern.

Ichthyostega, although unquestionably amphibian, retained a number of fish-like characteristics, among them the opercular bones—remnants of bones that in fish connect the gill covering to the cheek—and a tail fin supported by bony rays. But the limb and girdle structure of ichthyostegids had already fully reached the early amphibian condition; thus, the earliest amphibians (and land vertebrates) remain undiscovered and must be sought in even older deposits.

How did the transition to land come about? The classic explanation has been that the Devonian was a period of severe droughts. Fish with sufficiently strong fins could avoid stranding and death by crawling to available pools. According to this idea, land vertebrates could have evolved as a by-product of selection originally for increased agility in finding water, not land! New evidence casts doubt upon the scenario of periodic droughts, however, and it seems likely that the Devonian was a time of relatively continuous moist environments, at least in tropical regions.

Possibly some of the features associated with the first amphibians actually developed in the aquatic environment. For example, the development of a functional neck and the separation of the skull from the pectoral girdle to accomplish this may have developed in protoamphibians, permitting sudden sideways movement of the head to capture prey in water. Perhaps this change was a preadaptation later facilitating the capture of prey on land.

One or more of the following factors are believed to have led to the evolution of land vertebrates. During Devonian times aquatic environments, with their enormous diversity of fish and other organisms, contained many more competitors and predators than did the land, and land also may have been a safer place to deposit eggs and for juveniles to survive. The water of the warm Devonian swamps in which amphibians arose was probably poor in oxygen, especially in the shallows, but the fish ancestors of amphibians must have had lungs, as all of their living descendants do. Possibly these fish congregated in shallow waters, and ventured occasionally onto land. It might have been the more agile juveniles that did so, in order to exploit insect and other invertebrate food. Although this transition doubtless occurred over a period of millions of years, there is no known fossil record of these stages. Some have even argued that the fish-to-amphibian transition occurred more than once, making amphibians, including modern forms, members not of a single line, but of several that evolved independently.

In becoming terrestrial, amphibians overcame numerous challenges, although some changes could have occurred even in a shallow water habitat. On land, gravity became a key factor molding the development of the skeleton. Without the buoyancy of water, the body was suspended from the vertebral column which, in turn, had to be supported by the limbs and limb girdles. When the animal rested on the ground, a well-developed rib cage, as was present in *Ichthyostega*, prevented injury to internal organs. The elongated neural arches and articulating surfaces of the vertebrae distributed the gravitational forces more evenly along the vertebral column.

The skin of living amphibians, which is moistened by the secretions of numerous mucus glands, is not a passive outer layer but plays a vital and very active role in water balance, respiration and protection. It is highly permeable to water, especially in terrestrial species. Aquatic forms have reduced permeability to offset the inflow of water by osmosis.

Although most amphibians are restricted to moist habitats, there are specializations that permit many species to live in otherwise inhospitable environments. For example, desert toads create an osmotic gradient across their skin by retaining urea in their urine, thus permitting water uptake from extremely dry soils. Most terrestrial frogs possess a patch of skin, rich in blood capillaries, in the pelvic region that allows uptake of water even from a thin surface

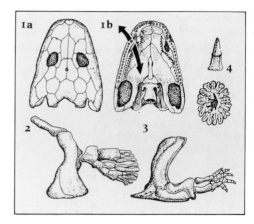

▲ **Anatomy of early amphibians.** (1) Skull of *Ichthyostega* from above (a) and below (b), showing internal nostril openings. (2) Shoulder girdles and fin of crossopterygian fish which had bony elements comparable to those of (3) primitive ichthyostegan amphibians. (4) Labyrinthodont tooth, whole and in cross section at base.

▼ **Giant amphibians of another age.** The Triassic (225–190 million years ago) saw crocodile-sized amphibians such as (1) *Mastodonsaurus*, 4m (13ft) from snout to tip of tail; (2) *Diadectes*, 3m (10ft), and (3) *Eryops*, 1.5m (5ft).

film. Other frogs and a few salamanders form a cocoon of shed skin to reduce water loss, and some tree frogs reduce evaporative water loss by wiping fat-like skin secretions over the body surface.

On the other hand, loss of body water through the skin is used in some species as a method of temperature regulation through evaporative cooling. In most species the skin and surfaces in the mouth cavity also serve a respiratory function, since dissolved gases pass across them; the numerous members of one family of salamanders (Plethodontidae) have lost lungs altogether and depend entirely upon this method of gas exchange.

Practically nothing is known about the skin of the earliest amphibians. By inference, it is often assumed that they too had soft naked skin, but recent fossil evidence suggests instead that scutes covered their undersides. Some types had osteoderms on the upper surfaces.

After the appearance of the first amphibians in the late Devonian, a period of rapid evolution occurred resulting in an enormous diversity of amphibian types. However, by the end of the Triassic, about 155 million years later, nearly all of them had become extinct. Some were truly enormous in size. The largest, *Mastodonsaurus*, had a skull 125cm (49in) long and a length estimated at 4m (13ft); the largest living amphibians, by comparison, are the Asiatic representatives of the giant salamanders, which reach 170cm (67.5in).

Many species were aquatic and possessed gills, whereas others were adapted to land. Although many were heavy-bodied and lizard-like in build, there were some truly bizarre types including legless, eel-shaped forms and others with extremely wide heads drawn back into peculiar horns.

These ancient amphibians were found on all land masses and were the dominant land animals of their day. Mammals and birds did not evolve until after most of these ancient amphibian types had become extinct, but the first reptiles evolved from amphibians very early in the Carboniferous period (about 345 million years ago). The earliest known reptiles resemble members of the amphibian order Anthracosauria.

As evidence of this close similarity, one anthracosaur (*Seymouria*) was long considered to be a primitive reptile. Recently, however, fossilized aquatic larvae were found, suggesting that seymouriamorphs did not lay shelled eggs. Nevertheless, the earliest reptiles were generally small and their great adaptive radiation did not begin

until late in the Permian (about 225 million years ago) at which time few of the ancient groups of amphibians still survived.

Modern Amphibians

In contrast to our knowledge about the origin of reptiles, the ancestry of modern amphibians is a puzzle, largely because there are no fossils linking the ancient Paleozoic forms to any of the three living orders. The earliest known fossil (*Triadobatrachus*, of the early Triassic) is already froglike in some of its features and the earliest true salamanders (from the late Triassic), true frogs (from the early Jurassic) and caecilians (from the early Tertiary, about 65 million years ago) are already as specialized, each in its own way, as modern forms.

Thus, the incomplete fossil record provides little help. Indeed, it prompts the question why these animals were not readily fossilized, since even very small and fragile labyrinthodont larvae have been recovered. The reason may be ecological: the ancestors of living amphibians probably occupied very shallow waters or rushing mountain streams where the large species of ancient amphibians could not pursue them and, coincidentally, places where fossilization is relatively rare.

Without critical fossil material, evolutionary relationships must be inferred from

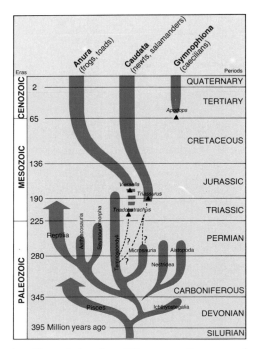

▲ **The evolution of amphibians.** ABOVE From fish to amphibian. (1) Crossopterygian fish, *Eusthenopteron*. (2) *Ichthyostega* one of the earliest amphibians (360 million year ago). (3) *Elpistostege*, remains of which were until recently believed to be those of an amphibian, with the form shown, but are now considered to be those of a fish. BELOW Chart showing the main evolutionary branches of amphibians and their ancestors.

AMPHIBIAN BODY PLAN

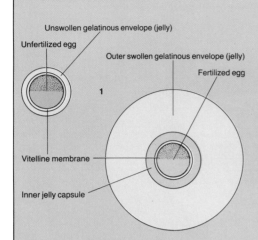

1. Unfertilized egg
- Unswollen gelatinous envelope (jelly)
- Outer swollen gelatinous envelope (jelly)
- Fertilized egg
- Vitelline membrane
- Inner jelly capsule

▶ **The heart** (3) has three chambers, two atria and a ventricle, which may be partly divided. Amphibians have paired lungs, but in four families of salamanders these are sometimes reduced or completely absent; in caecilians, the left lung is greatly reduced.

▼▶ **The skull** is flattened, and in the modern forms, eg frogs (4) and salamanders (5), articulates with the vertebral column by means of two knob-like occipital condyles (6), a condition found also in mammals; the extinct forms have a single condyle. Like fish, living amphibians have only ten pairs of cranial nerves. Primitive fossil forms had twelve, as do higher vertebrates. Living amphibians also have pedicellate teeth (7), with the crown attached to a narrow pedicel by uncalcified fibrous tissue, allowing the tooth to bend inwards.

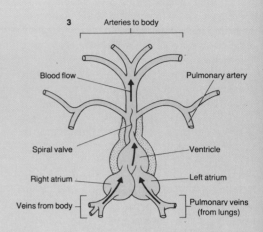

3
- Arteries to body
- Blood flow
- Pulmonary artery
- Spiral valve
- Ventricle
- Right atrium
- Left atrium
- Veins from body
- Pulmonary veins (from lungs)

▲ **Embryos** (fertilized eggs) of amphibians (1), like those of fish, have gelatinous envelopes but lack the protective membranes found in all higher vertebrates. Amphibian eggs also lack shells and therefore must be laid in fresh water or in moist places to avoid drying out, although a few species give birth to fully-formed young. Larvae, even those of the earliest extinct forms, possess external gills, and in frog tadpoles these become enclosed inside a chamber by a flap of skin (the operculum). The larva undergoes an abrupt metamorphosis (see pp10–11) to the adult stage, from which it often differs markedly in structure.

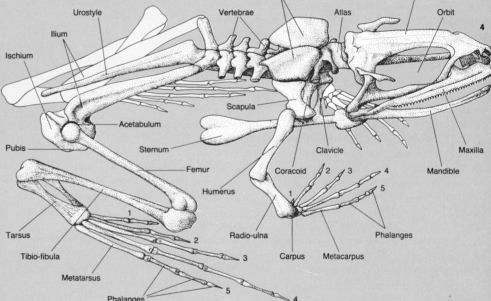

4
- Urostyle
- Ilium
- Ischium
- Pubis
- Acetabulum
- Sternum
- Femur
- Humerus
- Tarsus
- Tibio-fibula
- Metatarsus
- Phalanges
- Suprascapula
- Vertebrae
- Atlas
- Brain case
- Orbit
- Scapula
- Maxilla
- Mandible
- Clavicle
- Coracoid
- Radio-ulna
- Carpus
- Metacarpus
- Phalanges

▼ **Skin.** Living forms have a moist, glandular skin (2), without scales or true claws. Some caecilians, however, have scales embedded in the dermis of the skin and a few frogs have plates of bone (osteoderms) in the skin, as do many reptiles. Some species of frogs and salamanders have claw-like epidermal tips on the toes.

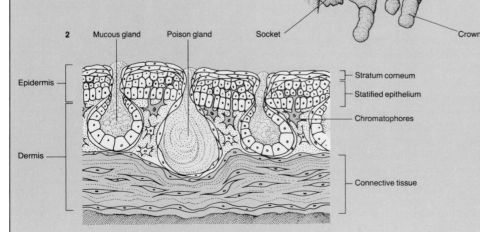

7
- Maxillary bone
- Pedicle
- Joint
- Socket
- Crown

2
- Mucous gland
- Poison gland
- Epidermis
- Stratum corneum
- Statified epithelium
- Chromatophores
- Dermis
- Connective tissue

Many of the features first developed by the amphibians relate to their crucial transition from water to land. Amphibians were the first vertebrates to possess true tongues (to moisten and move food), the first eyelids (which, together with adjacent glands, wet the cornea), an outer layer of dead cells in the epidermis that can be sloughed off, the first true ears—and a voice-producing structure, the larynx—and the first Jacobson's organ, a chemosensory structure adjacent to the nasal cavities that reaches its developmental zenith in snakes and lizards (see pp87, 114).

There were also striking changes in the nervous system related to life in a more complex terrestrial environment. The spinal cord is enlarged in the regions adjacent to the limbs, correlated with the more intricate movement of limbs compared to the fins of their fish ancestors. Invasion of the outer layer of the cerebral hemispheres by nerve cells, foreshadowing the tremendous enlargement of the mammalian cerebrum, also first occurred in amphibians.

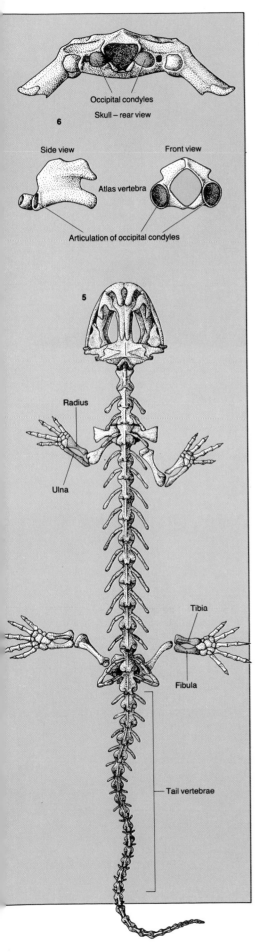

Occipital condyles

Skull – rear view

6

Side view

Front view

Atlas vertebra

Articulation of occipital condyles

5

Radius

Ulna

Tibia

Fibula

Tail vertebrae

comparisons of the living species. For a long time, given the enormous differences between frogs and salamanders, it was believed that each had descended from different orders of Paleozoic amphibians. More recently, it was suggested that despite their different appearances, frogs, salamanders and caecilians have many basic features in common, particularly in the skin, ears, skull and teeth.

The possibility that all of these features evolved independently was so unlikely, it was argued, that it was more reasonable to assume a common origin. Therefore, many scientists place the three living groups in one subclass (Lissamphibia). But since that time new evidence has come to light, particularly concerning the vertebral column, skull and jaw musculature, which raises anew the possibility that the living forms arose from different orders of ancient stocks. Until critical fossil material from the late Paleozoic is found, the question is likely to remain unresolved.

Locomotion

Whatever their true origins, modern amphibians do share numerous features, in particular their highly permeable skin and pedicellate teeth; but there has been a striking adaptive radiation among them in terms of locomotion and reproduction.

Salamanders and caecilians swim like fish, with side-to-side sinusoidal movements. Frogs, on the other hand, swim (and jump) in a totally different way. The vertebral column has become progressively shortened, the hindmost vertebrae have fused into a single element (the urostyle), and the bones of the hind legs have become elongated. Thus, frogs have rather inflexible bodies and swim by means of simultaneous thrusts of the legs (see p56).

Terrestrial salamanders move by means of lateral undulations, advancing diagonally opposite feet each time the body bends; some species use the tail as a fifth leg. Caecilians are legless and, except for a few completely aquatic species, live in burrows. Since the burrow walls greatly restrict lateral undulations, caecilians move by an alternating fold-and-extension progression in which only the vertebral column bends, producing momentary points of contact with the substrate which allows extension of other parts of the body, superficially resembling the locomotion of an earthworm.

Reproduction

Amphibians exhibit the greatest diversity of reproductive modes of any vertebrate group. Fertilization can be external or internal. In the most primitive families (the giant and Asiatic salamanders) it is external, the sperm being shed into the water near the eggs. However, most salamanders transfer sperm in small packets called spermatophores that are picked up by the female with her cloacal lips during courtship. The sperm can then be used at once or, in most species, stored in specialized glands (spermatheca) in the cloaca for use during the following season. In two North American mole salamanders (genus *Ambystoma*) the sperm merely activate the developmental process and do not contribute genetically (a form of parthenogenesis).

With few exceptions, frogs fertilize externally. Usually sperm is deposited as the eggs are laid, with the male clasping the female with his forelegs (amplexus). Some poison-arrow frogs have no amplexus at all, the males fertilizing the eggs after deposition. In some narrow-mouthed frogs the bodies are temporarily glued together, and in a few other species the male's cloaca is held next to the female's while sperm is transferred, so that fertilization is internal, but there is no intromittent organ. However, in the North American Tailed frog the tail is, in fact, an extension of the male's cloaca which is inserted into the female's cloaca to transfer sperm. All caecilians fertilize internally, the male everting his cloaca and using it as an intromittent organ.

Most amphibian species lay eggs (they are oviparous) in fresh water or on land. Others are viviparous: the mother retains the eggs in her body and the embryos are nourished either by food stored in their own yolk sac (this is sometimes called "ovoviviparous" reproduction) or by materials obtained directly from the mother. Clutch size in frogs varies from species to species and ranges from a single egg to about 25,000; in salamanders, the number is generally no more than a few dozen.

Fertilized eggs may be laid singly, in clusters, or in long strands, but are always enclosed in gelatinous envelopes. If laid in water (or near enough that hatched larvae can crawl or be swept into it by floods), the larvae have gills and lead an aquatic existence, eventually metamorphosing into miniature adults (see pp10–11).

Amphibians use a variety of sites for laying eggs, including still or running water, mud basins constructed by the male, cavities beneath logs or stones, debris or burrows, leaves overhanging water, or the water-filled axils of plants. However, each

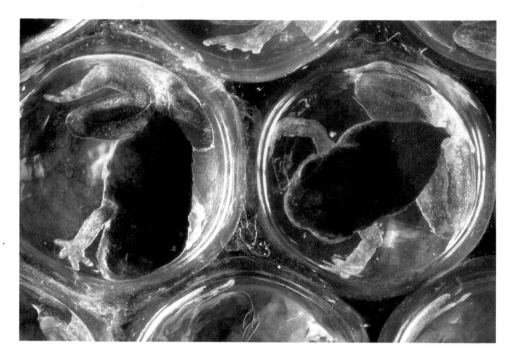

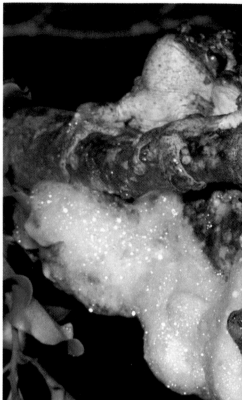

species generally has one preferred site. Those that lay eggs on land typically have no free-living larval stage and undergo direct development; this is true in many tropical frogs and in virtually all terrestrial species of salamanders. In many frogs and salamanders the eggs are defended by one of the parents and in several species of frogs the eggs or tadpoles are carried (see pp14–15).

Most amphibians giving birth to fully-developed young are ovoviviparous. In the Puerto Rican live-bearing frog, for example, only the embryo's own yolk is utilized; the embryo's tail is thin and rich in blood supply and may function in gas exchange. Several species of African live-bearing toads (genus *Nectophrynoides*) are ovoviviparous but in one, the West African live-bearing toad, the fetuses ingest a mucoprotein (uterine milk) secreted by the oviduct when the yolk supply is exhausted.

Two European species of salamanders are known to be viviparous. In the European Fire salamander the young are deposited as larvae into the water. In the Alpine salamander, a member of the same genus, only 1–4 young survive from as many as 60 fertilized ova. The survivors cannibalize their own siblings and they metamorphose before birth. The olm may also be viviparous under certain conditions. Although many caecilians lay eggs which are guarded by the mother, about half of the species are viviparous. After utilizing their own yolk, the large fetuses feed on uterine milk and also scrape material from the oviduct walls with their specialized teeth. Gas exchange occurs between the greatly-enlarged gills

▲ **Cooperative breeding.** Gray tree frogs (*Chiromantis xerampelina*), high in the branches of a tree on the South African savanna, beat a female secretion into a foam nest where eggs will stay moist.

◄ **Breaking out.** After hatching within their foam nest, tiny Gray tree frog tadpoles wriggle free, to fall into a seasonal pond below, where they will complete development.

◄ **Direct development.** ABOVE The young of Costa Rican rain frogs of the genus *Eleutherodactylus* have no free-swimming tadpole stage but hatch as tiny froglets.

and the wall of the oviduct, but the gills are resorbed before birth. These are all of the truly live-bearing amphibians, so far as is known. They should not be confused with those instances of parental care (see pp14–15, 47) in which parents only appear to give birth to fully-formed offspring.

The Amphibia are an astonishingly diverse class of vertebrates that has existed for at least 360 million years. Since at least the beginning of the Carboniferous period (about 340 million years ago) their lineage has been evolving independently. Thus, it

would be erroneous to think of modern amphibians merely as transitional forms between fish and reptiles, except in a very general way. There is a tendency to regard living amphibians as evolutionary losers, partly because of their diminished numbers and small size. Instead, one should think of them as descendants of an ancient lineage that has been extraordinarily successful in exploiting an extremely wide range of habitats and life histories and which often constitutes a dominant element in natural communities. KA

A Key Amphibian Event

Metamorphosis

Metamorphosis, the abrupt tranformation from larva to adult, is one of the distinctive characteristics of all amphibians, the only four-limbed animals in which it occurs. These morphological changes, and the modifications in physiology and behavior that accompany them, are far more remarkable in frogs than in salamanders.

The life-styles of larval frogs and toads (the only larvae properly called "tadpoles") and of larval salamanders are profoundly different. Salamander larvae are active carnivores that hunt large, individual prey items. Tadpoles, however, are mostly herbivores adapted either to a suspension-feeding way of life by filtering particles of food from the water or by tearing and scraping plant material. Tadpoles of some species can extract food items (eg blue-green algae) as small as one tenth of a micrometer (0.000004in) in diameter—an efficiency comparable to the best mechanical sieves. A few can filter water at a rate of more than eight times their body volume per minute. Larval salamanders look like miniature adults with external gills. Thus, besides the loss of gills and lateral line organs, and some internal changes in skeleton and musculature, metamorphosis in them is relatively subtle, involving resorption of tail fins, differentiation of eyelids, changes in thickness and permeability of skin to water.

In frogs and toads, metamorphic events are more dramatic because tadpoles are so different from the carnivorous adult stage. For example, they have large propulsive tails that are completely resorbed at metamorphosis. The larval "teeth" are shed and the mouth enlarges greatly. The hind limbs, which later become the primary means of locomotion, are tiny and nonfunctional in tadpoles until shortly before metamorphosis, and the forelimbs cannot be seen externally at all, because they develop inside the chamber housing the gills. Internally, the differences between larva and adult frog are equally extreme, especially in the digestive system. At metamorphosis, the tadpole's long, coiled intestine—required for its largely vegetarian diet—becomes greatly shortened, to as little as 15 percent of its original length in some species.

Metamorphosis is under hormonal control, as is development generally. Hormones produced in the pituitary (prolactin) and thyroid (thyroxine) are involved. Increased amounts of thyroxine (or, according to recent research, a changing sensitivity of the tissues to thyroxine) trigger metamorphosis.

The time to metamorphosis can vary

enormously. In some species of frogs the larvae overwinter and may not transform until the next summer, whereas tadpoles of some desert-dwelling toads complete the process in as little as eight days, an adaptation to the temporary nature of desert pools. But not all salamander larvae transform into a typical adult form; some retain larval characteristics, even though they become reproductive adults. This retention of juvenile traits in adults is called "paedomorphosis."

Paedomorphic characteristics in salamanders include a functional lateral line sensory system, absence of eyelids and the retention of external gills. One or more of these traits has been found in some species or populations of all families of living salamanders. In some families (the giant salamanders, the mudpuppy and olm, the amphiumas and the sirens) all species are paedomorphic. In lungless salamanders and in the olm paedomorphosis is associated with adaptation to life in caves. For all of these families it is usually a fixed genetic trait and the application of thyroxine by researchers does not cause metamorphosis.

In the other families of salamanders it is found only in some individuals or populations within a species and the application of thyroxine does cause metamorphosis. For example, in Lake Xochimilco of central Mexico, the axolotl becomes sexually mature in an otherwise larval state, although transformed adults have been found. Somehow the Xochimilco environment favors paedomorphosis, perhaps due to an insuffi-

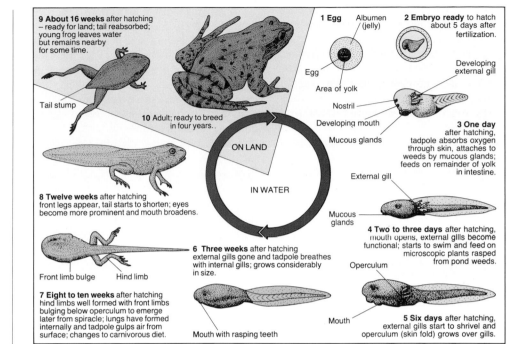

Life cycle of the European common frog, showing stages of metamorphosis.

1 Egg Albumen (jelly) / Egg / Area of yolk

2 Embryo ready to hatch about 5 days after fertilization.

Developing external gill

Nostril

Developing mouth

Mucous glands

3 One day after hatching, tadpole absorbs oxygen through skin, attaches to weeds by mucous glands; feeds on remainder of yolk in intestine.

External gill

Mucous glands

4 Two to three days after hatching, mouth opens, external gills become functional; starts to swim and feed on microscopic plants rasped from pond weeds.

Operculum

Mouth

5 Six days after hatching, external gills start to shrivel and operculum (skin fold) grows over gills.

Mouth with rasping teeth

6 Three weeks after hatching external gills gone and tadpole breathes with internal gills; grows considerably in size.

Front limb bulge / Hind limb

7 Eight to ten weeks after hatching hind limbs well formed with front limbs bulging below operculum to emerge later from spiracle; lungs have formed internally and tadpole gulps air from surface; changes to carnivorous diet.

8 Twelve weeks after hatching front legs appear, tail starts to shorten; eyes become more prominent and mouth broadens.

9 About 16 weeks after hatching – ready for land; tail reabsorbed; young frog leaves water but remains nearby for some time.

Tail stump

10 Adult; ready to breed in four years..

ON LAND

IN WATER

◄ Partially metamorphosed. This Costa Rican Bare-hearted glass frog (*Centrolenella colymbiphyllum*), just emerged from water, has not yet completely reabsorbed its tail.

▼ Tadpole giant. The Paradoxical frog gets its name because the tadpoles, up to 25cm (10in), can be four times as long as the adults. The largest of the pseudid frog family, this species occurs on Trinidad and in the Amazon.

cient quantity of iodine in the water, which is necessary to produce the hormone thyroxine. Or it may be due to cold lake temperatures, in which thyroxine has little effect, according to laboratory studies.

In the American Red-spotted newt, some coastal populations bypass the normal terrestrial (eft) phase, retain gills and become reproductively mature. Paedomorphosis is often found in high-elevation populations but is unknown in lowland populations of the same species. Several species of American mole salamanders, as well as the European Alpine newt and other *Triturus* species, and a Japanese salamander, *Hynobius lichenatus*, show the same pattern.

Ecologists suggest that aquatic habitats surrounded by hostile terrestrial ones ought to favor paedomorphosis. This circumstance is often true for species living in caves, in desert ponds, in streams running through arid areas, and in high-elevation ponds. Some species, however, do not fit this pattern. Sirens and amphiumas, for example, have lost the genetic capacity to metamorphose but have other adaptations such as the sirens' ability to aestivate in mud cavities or the amphiumas' to move overland whenever their aquatic habitat dries.

Unlike salamander larvae, tadpoles have apparently sacrificed reproduction in favor of feeding and rapid growth rates. They are "feeding machines" with head skeletons and enormous guts adapted to a herbivorous life-style. Space for complete differentiation of reproductive organs becomes available only at metamorphosis. KA

Kaleidoscopic Adaptation
The many uses of amphibian colors

Amphibians display a kaleidoscope of colors. These are produced by pigment granules in the epidermal (upper) layer of the skin, by specialized pigment-containing cells, collectively called chromatophores, in the dermal (lower) layer, and occasionally by pigment in even deeper tissues.

The green color of several tropical frogs results from the deposition of a green excretory product, the bile pigment biliverdin, in their soft tissues and bones. The colors seen arise from a combination of the differential absorption and reflectance of light (chemical color) as well as diffraction and other interference phenomena (physical color).

Many amphibians can change color, by concentrating or dispersing melanin or other pigments in the chromatophores, but since these changes are largely under hormonal control, they occur rather slowly, on a time scale of minutes. By changing color in this way amphibians, like many reptiles, can regulate body temperature, since dark-colored bodies absorb radiant energy more rapidly than light-colored ones do. Thus, frogs are pale in the hot sun. A dramatic example occurs when a frog's body is partly shaded and exhibits a two-tone color divided at the edge of the shadow. Melanin pigment is also an extremely effective filter for ultraviolet light, those wavelengths of sunlight potentially most damaging to body tissues and to genetic material.

Color and pattern in amphibians are often used for concealment (crypsis), either to allow them to avoid detection by would-be prey or, especially, to avoid becoming prey themselves. Although many amphibians possess skin toxins that are noxious or even fatal to predators, most species are cryptically colored. Many employ camouflage that allows them to match their background to varying degrees, or disruptive coloration that breaks up their body outline.

Certain forest-floor dwelling frogs (for example, the Malaysian horned toad, the Neotropical leaf toad and *Hemiphractus* of South America) resemble dead leaves, even to the detail of having fleshy projections like the edge of a leaf and a midrib-like stripe down the midline. Detailed studies show that the reflectance of a frog's back and that of its normal background correspond very precisely, even to minute variations at particular wavelengths. Certain species of neotropical frogs that sit on leaves match their background both in the visible spectrum as well as in the near infrared, which may conceal them from detection even by pit vipers searching with infrared-sensitive pit receptors. Many species are effectively countershaded, with a dark upperside but with light-colored bellies which render them less visible in water when viewed from below against the light sky.

In contrast, some species are strikingly colored and easily detected. Many of these, such as the poison-arrow frogs of the neotropics, have toxic skin secretions, and their bright coloration is believed to have evolved as a warning to potential predators (aposematic coloration). Some palatable species win protection by mimicking distasteful ones; in eastern North America the Red salamander avoids predation by color matching red efts, the land stage of the Red-spotted newt, which have skin toxins that are lethal to predators.

A few species combine crypsis and warning coloration, being cryptically colored when viewed from above but having a brightly colored belly that is exposed only when the animal is severely threatened by a predator. The fire-bellied toads of Europe and Asia, and Pacific or western American newts both have skin toxins and exhibit a so-called "unken" reflex when stressed (see pp34–35).

Other examples of intimidation of predators involving color and pattern include the flash colors of frogs. These bright colors

▲ ▼ ► Camouflage, warning and mimicry.
ABOVE The Oriental fire-bellied toad (*Bombina orientalis*) is camouflaged above but, when attacked, displays warning coloration on its belly. ABOVE RIGHT The vivid pattern of the Turquoise poison-dart frog (*Dendrobates auratus*) warns potential predators of its lethal skin secretion. BELOW LEFT The red eft of the Red-spotted newt is highly toxic, and is mimicked BELOW RIGHT by the harmless Red salamander. BELOW When the South American False-eyed frog is attacked, it faces away from its attacker and lifts its rump to display two dramatic eye spots that deter predators. BELOW RIGHT The fleshy "horns" and skin patterns of Brazilian toads of the genus *Proceratophrys* enable them to wait for their prey, camouflaged among leaves. With their huge mouths, they are able to eat large prey, including other frogs.

are restricted to surfaces, such as the flanks and posterior side of the thigh, that are hidden when the animal is at rest, but which appear and disappear as it jumps, possibly confusing predators that might attempt to capture the colored objects. The South American False-eyed frog has two large eye-like spots on its rump; when threatened, it aims the rump toward the predator. Some frogs have patterns that cannot be seen at all in the human visual spectrum. For example, White's tree frog from Australia has a large spot on its snout that can be seen only in the infrared range; the function of this is unknown.

Colors and patterns are also used for recognition between and within species. Different species sharing the same range tend to have distinctively different color patterns. In some species the sexes differ in color, sometimes markedly so (as in the Yosemite toad and the Golden toad); this sexual dimorphism might function in sex recognition in day-active species. In the Stream frog, a poison-arrow frog of Trinidad and Venezuela, calling males turn pitch black and fight only with other black males, and losers turn brown within a few minutes.

KA

Conscientious Parents
Parental care in amphibians

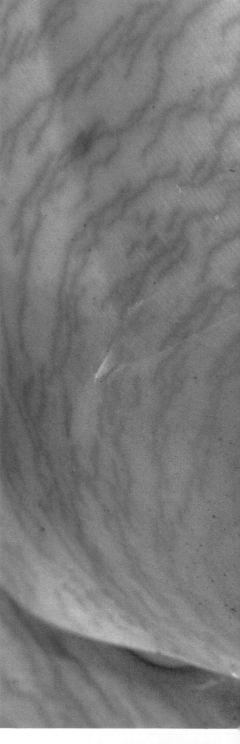

Amphibians display the widest array of reproductive modes of any of the vertebrate classes, and possess almost every conceivable type of parental care. In large measure, this diversity reflects the different trade-offs that different species make between numbers of offspring produced and the amount of care invested.

Since females produce fewer gametes (germ cells) than males, and at a greater energy expense, they normally invest more time in caring for their offspring, but there are many intriguing exceptions among the Amphibia. In the most primitive living salamander families (the giant and Asiatic salamanders) and in many frogs, nearly all of which have external fertilization, the eggs are laid within the territory of the male and are defended by him. This is the most common form of parental care, reducing predation and desiccation of eggs. Sometimes the male will simultaneously guard clutches of several females. In the most advanced group, the lungless salamanders, and the egg-laying species of caecilians, all of which fertilize internally, and in some frogs, the females guard the eggs on land or in the water.

Animals are rarely cared for by their fathers. Among vertebrates paternal care is most common in fish and amphibians. This may be due to the fact that fertilization is external; males can be certain which eggs they fertilized and their reproductive success can therefore be increased by caring for their offspring. Or it may be simply that males must be present for external fertilization and thus have the opportunity for care; in internally-fertilizing species mating and egg laying may be separated by a month or more, so male parental care is a less likely option.

Eggs or larvae of many amphibians are transported by one of the parents to protect them from temperature extremes, desiccation, predation or parasitism. In the midwife toads of Europe, the male carries strings of eggs, sometimes from more than one female, entwined around his hind legs, occasionally taking them back to water to keep them moist. When the eggs are ready to hatch, he carries them to water. In the Australian Pouched frog the tadpoles wriggle into the bilateral brood pouches on the male's flanks and later emerge as tiny froglets. In the mouth-brooding frogs, a family comprising just two South American frogs, the male carries as many as 20 larvae in his vocal pouch which must elongate to the full length of his body as the tadpoles grow in size. The males may carry the eggs from several different females at the same time.

In other species it is the female parent that carries the offspring. In the primitive aquatic Surinam toads of South America, males fertilize the eggs during a somersaulting bout in which the eggs are placed on the female's back. Each egg develops in a separate pocket, and the tail of the tadpole, rich in capillaries, serves the same purpose as a placenta. The young then emerge either as tadpoles or fully metamorphosed young, depending on the species.

There are about 640 species in the true tree frog family, Hylidae. In about 60—all tropical—the female carries the eggs on her back. In five genera the eggs either adhere to the back (*Cryptobatrachus*, *Hemiphractus* and *Stefania*) or are carried in open pouches (*Flectonotus* and *Fritziana*), and the larvae develop into froglets. In two genera (*Amphignathodon* and *Gastrotheca*) there is a marsupium-like pouch that opens just above the cloaca. The eggs are placed in the pouch after fertilization by the male and the young emerge as tadpoles or froglets, according to the species.

Perhaps the most bizarre case of egg-brooding in frogs is found in the Australian Gastric-brooding frog. The female ingests as many as 20 fertilized eggs which undergo development in her stomach and then are "vomited up" as tadpoles and froglets. During this time the parent does not feed; in fact, the digestive system is inhibited by the release of a hormone-like substance, a prostaglandin, secreted in the oral mucus of the larvae. It shuts down hydrochloric acid secretion and the peristaltic waves of the gut.

In the Neotropical poison-arrow frogs, the Seychelles frogs and Hamilton's frog of New Zealand, the eggs are laid on land and, after hatching, the tadpoles wriggle onto the parent's back and are then carried to water,

▲ **Watery nursery.** A South American Pygmy marsupial frog (*Flectonotus pygmaeus*) develops her eggs in an open pouch on her back, then releases the tadpoles into the water-filled hollow of a bromeliad.

◄ **Oral incubator.** A male Darwin's frog with a froglet that has just emerged from his vocal sac. This mouth-brooding species lives in South American forests.

▶ **Taxi service.** A female Red-and-blue poison-arrow frog from the rain forests of Costa Rica carries a tadpole on her back, in search of standing water where it can complete its development.

a journey that can last several days. In some species it is the male that performs the task and in some the female; in still others it may be both parents, but this needs to be confirmed by further detailed studies by scientists in the field.

In several species of poison-arrow frogs of the genus *Dendrobates* the female deposits tadpoles in water-filled axils of epiphytic bromeliads, but never more than one tadpole per axil. She then returns at intervals of one to two weeks, backs into the water, and lays a small clutch of unfertilized eggs on which her tadpole feeds and without which it would die. KA

CAECILIANS

Order: Gymnophiona (Apoda)
One hundred and sixty-three species in 34 genera and 5 families.
Distribution: SE Asia from S China, India and Sri Lanka to S Philippines; C Africa; Seychelles; C and much of S America.

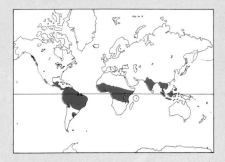

Habitat: moist loose soil and ground litter of tropical forests and plantations, often near streams; typhlonectids in lowland rivers and streams.

Size: variable; smallest species 7–11.4cm (2.4–4.5in) snout to tip of tail when mature, largest 1.5m (4ft 11in); many 30–70cm (11.7–27.3in); some stout-bodied (length/diameter ratio 15:1), some slender (length/diameter ratio 100:1).

Color: many species uniform blue-gray, some with lighter lateral or segmental stripes, some with blotched patterns; heads often lighter, to pink or light blue.
Reproduction: internal fertilization; some species laying eggs producing free-living larvae, others with direct development through metamorphosis before hatching; viviparous, the mother nourishing 2–25 young in her oviducts for 9–11 months.
Families: Caeciliidae (24 genera, 88 species); Ichthyophiidae (3 genera, 40 species); Rhinatrematidae (2 genera, 9 species); Scolecomorphidae (1 genus, 7 species); Typhlonectidae (4 genera, 19 species).

Mᴏʀᴇ likely to be mistaken for large earthworms, caecilians are long-bodied, limbless amphibians, with virtually no tail. Scientists are only beginning to understand the lives of these secretive tropical burrowers, which are difficult to observe and almost without a fossil history. The only fossil is a single vertebra from the Paleocene (65 million years ago) in Brazil, but the biology of the living species provides tantalizing clues to their evolution.

The bones, teeth, fat bodies and other structures of caecilians show that they are related to salamanders and frogs, and are thus members of the class Amphibia. They apparently underwent a major change early in their evolutionary history. With the elongation of their bodies they lost their limbs (no caecilians have limb or girdle rudiments) and their tails (only primitive caecilians have tails, of 4–12 vertebrae). Their skulls became massively bony and their eyes were reduced as they assumed an underground life-style.

Today, they appear to have a low density at many localities, but are abundant at others, especially in Ghana and some areas of Central America. Yet they have radiated throughout the tropics. They are difficult to observe, emerging infrequently from their burrows, although the aquatic species of South America are occasionally taken in fishermen's seines. Many look rather like large earthworms because of the segmental rings around their bodies.

Caecilians are very diverse in size. The smallest (*Idiocranium* of West Africa) is mature at 7cm (2.7in); the longest is *Caecilia thompsoni* of Colombia at 1.5m (4ft 11in). Other forms are shorter but stouter; *Caecilia nigricans* is 80cm (31in) long with a body diameter of 4cm (1.6in).

Most caecilians are generalized opportunistic feeders preying, for example, on earthworms, termites and orthopterans. Some of them appear to be specialists on termites (*Afrocaecilia*, *Boulengerula*) or earthworms (*Dermophis*, when worms are abundant) or beetle pupae (*Typhlonectes obesus*). Small lizards are occasionally eaten by *Dermophis*, and *Siphonops* eats baby mice in the laboratory. Caecilians themselves are preyed upon by snakes and birds.

Feeding involves a modified "sit-and-wait" strategy. Typically, caecilians slowly approach their prey then quickly seize it with a strong grab by the jaws. All caecilians have two rows of teeth on the upper jaw, and one or two rows on the lower. These inwardly curved teeth hold the prey, as successive bites and expansions of the mouth and throat propel it into the gut. Teeth are modified for cutting and holding, with sharp edges and sometimes two cusps. Some muscles have changed function from contracting the oral cavity to closing the lower jaw, to effect the strong bite.

Caecilians are burrowing animals, whether in soil or in the floor of a body of water. They use their heads as trowels for digging or to poke in mud for food. Their skulls are heavily boned for this use and the skin is very adherent, its underlying layers fused to the bones so that the skin does not shear away during digging. Locomotion is by body undulation, a wave of muscular activity from the head backwards. The curves formed by the body resist the soil or water and forward movement occurs. The segmental rings round the body seem to have little role in locomotion.

The skin is smooth, its outer layers somewhat toughened with keratin. The inner layer contains many mucus glands and variable numbers of poison glands. Their secretions can be quite toxic to predators, including humans. In many species there are also patches of scales in the segmental rings. They are like fish scales in structure and embryonic origin and unlike those of reptiles. There is a trend toward loss of the scales—primitive species have them the entire lengths of their bodies, others only in rear segmental rings and the most modern species lack scales altogether.

All caecilians have internal fertilization. The male extrudes the rear part of his cloaca and inserts it into the vent of the female, thus directly transferring sperm to the female's body, where fertilization takes place as in reptiles, birds and mammals. Virtually nothing is known of mate recognition and courtship, although aquatic species have been observed in an undulating "dance" before mating. Primitive species of caecilians

▲ Worm-like body form and covered eyes typical of caecilians. The eyes of caecilians are covered by skin or by skin and bone and adhere to these covering layers. The lens of the eye cannot move and some species have no eyeball muscles. The lens and retina are reduced in some species, but almost all have an optic nerve, suggesting that the function of the eyes is to sense light. This is *Gymnopis multiplicata* from Central America.

◄ Tentacle sensor. The sense of smell has been enhanced in these carnivorous animals by a small tentacle which develops at metamorphosis on the upper jaw behind each nostril. It carries chemical messages from the environment to the nasal cavity. The caecilian tentacle is unique in the vertebrate world, using structures normally associated with the eye. It is retracted by a muscle which, in other amphibians, retracts the eye, and its channel is lubricated by the Harderian gland, which provides fluid for the socket of the eye in other terrestrial vertebrates. Natural selection appears to have utilized raw material made available by reduction of the eyes. This is *Ichthyophis glutinosus* from Ceylon.

lay eggs in burrows near streams; gilled larvae hatch out and wriggle into the water. They become terrestrial after metamorphosis. Some species are direct developers— the eggs are laid underground, and the young develop within them through metamorphosis so that a miniature adult hatches. In apparently all the egg-laying species, the female provides parental care, lying coiled around her eggs.

Viviparity (live birth) is the most striking feature of caecilian reproduction. Perhaps half of the species will be found to retain the developing young in the female's oviducts through metamorphosis, nourishing the young with "uterine milk," rich secretions from glands in the oviducts, after the yolk supply is exhausted. Very few frogs and salamanders have evolved such a mechanism. The developing fetuses have many tiny teeth of a different shape in each species, associated with feeding on these glandular secretions of the oviduct. They acquire adult teeth just at birth. The fetal gills are thought to function in gaseous and perhaps nutrient exchange with the mother through transport of materials across the capillaries to the circulating blood of both fetus and mother. Gestation is long, 9–11 months, and the young are nourished by the maternal secretions most of that time. A clutch numbers

7–20 young, and their mass increases enormously; so the energy demand on the mother is very great.

The five families of caecilians are distinguished by combinations of characters, including those of the external body form, bones and muscles, and reproductive biology. These amphibians are so little known that there are no common names for the families and genera, nor for most of the species. The Ichthyophiidae include genera with several rings in each body segment (rather than just one or two), vertebrae (a "tail") extending beyond the anus, large numbers of skull bones, and an egg-laying mode of reproduction with free-living larvae. The Rhinatrematidae share these features but have fewer skull bones and differences in the musculature. The Caeciliidae have only one or two rings per body segment, no "tail" and fewer skull bones. They may be either egg-layers or live-bearing. The live-bearing Typhlonectidae have one ring per body segment and a slight to moderate dorsal "fin". They are aquatic, the only caecilians which are not terrestrial burrowers. The Scolecomorphidae also have only one ring per segment. They are live-bearers and have a reduced number of skull bones including the absence of the stapes, the middle ear bone.   MHW

SALAMANDERS AND NEWTS

Order: Urodela (Caudata)
Three hundred and fifty-eight species in 60 genera and 9 families.
Distribution: N America, C America, northern S America, Europe, Mediterranean, Africa, Asia, including Japan and Taiwan.

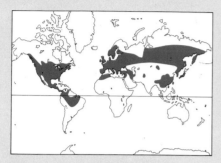

Habitat: aquatic, terrestrial or amphibious.

Size: length (snout to tip of tail) from 3–160cm (1.2–63in), but most are 5–15cm (2–6in).

Color: highly variable including green, brown, black, red, orange, yellow.

Reproduction: fertilization mostly internal: most lay eggs but in some eggs develop inside female.

Longevity: in captivity, sometimes 20–25 years, occasionally more than 50; very little known about longevity in nature, but some species do not breed until they are several years old.

▶ **Contrasts in life-styles.** Salamanders have life-styles that vary from wholly aquatic, through amphibious to wholly terrestrial. ABOVE The Cave salamander lives all its life on land, the female laying eggs under logs. This species lives in the twilight zone near cave entrances and is sensitive to the Earth's magnetic field. BELOW The axolotl normally spends all its life in water, and retains larval features such as gills throughout life. In periods of drought, however, it loses its gills and becomes terrestrial. This individual is an albino.

▶ **Watchful mother.** OVERLEAF A female Dusky salamander lays her eggs in grape-like clusters in a nest which she guards, even after the larvae have hatched.

THE life of the tailed amphibians— salamanders and newts—is secretive, and they are one of the least familiar groups of animals. Generally living in cool, shady places and typically active at night, few are more than 15cm (6in) long. Unlike frogs and toads, they do not advertise their presence by making loud sounds.

They can, however, be extremely abundant. In some mountain forests of eastern North America, it is estimated that the total mass of woodland salamanders exceeds that of all the birds and mammals put together. The newts of Europe and North America migrate from over a wide area to breed in ponds each spring and very large breeding populations can occur. In recent years, research has revealed a wealth of fascinating information about their habits. New species are still being discovered and described for the first time, particularly in tropical America.

Salamanders and newts comprise the order of amphibians known as the Urodela (or Caudata). They typically have elongated bodies, long tails and two pairs of legs of roughly similar size, although some forms have lost one pair of limbs. They thus resemble more closely the earliest fossil amphibians in terms of overall body shape than any other present-day group. They are largely confined to temperate climates, although one group, the lungless salamanders, has invaded the tropical zone in Central and South America.

Salamanders and newts live in a variety of habitats and include fully aquatic and fully terrestrial forms, as well as species that divide their time between water and land. Aquatic forms are found in rivers, lakes, mountain streams, ponds, swamps and underground caves. Terrestrial species commonly live under rocks and logs, but some burrow deep into the soil and some may climb to considerable heights in trees. Because salamanders and newts have a skin that is permeable to water, they cannot tolerate hot, dry conditions and, for many species, the summer is a time when they retreat into damp refuges, emerging only on cool nights. In cold weather they become inactive and species that live in temperate climates bury themselves in the ground or hide beneath large rocks and logs and become torpid.

The term "salamander" derives from the Latin *Salamandra*, in turn derived from the Greek for "fire-lizard." Salamanders were associated with fire because they crawled out of logs thrown onto a fire and it was thought they could crawl through fire—

asbestos was once called "salamander's wool." "Salamander" is applied generally to any tailed amphibian, but more especially to those with terrestrial habits. The term "newt," derived from the Anglo-Saxon *efete* or *evete* which became *ewt* in Medieval English, refers only to the European genus *Triturus* and the North American genera *Taricha* and *Notophthalmus*, all animals that return to water each spring to breed. The term "eft," from the same Anglo-Saxon derivation, refers to the young, terrestrial stage of *Notophthalmus* species.

In common with most other amphibians, salamanders and newts have a smooth, flexible skin that lacks scales and is usually moist. The skin acts as a respiratory surface, at which oxygen enters the body. For this

reason, salamanders and newts are restricted to damp or wet habitats. The outermost layer of the skin is frequently shed. In some species it comes off in bits and pieces, in others it peels off in one piece. The shed skin is usually eaten but sometimes a complete skin can be found hanging from water weed.

All salamanders and newts are carnivorous, feeding upon small, living invertebrates, such as insects, slugs, snails and worms. They possess a tongue which is used to moisten and move food in the mouth; in some species it can be flicked some distance forwards to capture small prey. The tail is well developed for swimming in many species, being laterally compressed, and may bear a dorsal fin. The two pairs of limbs both have digits, often fewer on the front than on

the hind limbs. In some species, such as the amphiumas of North America, the limbs are very small and serve no locomotory function. In others, such as the Palmate newt, the toes of the hind limbs have webbing between them that facilitates rapid swimming.

The eggs of tailed amphibians do not have a shell, but are coated with layers of protective jelly. They also lack the embryonic membranes typical of other amphibians and reptiles. Usually, the egg hatches into a wholly carnivorous larva, which grows until it metamorphoses into the adult form. Metamorphosis (see pp10–11) involves a number of complex changes which equip the salamander or newt for its adult life. This is especially true in newts, whose metamorphosis coincides with a dramatic change of habitat from water to land.

Because there is such a great deal of diversity, there is no "typical" life cycle for members of this order. However, three general types of life cycle can be distinguished: wholly terrestrial, wholly aquatic and amphibious. A typical terrestrial species is the Redback salamander, found in woodland areas of eastern North America. Mating takes place on land and the female retires to lay her eggs within a partly rotten log. A small number of large eggs (20–30) is produced and the embryos develop rapidly within them. The entire larval stage of development is passed within the egg, which hatches to produce a miniature version of the adult salamander. In some terrestrial salamanders, one of the parents guards the developing eggs, for example the American Dusky salamander. In a few species, such as members of the European genus *Salamandra*, the female retains her fertilized eggs within her body while they develop, later giving birth to live young which may be either larvae or juveniles.

In wholly aquatic species, adults mate in water, and some practice external fertilization. Clutches tend to be large (up to 500 eggs) and the eggs hatch into larvae. The adults of several wholly aquatic species, such as the olm of Yugoslavia and northern Italy and the mudpuppy of eastern North America, retain certain larval structures, such as external gills, into adulthood, a condition known as paedomorphosis (see pp10–11). The retention of gills throughout life is most common in those species, like the sirens, that live in stagnant water that is poor in oxygen. Paedomorphosis may be a permanent feature of all members of a species, as in the sirens, the olm and the mudpuppy, or it may be a temporary condition occurring in some individuals lacking a critical nutrient. The best-known example of this is the Mexican axolotl which retains its larval gills if it is deprived of the iodine it needs to produce the hormone thyroxine.

In the amphibious life cycle, the adult spends most of its life on land, but migrates to water in order to breed. Courtship may occur in dense aggregations of individuals, all coming to breed in the same pond at the same time, as in the Spotted salamander of North America. The female lays eggs that develop into aquatic larvae. Clutches are often large (100–400 eggs), but eggs tend to be small. The larvae metamorphose into juveniles, sometimes called efts, which leave the water to live on land until they have grown to reproductive age, a process that takes about 1–7 years. Newts of the family Salamandridae, such as the European Smooth newt and the North American Red-spotted newt, typify this type of life cycle.

The moist skin of newts and salamanders is, for most species, only one route by which oxygen and carbon dioxide enter and leave the body. Typically, larvae have feathery external gills and adults have lungs. Some species, including both aquatic and terrestrial forms, also use the inner surfaces of

their mouths, rhythmically sucking in and expelling water or air through the mouth or nostrils. This "buccal pumping" is very apparent as rapid vibrations of the soft skin under a newt's or a salamander's chin. It serves not only as a respiratory mechanism but also enables the animal continually to sample its external environment for odors.

The largest family, the lungless salamanders, have entirely lost the lungs of their ancestors and breathe only through their skin and mouth lining. Some live in fast-flowing streams, where oxygen is abundant, others are totally terrestrial. Salamanders and newts living in static water, where oxygen levels can become very low, have to breathe through their lungs, coming to the water surface at frequent intervals to take in a supply of fresh air, or through external gills, which they retain from the larval stage into adult life.

The aquatic newts have three ways of obtaining oxygen when they are living in water during the breeding season: through their skin, their mouth lining and their lungs. For most of the time, oxygen obtained from the water via the skin and mouth is sufficient to sustain their activity. However, if they become more active, for example during sexual behavior, they have to make frequent ascents to the water surface to gulp in air. Sometimes a newt will gulp in so much air that it is unable to sink back to the bottom of the pond. It can restore its negative buoyancy by expelling air bubbles, or "guffing," in the manner of a diver. Breathing ascents are potentially dangerous because newts are particularly conspicuous as they rise to the surface and it is then that predatory birds such as herons are most likely to catch them. Newts also have to breathe more often on very warm days, when the high temperature causes them to be more active but when oxygen levels in ponds become very low.

Many salamanders and newts are protected against predators by secretions from numerous poison glands in the skin (see p 34).

Families of Salamanders and Newts

Much the largest of all the salamanders, the **giant salamanders** live in rivers and large streams. They are generally nocturnal in their habits, spending the day beneath rocks. Despite their large size and ugly appearance, they are quite harmless to humans. In Japan and China, they are commonly caught with a rod and line and are considered very good to eat. Their diet consists of virtually any animal that lives in rivers and streams and includes fish, smaller

▶ **The Spotted salamander** may live for 25 years. Within its egg capsule there often grows a green alga, to the benefit of both organisms; eggs containing algae have larger embryos which hatch earlier and survive better. Acid rain pollutes many breeding ponds of this species, killing embryos or causing them to develop deformities.

▼ **Oxygen extractors.** The feathery external gills of this Smooth newt larva are essential for obtaining oxygen from the water.

◀ **Encapsulated life.** Eggs of the Two-lined salamander, with developing larvae.

▼ **Salamander and newt life cycles compared.** Many salamanders are totally terrestrial, while newts are amphibious. The axolotl is totally aquatic.

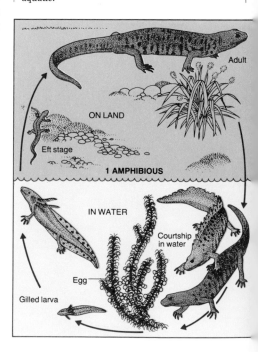

Adult

ON LAND

Eft stage

1 AMPHIBIOUS

IN WATER

Courtship in water

Egg

Gilled larva

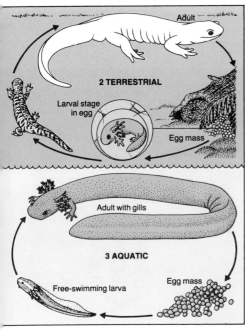

2 TERRESTRIAL

Adult

Larval stage in egg

Egg mass

3 AQUATIC

Adult with gills

Free-swimming larva

Egg mass

salamanders, worms, insects, crayfish and snails. Prey is usually caught from the cover of a rock or overhang by means of a very rapid sideways snap of the mouth. They feed mostly at night and rely on smell and touch to locate their prey. Their vision is poor; the eyes are small and, being positioned far back on the sides of the head, cannot both focus on the same object at the same time.

Giant salamanders never leave the water and, although they lose their gills quite early in life, they never completely lose all larval characteristics. They are probably very long-lived; one specimen has lived in captivity for 52 years. The Japanese giant salamander can reach a length of over 1.5m (5ft) and the American hellbender has a maximum length of about 70cm (28in). Their large size and lack of gills probably confine them to flowing water, where oxygen is in good supply. A conspicuous fold of skin along their flanks increases the sur-

face area through which oxygen can be taken in. They also breathe through their lungs and animals kept in an aquarium will make frequent ascents to gulp in air.

In the hellbender, breeding occurs in late summer. The male excavates a large space beneath a rock and defends it against other males. He also excludes females who have laid their eggs but allows any egg-bearing female to enter. The female lays her eggs in the male's nest in two long strings; the eggs are held together by a sticky thread that adheres to rocks and hardens soon after it comes into contact with water. A large female can lay as many as 450 eggs and several females may lay their eggs in the nest of a single male. The male fertilizes the eggs, covering them with a cloud of milk-like seminal fluid, and guards them throughout their development (10–12 weeks). The larvae then leave the male's nest and lead an entirely independent existence, feeding mainly on small aquatic animals.

Restricted to central and eastern Asia, the **Asiatic salamanders** are not well known. From both their form and their reproductive biology, they are clearly some of the most primitive tailed amphibians. They tend to live in mountain streams where oxygen is abundant and tend to have very small lungs or no lungs at all; large lungs could make it difficult to avoid becoming very buoyant and being swept away by the current. Some species have sharp, curved claws whose function is unknown.

During mating, the female produces paired sacs, each containing 35–70 eggs. The male grasps these as they emerge from her cloaca and, pressing them to his cloaca, sheds sperm onto them. In at least some species, the male guards the eggs until they hatch.

Of the nine families of tailed amphibians, the Salamandridae, including **newts, brook salamanders** and the **Fire salamander**, have the largest range—North America, Europe and parts of Asia. In terms of life history, they are a very diverse family and there is considerable variation between species in the proportions of their life spent in water and on land.

Fertilization is internal, sperm being transferred from male to female in a spermatophore, typically after a prolonged and elaborate courtship (see pp32–33). In most species, the female lays her eggs in water, where they develop into larvae, but in the European Fire salamander the female retains the fertilized eggs in her body until they are fully formed larvae. She then enters a pond or stream to give birth to her young, the only time that an adult returns to water.

Most newts, by contrast, spend nearly half of each year in the water once they become adult. It is in the water that they court, lay their eggs and then build up the fat reserves necessary to survive the winter on land. In some populations of the Crested newt, however, adults remain in the water all year round.

When, in the early spring, newts return to ponds, they undergo a number of physical changes representing a partial metamorphosis back to the larval condition. The skin becomes thin, smooth and permeable to oxygen, the tail becomes a deep, flattened structure that enables them to swim powerfully, and their eyes become a slightly different shape, for focusing under water. Within the skin, a large number of lateral line organs develop; these are sensitive to water vibrations and are important for detecting prey. Male Palmate newts acquire

webbing between the toes of their hind limbs during the breeding season. This probably enables them to swim a little faster than females.

Newt, brook salamander and Fire salamander larvae have external, feathery gills and, initially, no limbs. They grow rapidly during their first few months of life until, in the fall, they lose their gills and leave the water as tiny replicas of their parents. They enter a terrestrial phase, sometimes called the eft stage, which lasts from 1–7 years, depending on both species and locality. In the Smooth newt, for example, the eft stage is much longer in Scandinavia than it is in southern Europe.

Many members of the family are brightly colored and release noxious secretions from glands in their skin (see p34).

Whether they live on land or in water, newts, brook salamanders and the Fire salamander typically feed upon small invertebrates, including worms, slugs, insects and crustaceans. While in the

▲ **Largest of North American salamanders,** the hellbender may reach 70cm (28in) from snout to tip of tail, but this is less than one half of the size of some of its Asian relatives.

▶ **Magnetic navigator?** The Red-spotted newt returns to its breeding pond each year, often from a great distance. It is known to detect the axis of the Earth's magnetic field and may use this as a directional reference system.

▼ **Rock dweller.** The Green salamander (*Aneides aeneus*) lives in damp crevices on rock faces. Its green coloration gives it good camouflage against a background of lichens.

Finding Breeding Ponds

All newts and many salamanders return to water in the spring of each year in order to breed. They show remarkable powers of orientation and homing. It is not known how far they disperse from their breeding ponds, but newts in their terrestrial stage are commonly found several kilometers from the nearest suitable pond. Removal experiments with the Redbelly newt in California have shown that individuals are able to find their way back to the exact stretch of stream where they were caught, despite having been taken to streams several kilometers away and separated from their home stream by mountainous territory. A number of senses, some rather unusual, appear to be involved in this migration.

Vision and smell are important, although even blinded animals with their olfactory system destroyed are able to find their way to water. The pineal body, an outgrowth of the brain lying just beneath the bones of the skull, is also sensitive to light, particularly polarized light. It has been shown that some salamanders can perceive polarized light and can use it to determine the position of the sun in the sky, even when the sun itself is hidden by a cloud, so that they can use the sun as a "compass" to direct their movements. More recently, it has been demonstrated that some North American species, such as the Cave salamander and Red-spotted newt, can detect the earth's magnetic field, and use this cue as a directional reference system.

Newts and salamanders which breed in water frequently show very strong fidelity to the pond or stream in which they grew up, returning there to breed over several successive years, despite the fact that they may move a long way from their breeding site during the intervening months or years. This suggests that their nervous systems may be able to develop and store detailed "maps" of their environment.

aquatic phase, some species, such as the Smooth newt, are voracious predators of frog tadpoles. Prey detection is primarily visual and it is usually movement by a prey item that allows detection. Moving prey can also be detected through lateral line organs. The quarry is generally sniffed before it is snapped at.

Vision, smell and touch are also important in courtship. In newts, the male performs a variety of displays that send visual, olfactory and tactile stimuli to the female. The European newts are unusual among tailed amphibians in that, during courtship, the male does not capture and hold onto the female. Associated with this kind of courtship, males and females in these species are much more strikingly different in appear-

ance during the breeding season than in any other kind of tailed amphibian. The male develops a large crest that runs along the length of his body and tail and the Smooth newt has many large black spots on his body and tail. (See pp32–33.)

In some species, adults show a very strong tendency to return to the same breeding site in successive years. This is most striking in the Redbelly newt of western North America; individuals transported 15km (9mi) or more from their breeding site eventually returned there, despite having to cross high mountains to do so and despite crossing several streams where other members of their species regularly breed. Newts in the terrestrial eft phase also show a strong affinity for their natal ponds, but some do move to other ponds, and it is probably at this stage of the life cycle that newts disperse from one breeding site to another.

Because of their shape, the **amphiumas** used to be called "Congo eels." This was highly misleading; these animals bear only a superficial resemblance to eels, which are fish, and they are found in North America, not in Africa. There are only three species in the family, all found in the swamps of the southeastern United States. They have a long, thin cylindrical body, smooth slippery skin and limbs that are so small that they cannot be of any use in locomotion. In the larval stage, however, the limbs are larger, relative to the size of the body, and are used for walking. The Three-toed amphiuma can reach a length of 90cm (36in) and large individuals are capable of delivering a painful bite when caught. Adults have lungs and no gills, though they do possess the larval feature of one open gill slit.

Amphiumas lead a totally aquatic life, although they may make brief excursions onto the land following very heavy rain. For much of the time they live in a burrow and they are active by night, feeding on a variety of prey including frogs, snails and fish.

In the breeding season, females sometimes outnumber males and several females may be seen rubbing a male with their snouts to attract his attention. During mating, male and female coil around one another and sperm is transferred directly into the female's cloaca. She lays as many as 200 eggs, joined together in a long string, and guards them, her body coiled around them, until they hatch after about 20 weeks. Egg-laying often occurs when the water level is high and, as it falls, the female and her eggs may be left in a damp hollow beneath a log. When they hatch, the young have to find their way back to water.

The two genera in the family Proteidae lead entirely aquatic lives and possess a number of larval characteristics, notably feathery external gills, though they also have lungs. The **olm** lives in underground pools and streams in Yugoslavia and northern Italy and spends much of its time buried in mud or sand. Its skin lacks pigment, giving its body a white, pasty appearance, and its gills are bright red. It has short, feeble limbs and, lacking eyes, is totally blind. Olms grow up to 30cm (12in) long and are becoming increasingly rare, partly because of pollution, but also because they are collected for the aquarist trade.

All that is known of their reproduction is based on aquarium observations. The eggs are fertilized inside the female's body and, after fertilization, she may do one of two things with them. Sometimes (abnormally, it is argued by some authorities—as a response to high temperatures) she lays 12–70 eggs beneath a stone, where both male

▼► Representative species of eight families of salamanders and newts. (1) Japanese giant salamander (*Andrias japonicus*); Cryptobranchidae. (2) Hellbender (*Cryptobranchus alleganiensis*); Cryptobranchidae. (3) *Bolitoglossa schizodactyla*; Plethodontidae. (4) Red salamander (*Pseudotriton ruber*); Salamandridae. (5) Tiger salamander (*Ambystoma tigrinum*); Ambystomatidae. (6) Olm (*Proteus anguinus*); Proteidae. (7) Mudpuppy (*Necturus maculosus*); Proteidae. (8) *Batrachuperus pinchonii*; Hynobiidae. (9) *Onychodactylus japonicus*; Hynobiidae. (10) *Tylotriton taliangensis*; Salamandridae. (11) Red-spotted newt, red eft stage (*Notophthalmus viridescens*); Salamandridae. (12) Smooth newt (*Triturus vulgaris*); Salamandridae. (13) Greater siren (*Siren lacertina*); Sirenidae. (14) Two-toed amphiuma (*Amphiuma means*); Amphiumidae.

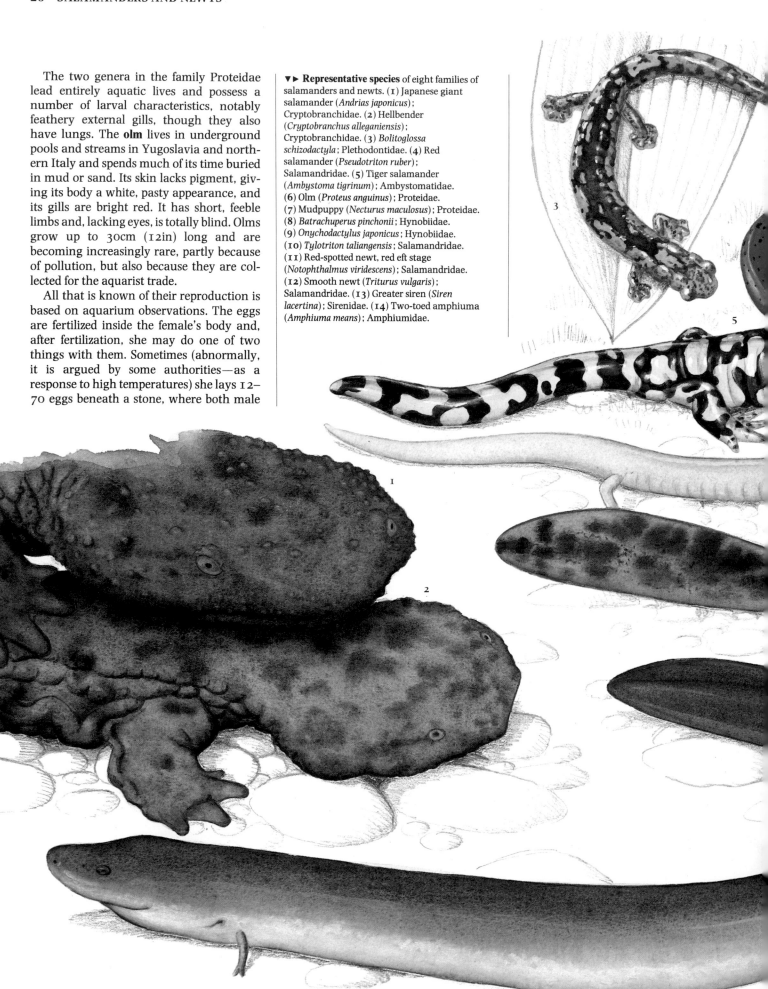

D.M.Dennis

and female guard them during their development; or just one or two eggs may develop within her body, the rest breaking down to provide nutrients for them, and the mother eventually giving birth to well-developed larvae.

The **mudpuppy** and the **waterdogs** of eastern North America are much stouter animals, with pigmented skin, that live in ponds, lakes and streams. The mudpuppy is in the northern part of the range; waterdogs are found farther south. Both names reflect the erroneous belief that these animals produce a noise like barking.

They have red or purple external gills that resemble miniature ostrich plumes; these vary in size depending on the oxygen content of the water. In stagnant water where oxygen is scarce, the gills are very large, but in well-oxygenated running streams they are quite small. Mudpuppies and waterdogs feed on a variety of animals, including insects, crayfish and fish, and they take several years to reach maturity. They mate in the fall, the eggs being fertilized internally but not laid until the following spring. A female lays 20–190 eggs, sticking them individually to logs or rocks, and the male guards them for the 5–9 weeks it takes them to develop.

The **mole salamanders** are so named because they live in burrows for much of their lives. They are rarely seen, except in the breeding season, when they migrate to ponds to mate and deposit their eggs. Found only in North America, the majority of mole salamanders are terrestrial, but all have aquatic larvae. They have heavily built bodies, broad heads and a smooth, shiny skin. Many of them have bold, colored markings.

During early spring, the Spotted salamander shows spectacular breeding migrations, converging in very large numbers on ponds where, over 2–3 days, it engages in mass mating. Females lay up to 200 eggs in the water and then return to their terrestrial life, leaving the eggs to hatch into larvae that metamorphose into the adult form 2–4 months after hatching, leaving the water in late summer or fall. By contrast, the Marbled salamander lays its eggs in the fall in dry pond beds, the female coiling herself around the eggs and guarding them until the winter rains, when they hatch into larvae.

In some parts of the United States, there are populations of various species of mole salamander in which adults are paedomorphic, remaining in the larval form even when they reach sexual maturity. The most celebrated example of this is the Mexican

axolotl which exists in both larval and terrestrial forms. The larval form will metamorphose into the terrestrial if it is injected with thyroid extract (see p10).

The Pacific giant salamander and the Olympic salamander were, until recently, included in the mole salamanders but are now placed in a small family of their own, the **Pacific mole salamanders**. They live in or near mountain streams near the west coast of North America and have lungs that are reduced in size, preventing them being buoyant and thus likely to be swept away. A large, paedomorphic form, Cope's giant salamander, may be a variant of the Pacific giant salamander or a separate species.

Much the largest family of tailed amphibians, the **lungless salamanders** are arguably the most successful group, in terms of number of individuals, among all the amphibians. In the northeastern United States they are extremely numerous.

This success is paradoxical in view of the fact that, during their evolution, they have lost one of the most basic features of all terrestrial vertebrates, their lungs. They can absorb oxygen only through their skins and mouth lining. This potentially imposes severe constraints on where they can live, how active they can be and the size to which they can grow. Large animals have a small surface area in proportion to their volume, and so have greater difficulty than small animals in supplying all their tissues with oxygen if they are dependent on their skin for respiration. Despite this, some lungless salamanders are more than 20cm (8in) long.

The most important factor in using the skin for respiration is that it must be moist at all times in order that oxygen can be taken up by the blood in capillaries beneath the skin. For this reason, lungless salamanders are confined for most of their lives to damp hiding places and they can only emerge from these in wet weather, typically at night, to mate or to find food.

The life of a lungless salamander thus consists of brief periods of activity, interspersed with often very long periods of inactivity. They are able to survive the inactivity because, having a very low metabolic rate, they have very low energy requirements. They do not need to feed very often and, when they do feed, they are able to store much of what they eat as fat. Some species are territorial, defending an area around their retreat where they feed and mate.

Lungless salamanders typically have slender bodies, long tails and prominent eyes. A distinctive feature of the family is a

► **Breathing through the skin.** The skin of lungless salamanders must be moist at all times so that the blood in capillaries beneath the skin can take up oxygen. This system of respiration confines lungless salamanders, such as this Redback salamander, to damp hiding places for much of their life.

▼ **Red-legged race** of Jordan's, or the Appalachian woodland, salamander.

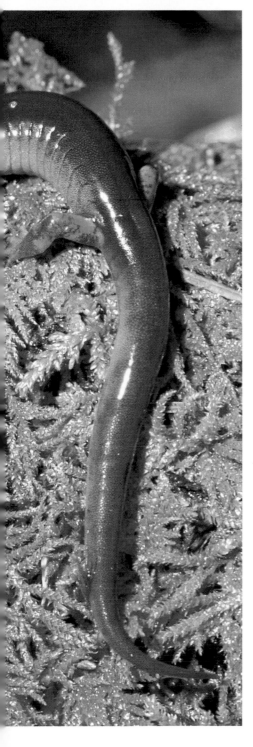

shallow groove, the nasolabial groove, running from each nostril to the upper lip. The function of this is to carry water-borne odors from the ground to the nose.

The lungless woodland salamanders are wholly terrestrial and have no aquatic larval stage. Their eggs, laid in moss or rotting logs, hatch directly into tiny replicas of their parents. Hiding by day in burrows or under logs or stones, they emerge on damp nights to feed on a wide variety of invertebrate prey, including slugs, worms and beetles. Jordan's or the Appalachian woodland salamander occurs in a wide variety of color patterns, varying from one locality to another. The basic body color is black and, while some populations are totally black, others have various combinations of red legs, cheeks and dorsal stripes. When handled, woodland salamanders produce a sticky slime that is difficult to remove from the hands. Predators such as snakes may find their jaws glued together.

The dusky salamanders are typically found near streams, where they lay their eggs. They wander far afield, however, and sometimes climb up trees and shrubs in search of food. The Mountain dusky salamander is very variable in appearance and much of this variation is due to the fact that, in some localities, it mimics the local form of Jordan's salamander; such mimetic forms are called "imitator" forms. The Pygmy salamander, whose maximum length is about 5cm (2in), lives at high altitudes, is totally terrestrial and goes through its larval stage within the egg. It is sometimes found high above the ground among foliage.

Many lungless salamanders are specialized for life in specific kinds of habitat. The Spring salamander, a brightly colored animal with a red, salmon pink or orange skin spotted with black or brown, lives in mountain streams where its wedge-shaped head enables it to push itself between rocks. The Red salamander, also bright red, burrows into the mud near springs and streams. The Cave salamander lives inside the entrances to caves where its long, prehensile (grasping) tail enables it to climb among rocks with great agility.

Perhaps the most bizarre lungless salamanders are those that live in deep caves and underground bodies of water. The Texas blind salamander of the southwestern United States bears a remarkable resemblance to the European olm, a member of another family, the Proteidae. It has thin, feeble legs, a flattened snout, vestigial eyes, pink external gills and an otherwise white body. The Grotto salamander, found in the Ozarks region of the United States, is pale pink to white in color, has vestigial eyes but has no external gills. Its life history is unique. As a larva, it lives in ordinary streams and has a typical salamander form with fully functional eyes, external gills, a large tail fin and gray or brown coloration. At metamorphosis, however, it retreats into caves and loses the tail fin, gills and skin pigmentation. Its eyes cease to grow and become covered by skin.

There are only three species of **sirens**, which are found in the southern and central United States and northeastern Mexico. They live in shallow water in ditches, streams and lakes, feeding on such animals as crayfish, worms and snails, and spending much of their time buried in mud or sand. They resemble overgrown larvae with their long eel-like bodies and external gills; they lack hindlimbs but have small, weak forelimbs positioned close behind the gills. The Greater siren can reach a length of 90cm (36in), making it one of the largest of the tailed amphibians, but the Lesser siren rarely exceeds 25cm (10in). The tiny Dwarf siren can be very numerous, particularly when it lives among water hyacinths, a water weed that has become very abundant since its introduction to North America. When grasped, sirens commonly emit a yelping sound.

Many of the ponds and ditches where sirens live dry up in the summer but they are able to survive periods of drought by going into a state called aestivation. As the sand or mud dries out, the mucous coat covering their skin hardens to form a parchment-like cocoon that covers the entire body except the mouth. They can survive in this condition for many weeks until their habitat becomes flooded once again.

Siren reproduction is something of a mystery, since mating has never been observed. The absence in males of the glands that secrete the spermatophores in many other tailed amphibians, and the absence in the female of a receptacle in which sperm could be stored, suggests that they practice external fertilization.

However, the female lays her eggs singly, dispersing them widely on aquatic vegetation, suggesting that they are fertilized before they are laid. Either sirens show a form of internal fertilization quite unlike anything seen in other tailed amphibians or the male follows the female around during egg-laying, fertilizing each egg individually as it is deposited. This requires further detailed study. TRH/PV

THE 9 FAMILIES OF SALAMANDERS AND NEWTS

Abbreviations: Length = length from snout to tip of tail. * CITES-listed E Endangered I Threatened but status indeterminate K Threat suspected but status unknown R Rare V Vulnerable. Total threatened species = numbers endangered, vulnerable, rare or of indeterminate or unknown status. Approximate nonmetric equivalents: 10cm = 4in.

The order Urodela is divided into 9 families on the basis of a wide variety of characters, some of which relate to details of the positions of the skull bones relative to one another and to the detailed distribution of teeth in the skull bones. The 9 families are sometimes grouped into three superfamilies, but some authorities place the family Sirenidae in an order, called the Meantes, separate from the other families.

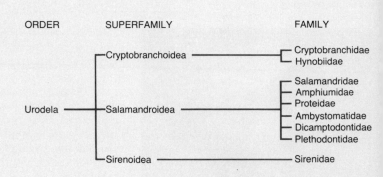

ORDER	SUPERFAMILY	FAMILY
Urodela	Cryptobranchoidea	Cryptobranchidae Hynobiidae
	Salamandroidea	Salamandridae Amphiumidae Proteidae Ambystomatidae Dicamptodontidae Plethodontidae
	Sirenoidea	Sirenidae

Superfamily Cryptobranchoidea

Giant Salamanders
Family: Cryptobranchidae
Three species in 2 genera.

Distribution: E and C USA, E China, Japan. Length: 60–160cm. Color: brown or gray. Body form: body and head massive and squat, tail short; folds of skin along flanks; eyelids lacking; lungs present; 4 fingers and 5 toes. Fertilization external. Wholly aquatic, living in flowing rivers and streams. Species include: **Chinese giant salamander** * I (*Andrias davidianus*), **hellbender** (*Cryptobranchus alleganiensis*), **Japanese giant salamander** * R (*Andrias japonicus*). Total threatened species: 2.

Asiatic Salamanders
Family Hynobiidae
Thirty-three species in 9 genera.

Distribution: C and E Asia, including Japan and Taiwan. Length: 10–21cm. Color: various. Body form: slender; tail long; eyelids movable; lungs small or absent; 4 fingers and 4–5 toes. Fertilization external. Wholly aquatic, living in fast-flowing streams with abundant oxygen. Species include: **Siberian salamander** (*Hynobius keyserlingii*).

Superfamily Salamandroidea

Newts, Brook Salamanders and Fire Salamanders
Family Salamandridae
Fifty-three species in 14 genera.

Distribution: W and E N America, Europe, Mediterranean Africa, W Asia, China, SE Asia, Japan. Length: 7–30cm. Color: brown, black or green above, yellow, orange or red below; often with dark spots. Body form: slender with long tail; rough-skinned except when in water; eyelids movable; lungs present; 4 fingers and 4–5 toes; differ from other members of Salamandroidea in lacking vertical rib grooves on the side of the body. Fertilization internal. Most breed in water and are terrestrial as adults. Species and genera include: **Alpine newt** (*Triturus alpestris*), **brook salamanders** (genus *Euproctus*), **Crested newt** (*Triturus cristatus*), **Fire salamander** (*Salamandra salamandra*), **Gold-striped salamander** V (*Chioglossa lusitanica*), **Pacific newts** (genus *Taricha*), **Palmate newt** (*Triturus helveticus*), **Redbelly newt** (*Taricha rivularis*), **Red salamander** (*Pseudotriton ruber*), **Red-spotted newt** (*Notophthalmus viridescens*), **Sharp-ribbed newt** (*Pleurodeles waltl*), **Smooth newt** (*Triturus vulgaris*), **Spiny newt** (*Echinotriton andersoni*). Total threatened species: 1.

Amphiumas
Amphiumas or "Congo eels"
Family Amphiumidae
Three species in 1 genus.

Distribution: SE USA. Length: 22–76cm, occasionally up to 116cm (46in). Color: dark brown or black above, gray below. Body form: long, eel-like and flexible; limbs very small; eyelids lacking; lungs present; 1–3 fingers and toes; vertical rib grooves along the side of the body. Fertilization internal. Wholly aquatic, living in stagnant waters and swamps. Species. **One-toed amphiuma** (*Amphiuma pholeter*), **Three-toed amphiuma** (*A. tridactylum*), **Two-toed amphiuma** (*A. means*).

Olm, Mudpuppy and Waterdogs
Family Proteidae (Necturidae)
Six species in 2 genera.

Distribution: Yugoslavia and N Italy (olm), E and C N America. Length: 11–33cm. Color: gray or brown above, gray below; olm—creamy white. Body form: head large and flat, body stout, tail short, limbs small; olm has elongated body, pointed head; eyelids lacking; lungs and external gills present; 4 fingers and 4 toes or 3 fingers and 2 toes (olm); vertical rib grooves along the side of

the body. Fertilization internal. Wholly aquatic, living in mud or stagnant water. Species include: **Gulf Coast waterdog** (*Necturus beyeri*), **mudpuppy** (*N. maculosus*), **olm** V (*Proteus anguinus*). Total threatened species: 1.

Mole Salamanders
Family Ambystomatidae
Thirty-five species in 4 genera.

Distribution: N America. Length: 8–22cm. Color: brown or black, spotted, mottled or striped with white, yellow, green, pink, orange, red or blue. Body form: sturdy, head broad, tail laterally compressed; eyelids movable; lungs present; 4 fingers and 5 toes; vertical rib grooves along the side of the body. Fertilization internal. Most breed in water, adults terrestrial. Species include: **axolotl** * R (*Ambystoma mexicanum*), **Marbled salamander** (*A. opacum*), **Santa Cruz long-toed salamander** E (*A. macrodactylum croceum*), **Spotted salamander** (*A. maculatum*), **Tiger salamander** (*A. tigrinum*). Total threatened species: 4; subspecies: 1.

Pacific Mole Salamanders
Family Dicamptodontidae
Three species in 2 genera.*

Distribution: Pacific coast of N America. Length 4–27cm; Pacific giant salamander largest terrestrial

salamander, reaching 27cm. Color: brown or gray, mottled with black (*Dicamptodon*) or brown above, yellow or orange below. Body form: sturdy, head broad, tail laterally compressed; eyelids movable; lungs small; 4 fingers, 5 toes; vertical rib grooves along side of body. Fertilization internal. Breed in water, adults terrestrial; Cope's giant salamander is paedomorphic. Species include **Cope's giant salamander** (*Dicamptodon copei*), **Pacific giant salamander** (*D. ensatus*), **Olympic salamander** (*Rhyacotriton olympicus*).

*Sometimes included as subfamily in family Ambystomatidae

Lungless Salamanders
Family Plethodontidae
Two hundred and nine species in 24 genera.

Distribution: E and W N America, C America, N S America, with two species of *Hydromantes* in SE France, Italy, Sardinia. Length: 4–21cm. Color: brown, black, red, yellow or green, many spotted, mottled or striped with red, yellow or white. Cave species, such as *Typhlomolge*, *Haideotriton* and *Typhlotriton*, white. Body form: long and slender, head narrow, tail long and cylindrical; eyelids movable; lungs absent; typically 4 fingers and 5 toes; vertical rib grooves along the side of the body. Fertilization internal. The most evolutionarily advanced salamanders, living in woodland, caves or mountain streams. Eggs mostly laid in water, adults mainly aquatic, but some terrestrial and tree-living forms. Species include: **Cave salamander** (*Eurycea lucifuga*), **Desert slender salamander** Ⓔ (*Batrachoseps aridus*), **Dusky salamander** (*Desmognathus fuscus*), **Grotto salamander** Ⓚ (*Typhlotriton spelaeus*), **Jordan's** or **Appalachian woodland** or **Red-cheeked salamander** (*Plethodon jordani*), **Mountain dusky salamander** (*Desmognathus ochrophaeus*), **Spring salamander** (*Gyrinophilus porphyriticus*), **Pygmy salamander**

(*Desmognathus wrighti*), **Red salamander** (*Pseudotriton ruber*), **Redback salamander** (*Plethodon cinereus*), **Slimy salamander** (*P. glutinosus*), **Tennessee cave salamander** (*Gyrinophilus palleucus*), **Texas blind salamander** Ⓔ (*Typhlomolge rathbuni*), **Two-lined salamander** (*Eurycea bislineata*). Total threatened species: 13.

Superfamily Sirenoidea

Sirens
Family Sirenidae
Three species in 2 genera.

Distribution: E and C USA, NE Mexico. Length: 10–90cm. Color: olive green or dark gray with pale spots. Body form: eel-like, with external gills and tiny forelimbs close

▲ **Miniature salamander.**
Several species of tiny lungless salamanders of Central America are highly arboreal, their small size enabling them to crawl about on foliage. Small size has been achieved by halting development at an early stage, when hands and feet are not as fully developed as they are in typical adult salamanders. The fingers and toes are short and they retain webbing which, in other salamanders, disappears in the later stages of limb development. This is *Bolitoglossa lignicolor*.

to gills; eyelids lacking; eyes very small; lungs present; 3–4 fingers; no hind limbs. Fertilization mode uncertain. Live permanently in muddy pools. Species: **Dwarf siren** (*Pseudobranchus striatus*), **Greater siren** (*Siren lacertina*), **Lesser siren** (*S. intermedia*).

Courtship

Twists and turns in salamanders and newts

The great majority of newts and salamanders show an unusual form of mating. Fertilization is internal, the sperm meeting the eggs inside the female's body, but the male has no penis to introduce the sperm into the female's body. Instead, sperm is passed from male to female in a capsule called a spermatophore: this has two parts, a broad base surmounted by a sperm-filled cap. In salamanders mating on land the base is rigid and hard; in newts, all of which mate in water, it is a soft, fluid-filled sac. In both situations the function of the base is to hold the sperm cap above the ground or the floor of the pond, where it can be picked up by the female's cloaca. The base is secreted by a variety of glands that open into the male's cloaca.

The transfer of sperm involves complex and elaborate forms of behavior. In many salamanders, the male captures the female and clasps her in a firm grip called amplexus. Species vary as to which limbs they use; various combinations of limbs and tail may be involved (see BELOW). In salamanders such as the European Fire salamander and the mountain salamanders of

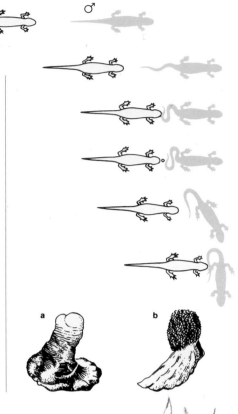

► **Spermatophore transfer behavior** in the Smooth newt. The spermatophore is visible in the fourth position shown. Spermatophores of (**a**) the Dusky salamander and (**b**) the Two-lined salamander.

▼ **Amplexus in three salamanders and newts.** (**1**) The Fire salamander, a terrestrial European species. The male clasps the female from below; he deposits a spermatophore on the ground and then flicks his body and tail to one side so that the female's cloaca falls onto it. (**2**) An aquatic European brook salamander. The male captures the female with his tail and the spermatophore is transferred from the male's cloaca directly to the female's. (**3**) The Red-spotted newt, an aquatic North American species. The male clasps the female's neck with his powerful hind limbs; in this position he rubs large glands on his cheek over her nostrils.

Corsica, Sardinia and the Pyrenees, amplexus is maintained throughout mating, and the spermatophore is transferred directly to the female. In species like the North American Red-spotted and Redbelly newts, the male clasps the female initially but releases her just before the transfer of the spermatophore. In the European Smooth newt and in the North American woodland salamanders, there is no amplexus and the female is free to move about at all stages of courtship.

Amplexus fulfills two functions; the male can hold the female while stimulating her with secretions from various glands and it is a means by which he can prevent other males reaching and attempting to court her. In species in which the female is free to move during mating, she must be stimulated by the male before she will behave appropriately. Male newts and salamanders possess a variety of glands producing secretions for this purpose, applied to the female in a variety of ways (see ABOVE).

In contrast to the variety between species in the behavior they perform in the initial phases of courtship, many show very similar behavior during spermatophore transfer. The male creeps in front of the female and then stops, quivering his tail. The female touches his tail and the male responds by depositing a spermatophore. He then creeps away from it, moving through an arc so that he takes up a position perpendicular to his previous direction. He then stops and prevents the female, who has followed him, from moving further. She nudges his tail again and she is now positioned with her cloaca directly above the spermatophore. The sperm mass is taken up by the female's cloaca, leaving the spermatophore base behind. TRH

▲ **Application of sexual stimulants** in salamanders and newts. (1) The Two-lined salamander, a semi-aquatic North American species. The male has protruding teeth (1a) with which he lacerates the female's skin, after first covering it with secretions from his chin gland. (2) Jordan's salamander, a terrestrial woodland species from eastern North America. The male leads the female, repeatedly turning to slap a gland under his chin against the female's snout. (3) The Redbelly newt, an aquatic species from western North America. The male clasps the female with both fore- and hind limbs and rubs a gland under his chin over her nostrils. (4) The Smooth newt. The male fans his tail to generate a water current that carries odor from numerous skin glands to the female's nose.

Repellent Defenders
Antipredator mechanisms in salamanders and newts

Salamanders and newts are attacked and eaten by shrews, birds, snakes, other salamanders and even beetles, centipedes and spiders. Heavy pressure from these predators has led to the evolution of antipredator mechanisms which combine repulsive or toxic secretions of skin glands with other defensive devices.

Certain species have concentrations of glands at the back of the head (paratoid glands) producing unpalatable secretions. A number of these, such as the Spotted salamander, bend their heads down or hold them flat against the ground when attacked, thus presenting a predator with the most distasteful part of their bodies. More complex is the head-butting behavior of some mole salamanders and newts, eg the Sharp-ribbed newt of Spain, Portugal and Morocco. The body is held high off the ground, the head is bent down and the back of the head, bearing well-developed glands, is swung or lunged into the predator, an effective way of repulsing shrews. Most species vocalize while head butting, and in several the glands are brightly colored with spots of yellow or orange as a warning to experienced attackers. Predators without color vision, such as shrews, probably learn to recognize the distinctive odors or vocalizations of these salamanders.

Tail lashing is characteristic of species with well-developed tail muscles and concentrations of poison glands on the upper surface of this appendage. The Sharp-ribbed newt is once again an example, and shrews are typical of the predators repelled. This behavior draws the attention of the attacker to a repellent part of the anatomy which is also one that can receive wounds without debilitating the defender. There is sometimes warning coloration on the upper surface.

Many species have concentrations of skin glands on the upper surfaces of long, slender tails which are not strong enough to lash at attackers. Some of these species undulate their tails, usually in a vertical position, while holding their bodies still. This is most common among the lungless salamanders, which are also often capable of shedding their tails. The distastefulness of the object to which the attack is directed deters future attacks, and its wild thrashings after it breaks off distract the predator while the salamander escapes to grow a new one.

Some newts are also tail undulators, but under intense attack shift to the "unken reflex" which is more characteristic of their family: they hold themselves rigidly immobile with tail and chin elevated, showing brightly colored undersides. Birds quickly learn to avoid species such as the Alpine newt of Europe, an inedible animal with an upper surface abundantly supplied with poison glands, and a deep yellow to red belly. Imitators in the genera *Desmognathus*, *Gyrinophilus*, *Pseudotriton* and *Eurycea* take advantage of this successful form of defense by mimicking the warning colors of poisonous species. The immobility of a salamander showing the unken reflex has the effect of inhibiting the attack reflexes of predatory birds, so that the likelihood is reduced of a serious wound from a bird that has not yet learned that the salamander, or a species it is mimicking, is inedible.

Perhaps the most remarkable antipredator mechanism belongs to the Sharp-ribbed and Spiny newts which, in addition to their other defenses, have elongated, sharp ribs whose tips protrude through pores in the skin when these animals are grasped. The rib tips of Spiny newts pass through clusters of enlarged glands on the side of the body, and skin secretions causing intense pain are injected into the mouths of would-be predators.   EDB

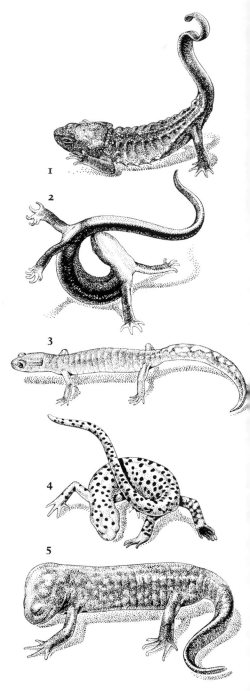

▲ **Defensive postures.** (1) Low-intensity unken reflex in the Spiny newt. (2) High-intensity unken reflex in the Redbelly newt. (3) Tail lashing in the ensatina (*Ensatina eschscholtzii*). (4) Undulating tail posture in the Cave salamander. (5) Head-butting in the Mole salamander (*Ambystoma talpoideum*).

▶ **Unken reflex.** A Roughskin newt (*Taricha granulosa*) of North America lifts its head and tail, to reveal its brightly colored ventral surface, and becomes immobile.

◀ **Poison-rib defense.** The Spiny newt, a Chinese species, has long, sharp-pointed ribs. If it is grasped by a predator, the ribs push out through poison glands in the skin.

FROGS

Order: Anura (Salientia)
Three thousand four hundred and ninety-four
species in 303 genera and 20 families.
Distribution: all continents except Antarctica.
Nearly all habitat types colonized. Absent from
the polar regions and very dry deserts. Adults
terrestrial, amphibious or aquatic.

Size: snout-to-vent length from 1–35cm
(0.4–14in), but most are in the range 2–12cm
(0.8–4.8in).

Color: extremely variable including green,
brown, black, red, orange, yellow, white.

Reproduction: fertilization mostly external;
eggs may be laid in water or on moist ground
or develop in or on one of the parents. Embryos
of most species pass through a free-swimming
and feeding tadpole stage but in some they may
be immobile, feeding only on the yolk sac and
developing directly into froglets.

Longevity: in captivity adults commonly live 1–
10 years; some true toads reported to live over
30 years in captivity; very little is known about
longevity in the wild.

FROGS and toads are the most numerous
and diverse of the amphibians—about
3,500 species occupy habitats ranging from
deserts, savannas and high mountains to
tropical rain forests. Although most live
both in water and on land at least for parts
of their lives, some are entirely aquatic and
others entirely terrestrial.

The richest variety is found in the tropics
and subtropics (more than 80 percent of all
species), but even so, a great many have successfully colonized the temperate zones.
They are found on most islands and on all
continents except Antarctica. The European
common frog and the Wood frog of North
American have ranges extending north of
the Arctic Circle.

The Body Plan of Tail-less Amphibians
The main feature that distinguishes frogs
and toads from other living amphibians is
the absence of a tail in the adult stage. They
have evolved a jumping life-style in which
a tail would be a hindrance (see pp56–57).
The body is very much shorter than in other
amphibians; there are at most nine
vertebrae in the backbone compared with
30–100 in newts and salamanders, and up
to 250 in caecilians. A short, rigid backbone
has proved essential to withstand the forces
involved in leaping, landing and burrowing
in soil.

"Frogs" are smooth-skinned, long-limbed
and living in water, and "toads" are ugly,
stout-bodied, warty-skinned creatures living in dark, damp places away from water.
However, these two body types have evolved
several times as adaptations to two ways of
life and do not reflect any important separation between evolutionary lines: there are
many families containing both "frog" and
"toad" species. No scientific distinction is

blurred by referring to all simply as frogs.
Frogs which live mainly in water tend to
have slender, elongated bodies, long heads
with tapering snouts and extremely long
hind legs. Such a streamlined body form is
ideal for jumping and swimming. On land,
these frogs tend to be very shy, and when
disturbed, immediately leap into water and
swim away very quickly. Those which live
on land or burrow underground tend to
have short, squat bodies and very short legs.
Their feet are usually broad, with spade-like
digits and horny lumps of skin (tubercules)
to assist in burrowing. Some species also
have sharp ridges on the head and snout
which act as cutting edges for digging into
hard earth. Tree-dwelling frogs have rather
flattened bodies for resting and maintaining

▲ **Belligerent and big-mouthed,** this horned toad, *Ceratophrys dorsata* from Surinam, snaps at almost any moving object and can feed on other frogs.

◄ **Toe pads and loose belly skin** enable tree frogs, like this strikingly marked South American species, *Hyla leucophyllata*, to cling to vertical surfaces.

balance on the flat surfaces of leaves and tree trunks. The skin of the belly is loose and can be pressed tightly against any surface. Many tree frogs have large areas of sticky webbing between their fingers and toes which serve a similar purpose to the loose belly skin. Some species have extra bones or cartilages in their toes which enable them to grip onto thin twigs, and the ends of their toes are expanded into circular, adhesive disks, enabling them to climb up smooth, vertical surfaces.

The head of a frog is flush with its body; there is no constricted neck. The nostrils and eyes are usually on top of the skull so that, when sitting in water, the animal can breathe and watch, with the rest of the body hidden from view. Adults have lungs for

breathing air on land, and they also obtain oxygen directly through the skin. Some frogs living in water which is very low in dissolved oxygen have extremely baggy skin or hair-like projections enriched with blood capillaries; these modifications increase the area of the respiratory surface and make the most of a poor oxygen supply.

The eyes are large and in most species inclined very slightly forward. The area just in front of the snout is a blind spot, so when feeding on prey (usually small arthropods) just in front of the snout, a frog must turn its head slightly to one side. Some species have specialized receptors in the retina and brain to detect small moving objects—so-called "bug detectors." The eyes have special glands to keep them moist and they are protected from dust and soil by movable lids. Just behind the eye of most species is a large and conspicuous eardrum (tympanum). Frogs are the most primitive vertebrates to have a middle ear cavity for transferring sound vibrations from the eardrum to the inner ear. Correlated with this development of the ear is the appearance of a true voice box (larynx) and a large, expandable vocal sac, making possible a wide variety of vocalizations (see pp58–59).

Temperature and Water Regulation

Frogs are "cold-blooded" animals (ectotherms) and although they produce some internal heat by metabolism, they are primarily dependent on environmental sources of heat to regulate body temperature. Their body temperature is usually very close to that of their surroundings and ranges from 3–36°C (37–97°F) depending on climatic conditions. At low temperatures during temperate zone winters, it is impossible for them to maintain activity and their only option is to enter torpor. Most species can survive temperatures between 0–9°C (32–48°F) for long periods during torpor, and some, such as the European common frog and the Wood frog in North America can survive temperatures as low as –6°C (21°F). Some frogs increase their body temperature during the day by basking in the sun with their bodies and legs outstretched, but as this involves water loss, basking is restricted to species which live close to permanent water. Frogs living in very hot climates avoid heat by burrowing during the day and only come to the surface at night.

In general, frogs have not been able to escape the need to spend at least some stage of their life cycle in water, and on land they face a potentially hostile world from the point of view of water retention. This is especially true in deserts. When submerged in water, these animals can absorb water and salts through the skin and the surfaces lining the mouth cavity and lungs, but they have no physiological ability to control evaporation of body water on land.

Desert-living species are the most tolerant of water loss. The Western spadefoot toad of the dry plains and deserts of North America can tolerate up to a 60 percent reduction in body water, whereas the aquatic Pig frog will only tolerate a 40 percent loss. Arid-zone species can also rehydrate more rapidly than species from wetter regions. Some toads, such as true and spadefoot toads, can absorb water simply by sitting on an area of damp soil. The skin on the lower surface of the body is thin and rich in blood vessels: they have an absorbent seat-patch.

Many burrowing frogs can store water in the bladder, which enables them to remain underground for long periods without drying out. When water is needed it simply moves through the bladder walls into the body. The Australian Water-holding frog has large, baggy lymph glands beneath the skin and appears bloated when fully hydrated, water making up half its weight. This and other burrowers secrete a special outer layer of skin which separates from the remainder in one piece and acts as a water-retaining cocoon. Burrowing frogs may remain inactive during dry periods lasting for many months, even several years. In spadefoot toads, emergence from below ground after a dry spell is triggered by the sound of rain pit-pattering on the surface; no increase in soil moisture is needed.

Some frogs living in dry regions combine unusual anatomy with remarkable behavior to avoid water loss. The casque-headed tree frogs have skulls heavily ornamented with crests, ridges and flanges. They use their peculiar heads for "phragmosis," filling cavities and blocking holes where moisture might escape from their refuges. A few frogs are known to excrete uric acid in a semisolid form rather than urea which is water soluble and involves a much greater water loss.

Reproduction and Development

Frogs and toads are most conspicuous during the breeding season. Then they gather together, often in aggregations numbering hundreds or thousands of individuals, and produce an impressive noise (see p58) which may be heard from a great distance. Most frog populations are scattered over a wide area when they are feeding and they must migrate to a suitable breeding site when conditions are right. The length of daylight, temperature and rainfall seem to be the three main factors which trigger breeding activity.

Migrations to breeding areas are often highly synchronized and may involve large numbers of animals. This is especially true in arid zones, simply because there are not many occasions when conditions are suitable for breeding. The spring migration of Australian Water-holding frogs to their breeding sites was once so enormous that it interfered with the services of the transcontinental railway in central Australia. So many frogs were squashed on the rails that train wheels were unable to gain traction on the slippery surface.

▲ **Digging backwards.** Typically of burrowing frogs, a Meeoioing frog (*Neobatrachus pictus*) of Australia uses its hind feet to excavate a vertical shaft into the mud.

▼▶ **Mating grip – amplexus.** Most frogs and toads mate in water, the male grasping the female tightly in a position called amplexus. BELOW In many of the more primitive frogs the male clasps the female around her waist (inguinal amplexus), as in the Gold frog from southeastern Brazil. RIGHT In advanced species the male usually clasps the female under her armpits (axillary amplexus), as in these Golden toads in Costa Rica. In all amplexus, the clasping reflex of the male depends on the female's size and shape; males will not often clasp females who have already laid their eggs, but if they do, the female gives a special release call to indicate that she is spent. With very few exceptions, fertilization takes place outside the body as the female extrudes the eggs.

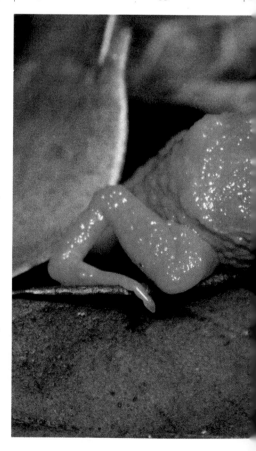

Some species which breed in permanent ponds or lakes show remarkable site-fidelity, returning to exactly the same pond year after year. Even if individuals are transported to other suitable ponds in the area, they will attempt to return to the pond which they have visited before. Several environmental cues are probably involved in migration to breeding ponds, including smell, humidity gradients, landmarks, the position of celestial bodies, magnetic fields and the calls of other frogs. For a long time it was thought that European common frogs find their "home" pond by smell, but this cannot be the only cue used because there are frequent reports of frogs returning to sites where ponds have been drained, filled in or built over.

The egg masses of frogs and toads deposited in water vary enormously in size and shape. In cold water, egg masses tend to be globular in shape, whereas in warmer water where oxygen levels are low, the eggs form a thin film over the surface so that each embryo can obtain sufficient oxygen. Frogs belonging to several families lay their eggs not directly into water but in elaborate foam nests floating on water or suspended from vegetation overhanging water. Egg laying sites may be situated above water-filled depressions in branches of trees, or in ponds specially constructed by males. The foam is made from a small amount of fluid secreted by the female and is whipped up by the female's energetic kicking until it sets and hardens like a meringue. In some tree-nesting species, one or more males assist in whipping up the foam. When the tadpoles hatch, the foam nest begins to dissolve and they fall into the water below.

Instead of abandoning many small eggs in water, some species have adopted the habit of laying fewer, larger eggs and looking after them carefully. Parental care in frogs is often, though not always, part of a shift towards laying eggs on land. Parental duties frequently involve sitting on the eggs, to keep them moist and to protect them from predators, or transporting eggs or tadpoles to water on their backs. In a few species the tadpoles complete their development with one of the parents in special, sometimes bizarre, brood pouches (see pp14–15, 47). Female West African live-bearing toads nourish the developing embryos within their oviducts in a way that compares with placental mammals (see p8).

Frog tadpoles are a contrast to larvae of other amphibians. Tadpoles have short backs and almost spherical bodies. Their mainly vegetarian diet requires a long gut

with large absorbing surfaces, coiled up into a tight ball. Most are herbivorous grazers or browsers, rasping off vegetable matter from algae and other water plants. Sometimes herbivorous tadpoles scavenge on the carcasses of dead or dying animals, but the tadpoles of a few species, such as the South American bullfrog, are truly carnivorous and have a much shorter gut than the herbivores. Most tadpoles are also capable of filter-feeding and can survive for months without visible food, as they take algae and other small particles from the water surrounding them. Water is taken in through the mouth, passed over the gills to filter out plankton and finally expelled to the outside through a tube—the spiracle. By gargling it past the gill chamber surfaces, tadpoles also extract oxygen from the water.

The mouthparts of most tadpoles consist of a pair of fleshy lips with rows of horny teeth arranged upon them like the teeth of a comb. The number and appearance of the teeth (which are unlike the jaw teeth of adults) varies and is an important feature in the identification of species. Some tadpoles have a sharp extension of the upper jaw (called a beak) and fleshy, tubular, sensory extensions of skin (barbels or tentacles).

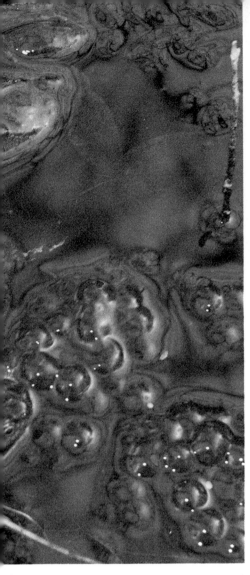

▲ **Breeding group** of the European common frog around a communal spawn site. Eggs laid close together gain some safety in numbers from predators and maintain a higher temperature than the surrounding water.

◄ **Paternal care.** A male Stream frog, a poison-arrow frog of Trinidad and Venezuela, carrying tadpoles on his back.

▼ **Shoaling tadpoles** of the Map tree frog (*Hyla geographica*) in Trinidad gain safety in numbers from predators and, through vigorously spiralling, sometimes stir up food from the bottom of the pond. In some species, individuals shoal with their siblings.

For detecting pressure changes and vibrations in the water, tadpoles possess lateral-line organs: a series of special sensory cells (neuromasts) lying in orderly rows on the head and body. In some totally aquatic frogs (eg the clawed toads) the lateral line system is retained by adults.

The tadpole stage lasts from a few days in some species to over three years in others. The trend towards rapid development is taken furthest in species which breed on land. Embryos of terrestrial breeders often undergo "direct" development: instead of having a free-swimming, free-feeding tadpole stage, the tadpoles are immobile and only feed on the nutrients provided in the yolk sac. In species with direct development, many stages which aquatic tadpoles normally pass through seem to be absent. For example, the embryonic stages of frogs in the genus *Eleutherodactylus* lack many tadpole characters and hatch from terrestrial eggs as fully formed miniature frogs.

Clutch sizes vary from 2–20,000 eggs. The smallest clutch sizes are found in species with parental care or direct development and the largest in those which lay aquatic eggs and then abandon them.

Frogs and Man

Frogs are eaten in many parts of the world, but they have mostly been considered a delicacy by gourmets rather than a major source of nutrition. In Europe, the Edible frog, a hybrid of the Marsh and Pool frogs, is the main table species, but recently there has been a trend towards importing frogs' legs (often inhumanely collected) from the developing countries. Most species are edible, but it is only economical to market the larger ones, eg the American and Asian bullfrogs. In the South American Andes, local people collect giant leptodactylid frogs and roast them whole. Although the flesh of a frog has a high protein content, a slow rate of development has meant that frog farming has never really caught on.

Frogs are widely used for teaching and research, and studies of the anatomy and functions of organs and organ systems in frogs have contributed immeasurably to our understanding of the evolution of vertebrates. Experiments on frogs have shed light on suitable methods for organ transplants and they were widely used for human pregnancy tests until better methods were devised. Techniques have also been developed to extract certain alkaloids from poisonous species for use in therapeutic drugs.

Despite the benefits man has gained through the study of frogs, the effect of human activity on these animals has usually been negative. In some areas, a threat has arisen due to over-collecting certain species for use in laboratories and for food, but much more harmful is man's indirect effect through habitat destruction. Over three-quarters of all species occur in tropical rain forests which are being destroyed at an ever-accelerating rate. The clearing of land for buildings, the drainage of swamps and marshes, the damming of rivers to form lakes, acid rain and the heating of water as part of the cooling process of nuclear power plants have all had adverse effects on frog populations. The use of pesticides and herbicides on crops has also contributed to the demise of some populations: adults are affected when they eat contaminated arthropods, and run-off makes ponds, streams and lakes unsuitable for developing tadpoles.

Families of Frogs and Toads

Adults of the **Tailed frog** from northwestern North America and of the **New Zealand frogs** share a number of primitive features and together make up the family Leiopelmatidae. Both have a small prepubis bone projecting forward from the pelvis (in most frogs it is fused with and not distinct from the pelvis) and a backbone with nine vertebrae, the maximum for living frogs and toads. However, they are widely separated geographically and have different life-styles and embryonic development.

The Tailed frog, found in fast-flowing mountain streams, is one of the few frogs known to have internal fertilization. Its name comes from the male's small, 5–6mm (0.2–0.24in) tail-like appendage, really a cloaca turned inside out, for fertilizing the female; because this species mates in fast-flowing water, external sperm would be swept away before reaching the eggs. The voiceless male finds a mate by swimming along the bottom of the stream. The tadpoles possess large suckers on the mouth for clinging onto rocks when feeding.

Adult male New Zealand frogs do not possess a tail but retain apparently redundant tail-wagging muscles from their tadpole stage. They live on mountainsides where streams and pools of water are scarce. Fertilization is external, and the females lay small clutches of unpigmented, heavily-yolked eggs (1–22) in damp crevices under rocks and logs. The male provides parental care by remaining with the eggs, and in Hamilton's frog the tadpoles climb onto his back, where they are kept moist.

The **disk-tongued toads** are a small, rather

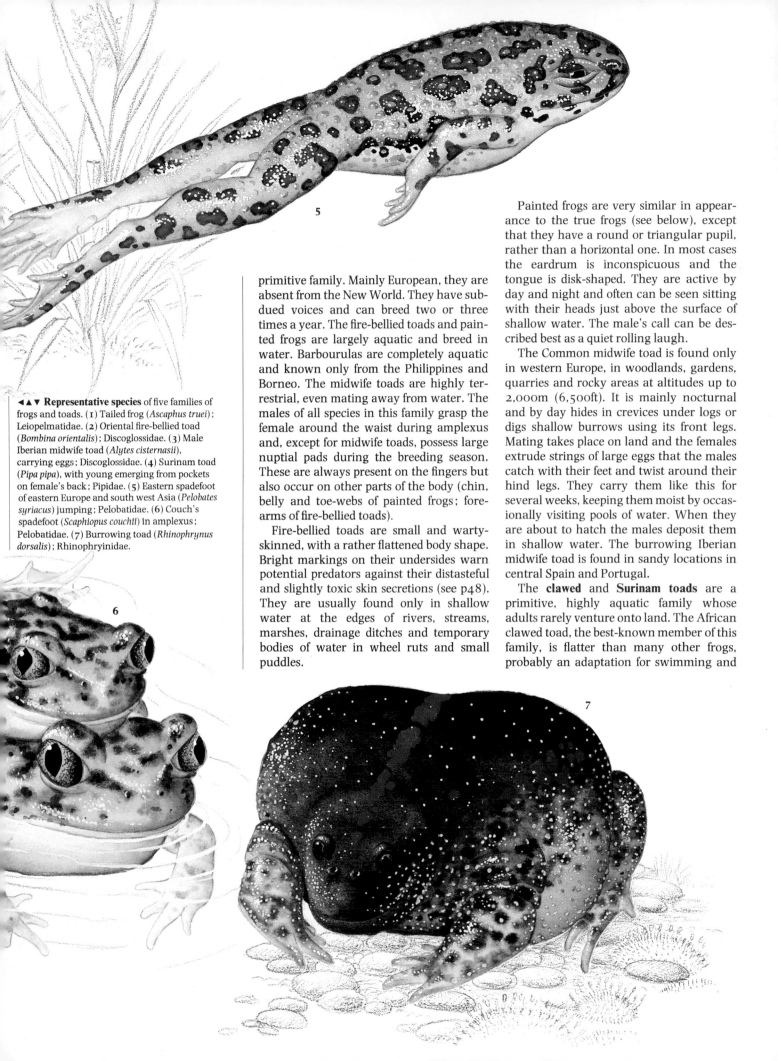

◄▲▼ **Representative species** of five families of frogs and toads. (1) Tailed frog (*Ascaphus truei*); Leiopelmatidae. (2) Oriental fire-bellied toad (*Bombina orientalis*); Discoglossidae. (3) Male Iberian midwife toad (*Alytes cisternasii*), carrying eggs; Discoglossidae. (4) Surinam toad (*Pipa pipa*), with young emerging from pockets on female's back; Pipidae. (5) Eastern spadefoot of eastern Europe and south west Asia (*Pelobates syriacus*) jumping; Pelobatidae. (6) Couch's spadefoot (*Scaphiopus couchii*) in amplexus; Pelobatidae. (7) Burrowing toad (*Rhinophrynus dorsalis*); Rhinophryinidae.

primitive family. Mainly European, they are absent from the New World. They have subdued voices and can breed two or three times a year. The fire-bellied toads and painted frogs are largely aquatic and breed in water. Barbourulas are completely aquatic and known only from the Philippines and Borneo. The midwife toads are highly terrestrial, even mating away from water. The males of all species in this family grasp the female around the waist during amplexus and, except for midwife toads, possess large nuptial pads during the breeding season. These are always present on the fingers but also occur on other parts of the body (chin, belly and toe-webs of painted frogs; forearms of fire-bellied toads).

Fire-bellied toads are small and warty-skinned, with a rather flattened body shape. Bright markings on their undersides warn potential predators against their distasteful and slightly toxic skin secretions (see p48). They are usually found only in shallow water at the edges of rivers, streams, marshes, drainage ditches and temporary bodies of water in wheel ruts and small puddles.

Painted frogs are very similar in appearance to the true frogs (see below), except that they have a round or triangular pupil, rather than a horizontal one. In most cases the eardrum is inconspicuous and the tongue is disk-shaped. They are active by day and night and often can be seen sitting with their heads just above the surface of shallow water. The male's call can be described best as a quiet rolling laugh.

The Common midwife toad is found only in western Europe, in woodlands, gardens, quarries and rocky areas at altitudes up to 2,000m (6,500ft). It is mainly nocturnal and by day hides in crevices under logs or digs shallow burrows using its front legs. Mating takes place on land and the females extrude strings of large eggs that the males catch with their feet and twist around their hind legs. They carry them like this for several weeks, keeping them moist by occasionally visiting pools of water. When they are about to hatch the males deposit them in shallow water. The burrowing Iberian midwife toad is found in sandy locations in central Spain and Portugal.

The **clawed** and **Surinam toads** are a primitive, highly aquatic family whose adults rarely venture onto land. The African clawed toad, the best-known member of this family, is flatter than many other frogs, probably an adaptation for swimming and

burrowing into mud at the bottom of ponds. It has very long hind legs with long webbed toes splayed out sideways. The shorter front legs also project out from the sides of the body and are unable to support the toad on land, where it cannot survive long periods; when occasionally it does have to cross land, it can move quite quickly by making a series of clumsy leaps, landing flat on its belly and slithering forward. The flat head appears small relative to the rest of the body, and the eyes are very small and directed upwards rather than forwards, an advantage to an animal which spends much of its time lying on the bottom of pools watching for predators and prey to approach from above. The smooth skin is covered by a layer of unpleasant-smelling slime which may help to deter predators.

The African clawed toad typically lives in stagnant pools where oxygen concentrations are very low. It has a poor supply of blood vessels to the skin, but the lungs are much larger in proportion to its body size than those of many other frogs. It seems that this species has little respiration through the skin, but instead obtains oxygen by coming to the surface regularly to gulp air.

Another species, *Xenopus borealis*, has a sound production mechanism unique among vertebrates, allowing it to produce underwater calls at very high intensities; more than 300 clicks can be produced per minute in 5–15 minutes between breaths. The male's voice box lacks vocal cords and is divided into 4 air-filled chambers. Besides the glottis (the opening at the top of the windpipe), the only movable structures are two cartilage disks controlled by large muscles. As the disks are moved apart, a vacuum is created and air rushes into the gap producing a loud, implosive click. The voice box acts as a tuned internal vocal sac and radiates the clicks into the surrounding water.

The Surinam toads are easily recognized because they are shaped somewhat like squarish pancakes. The head is flat on top but there are peculiar flaps of skin around the jaws which break up the toad's outline. The nose is pointed, and the tiny, lidless black eyes look like minute beads. Their color tends to be a uniform blackish brown, almost invisible against the black mud of the Amazon and Orinoco Rivers where they live. Their star-shaped fingertips are covered in glandular hairs; even in thick mud or at

▲ **Leaf imitator.** The Casque-headed frog (*Hemiphractus proboscideus*) of Ecuador is protected from predators by its resemblance to dead leaves. Wholly terrestrial in its habits, this species carries its eggs on its back, where they hatch directly into young frogs.

▼ **Lateral-line organs,** resembling small white stiches in the skin along the side of this clawed toad's body, detect water-borne vibrations created by prey and enemies. This is *Xenopus muelleri,* an inhabitant of ponds and rivers in South Africa.

flood time, when the rivers are opaque with silt, these toads can find food by sweeping the mud with their fingers and seizing any small animals that they find.

The eggs of Surinam toads develop in special pits in the soft skin of the female's back. The way in which the eggs are transferred onto the female's back has been observed in the best-known species, the Surinam toad (see p14).

The **Burrowing toad** is the only living member of its family. It shares several anatomical features with the clawed and Surinam toads but leads a terrestrial life. An egg-shaped, short-legged, toothless creature, its hind feet are specialized for digging and the first toe on each foot is a single, shovel-shaped bone. Alongside this toe is a bony projection (prehallux) which is covered with thick skin and acts as a spade. The front of the tongue is not attached to the floor of the mouth and, when feeding, this toad can protrude its tongue slowly like a mammal, rather than flick it out in the usual frog fashion. It feeds almost exclusively on ants and termites. The tadpoles do not possess lips or a beak but have instead a large number of sensory barbels (tentacle-like projections) radiating from a simple, slit-like mouth.

The Pelobatidae, comprising the **spadefoot toads, horned toads** and **parsley frogs,** possess a combination of primitive and advanced characteristics, mainly skeletal features, and are considered intermediate between the primitive and advanced families. The adults are specialized for burrowing and tolerate high levels of water loss. Tadpoles reach metamorphosis quickly in temporary pools.

Spadefoot toads (subfamily Pelobatinae) are usually confined to dry areas with sandy soils. There are two genera, *Pelobates* in Europe and Asia and *Scaphiopus* in North America. Adults are strictly nocturnal, and during the day and during long dry periods they hide in deep, almost vertical burrows. They dig these using the spades on their hind feet alternately. On warm, moist nights during the summer they emerge to feed, eating almost any kind of terrestrial arthropod. Outside the breeding season the adults do not move very much, but sit and wait for prey to come to them. The home range of the Eastern spadefoot is estimated at no more than 9sq m (100sq ft).

Breeding usually occurs during the spring with the onset of the first heavy rains following several warm days. Toads sometimes appear in great numbers. In two days, the females have finished laying their eggs and

Marine Toads in Australia

In the 1930s, Australian sugar cane growers greeted with enthusiasm reports about a toad from Central and South America which had been introduced to Puerto Rican cane fields in 1920. Up to 23cm (9in) from snout to vent, it was variously called the Giant, Marine or Mexican toad. In Puerto Rico it was said to have eaten large numbers of sugar cane pests and there was hope that it could help to control the Grayback cane beetle (*Dermolepida albohirtum*) BELOW LEFT which menaced Australian sugar cane.

In spite of warnings that without natural enemies, and breeding all year round, the toad would soon become as much an imported pest as the rabbit or the cactus, 100 adult toads were imported in 1935. Of more than 1.5 million eggs laid by these, 62,000 reached the young adult stage and were released into selected sugar growing areas of Queensland, where they became known as the Cane toad.

Despite their voracious appetite, the toads did not live up to farmers' expectations. Queensland cane fields provided inadequate cover for daytime hiding and the toads quickly moved out to surrounding countryside and into gardens. Here they achieved an extremely rapid population increase of near-plague proportions. Today they are so abundant in some places that nighttime gardens become a slowly moving, dark, shuffling sea of toads, and in the morning roads are littered with squashed bodies run over in the night.

More troubling is the evidence that these toads eat just as many creatures that are beneficial to agriculture as they eat pests, and naturalists are worried that the toads may be numerous enough to have a damaging effect on the populations of native frogs which contribute to their diet.

One unexpected benefit of the Marine toad's introduction, however, is its usefulness as a laboratory animal in schools, universities and hospitals.

Shown here is a holding pen awaiting shipment BELOW are some of the 100,000 used every year in Australia for research and teaching. In addition, large numbers are exported to other countries for these purposes. Raw marine toad skins are tanned for leather BELOW RIGHT.

the toads are nowhere to be seen. The voice is a loud and harsh clucking which can be heard from more than 2km (1.25mi) when many males are calling together. Sometimes males fight for females, which may be wounded by the sharp spades on the struggling males' hind feet. In Swedish populations of the European common spadefoot, females are often found during the breeding season with oblong wounds on the belly; some die through infection or loss of blood.

Spadefoots lay their eggs in short, thick bands wound around the stems of water plants. They hatch in as little as 1.5 days and tadpoles may reach metamorphosis in 15–20 days. The feeding tadpoles sometimes swim about in huge aggregations, creating whirlpools which suck up and concentrate plankton and organic material from the bottom of the pool. The tadpoles filter out food by passing water over their gills. Some tadpoles of desert-dwelling spadefoots develop different jaws and teeth from algae-eating tadpoles of the same species and become cannibals, growing to an enormous size, often reaching 10cm (4in) in length and occasionally 18cm (7in). With two types of tadpole in a breeding pool, the desert spadefoots are prepared for different eventualities. If more rain falls, algae-eaters will thrive. If there is no more rain, the cannibals will feast on stranded herbivores.

The horned toads (subfamily Megophryinae) occur in Southeast Asia. There are 76 species, some quite spectacular. The Malaysian horned toad has flexible extensions of skin on each upper eyelid and on the snout so that it appears to have three horns. The body is mottled with various shades of brown and the skin is ribbed so that it takes on the appearance of a dead leaf. This species is almost impossible to find when it is resting on the forest floor, but the males become conspicuous during heavy rain when they sit in shallow streams and produce very loud mechanical-sounding "clanks." The tadpoles of some horned toads have many horny teeth radiating from the large mouth aperture like spokes on a wheel. They swim upright as if suspended on the surface film by their large mouths.

The parsley frogs (subfamily Pelodytinae) are so called because the speckled green on the backs of some species resembles chopped parsley. They are confined to Europe and resemble the true frogs in appearance.

Adult **true toads** are mainly terrestrial and many are excellent burrowers. Some do not burrow but shelter during the day in holes made by other animals. Species of the largest genus, *Bufo*, are the most toad-like of all tail-less amphibians. Locomotion in most species is by short hops. Some, such as the Natterjack toad, run. None has the ability to escape from predators by leaping, but skin poisons compensate. Protective skin secretions are concentrated in the prominent parotoid glands just behind the head and some large species have poison glands on the legs.

In *Bufo* species with very short breeding seasons ("explosive" breeders), the males jump on and attempt to clasp any small object which moves by. They fight vigorously for paired females, and have several adaptations, including very muscular forearms, for maintaining a secure grip once amplexus is achieved. Explosive-breeding European common toads and Golden toads do not have the large vocal sacs typical of many frogs and can only produce weak calls. By contrast, in *Bufo* species with prolonged breeding seasons, eg the Natterjack toad, males call loudly at the edge of temporary pools to attract females. Small "satellite" males are sometimes observed quietly intercepting females near larger, calling males.

Typically, in *Bufo* species many small eggs (over 20,000 per clutch in the Marine toad) are laid in necklace-like strings in the water, usually wrapped around vegetation. There is a free-swimming tadpole stage followed by metamorphosis, and species which live in temporary pools usually complete development much quicker than those which live in permanent water. Other true toad genera often follow different patterns. The Short-legged toadlet of Southeast Asia, for example, lays a few large-yolked eggs which develop in small rain-filled depressions on the forest floor. The tadpoles have reduced mouthparts and a weakly coiled gut, suggesting that they probably do not feed. They possess large leaf-like gills.

The harlequin frogs are often brilliantly colored, rivalling the poison-arrow frogs for

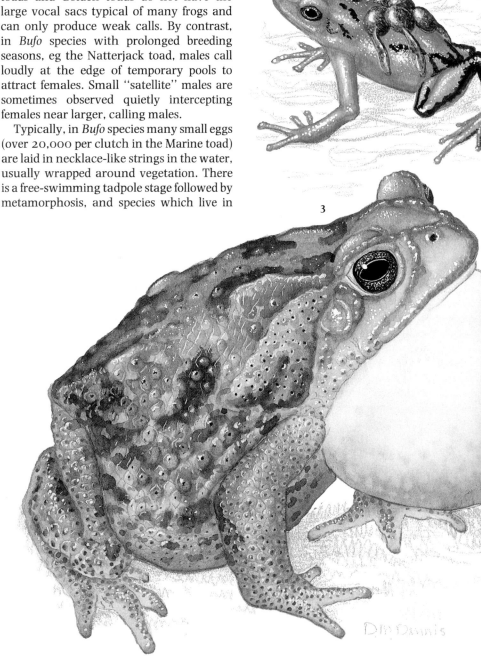

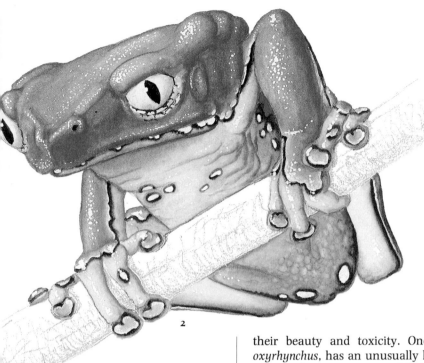

◄▲▼ Representative species of four families of frogs and toads. (1) Male Koikoi poison-arrow frog (*Phyllobates bicolor*) carrying developing tadpoles; Dendrobatidae. (2) A leaf frog, *Phyllomedusa bicolor*; Hylidae. (3) Marine toad (*Bufo marinus*), with the characteristically stout body and warty skin of true toads; Bufonidae. (4) Ornate, or Painted, horned frog (*Ceratophrys ornata*); Leptodactylidae.

their beauty and toxicity. One, *Atelopus oxyrhynchus*, has an unusually long period of amplexus. A record-holding pair remained in amplexus for 125 days. Males frequently outnumber females by ten to one, and to ensure mating success, a male must clasp a female early in the season and guard her until she is ready to spawn.

The **Gold frog family** includes just two genera of South American frogs, *Brachycephalus* and *Psyllophryne*, and takes its name from the beautiful Gold frog of Brazil, a species with a brilliant gold-yellow body and glossy black eyes that resemble tiny buttons. On its back there is a peculiar cross-shaped bony shield, flush with the skin but fused to its backbone. This shield is probably used in phragmosis—to plug the entrance to its burrow and prevent moisture escaping. It lives on the forest floor among dead

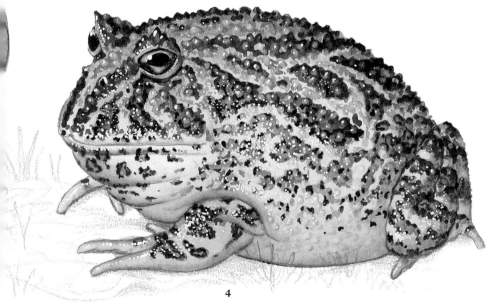

leaves and is common on wooded mountain peaks that rise near the heart of the city of Rio de Janeiro.

The **mouth-brooding frogs** of South America include only two known species, and only Darwin's frog is well known. It has an unusual form of parental care. The female lays 20–30 eggs on land, and the egg clusters attract several males which gather round and wait until they begin to hatch (in 10–20 days time). Movement of young tadpoles within the egg capsules elicits a snapping reflex, each male picking up several eggs with his tongue and sliding them into his vocal sac. The vocal sac is greatly enlarged into a pouch, reaching back to his groin before turning under on itself and continuing forward up to the chin. In this strange nursery, the eggs hatch and the tadpoles complete their development. Nourished by the yolk sac, they metamorphose as small froglets, about 1cm (0.4in) long, and emerge from the male's mouth. The presence of 5–15 tadpoles in the male's brood pouch does not interfere with his feeding. However, the pressure on his organs is enough to displace his shoulder girdle and make him walk with a stumbling gait. The vocal sac can still be used for calling, but produces only a faint bell-like sound.

The rare **ghost frogs** of South Africa mostly live close to fast-flowing mountain streams and frequently take to the water. The adult Table Mountain ghost frog is about 6.5cm (2.5in) from snout to vent, green above with a reddish network of lines. The white belly skin is so thin that the abdominal muscles and organs can be seen through it. The skin is covered in small hooks, just visible to the naked eye, which may help the frog to climb over slippery rocks. In spite of its disked fingers and toes, the adult does not live in trees but is usually found sitting in damp crevices under stones. Another species, *Heleophryne purcelli*, has sharp spines on its skin. It is partly arboreal and leaps after flies. Tadpoles of ghost frogs have a huge flattened head with a wedge-shaped outline when seen from above. An enormous suction disk around the mouth enables them to cling to submerged rocks while browsing on algae.

The **myobatrachid frogs** of Australia and New Guinea show the greatest adaptive radiation of all the frogs in their region. Some live in arid deserts, others on cold, moist mountains. Their life histories range from aquatic egg-laying with free-swimming tadpoles through foam-nesting, direct development and elaborate forms of parental care.

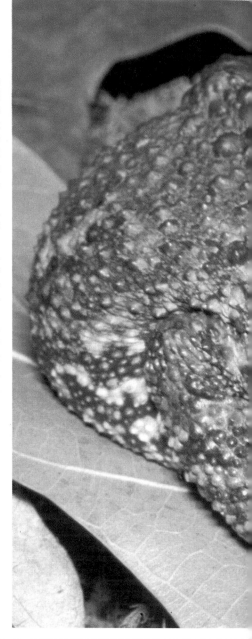

Among the smallest are the toad-like members of the genus *Pseudophryne*. These are rarely more than 3cm (1.2in) long and often have brightly colored bellies. Some species also have bright colors on the back. Bibron's toadlet lays its eggs in damp cavities under stones and males are often found sitting next to several clutches of eggs. Breeding may take place any time during the 6–7 months of the year when rain is sufficient to wet the ground. If a drought occurs after egg-laying, the eggs may not hatch for over three months, but the tadpoles must eventually swim to and complete their metamorphosis in standing water.

The Australian shovelfoots are medium-sized, globular myobatrachids with warty skin and short, stubby limbs. They possess sharp, fleshy outgrowths on the soles of their feet for burrowing into loose soil. The Desert shovelfoot can survive in the arid interior of Australia and is only seen above ground after rain. This species is quite remarkable in that it exploits the constant temperature and humidity inside nests of the Bulldog ant (*Myrmecia regularis*), living there in harmony with its insect host. The Australian shovelfoots, when molested, can puff out their bodies to an absurd size, while rising on all fours and facing the intruder. All species exude a thick, white, smelly poison when aroused, which dries to a strong elastic material. The stout-bodied frogs in the genus *Neobatrachus*, the Trilling, Humming, Meeowing and Shoemaker frogs, are burrowers famous for their unusual calls.

One of the most successful groups of myobatrachids are members of the genus *Limnodynastes*. Several species inhabit marshes and swamps, and some burrowing forms live in dry areas. Most are large, well-built frogs with broad heads, smooth skins and drab coloration. All of them lay their eggs in foam nests. The myobatrachid family includes species with parental care, including the Pouched and Gastric brooding frogs (see pp14–15).

The **leptodactylid frogs** of South and Central America include the wide-mouthed toads (subfamily Ceratophryinae), which sometimes have a very bizarre appearance. The Brazilian horned toad, for example, gets its name from horn-like flanges of skin projecting from its upper eyelids.

In the West Indies and tropical America *Eleutherodactylus* species of the subfamily Telmatobiinae mostly lay terrestrial eggs, but one, the Puerto Rican live-bearing frog, gives birth to small froglets after the tadpoles have completed development within the female's oviducts. The genus *Telmatobius* contains about 30 species mostly confined to the Andean highlands, some of which are completely aquatic. The Lake Titicaca frog is adapted to life on the oozy bottom of deep lakes, where there is very little dissolved oxygen. This species has no lungs, but has an extremely baggy skin which acts as a respiratory organ.

The subfamily Leptodactylinae, also from South America, includes many species which build foam nests. One leptodactyline, the White-lipped frog of Puerto Rico, has an unusual method of communication. The males, as well as producing audible chirp-like calls, produce seismic waves by pounding the vocal sac on the ground as they call. Neighboring males have acute sensitivity to ground-borne vibrations and, when they detect them, respond by producing calls at a faster rate. The waves are probably used by males to assess their distance from rival callers.

While nearly all frogs and toads have at least a trace of poison in their skin glands (see box), toxins are most highly developed in some of the **poison-arrow frogs.** These small, often brightly colored terrestrial frogs are found in the rain forests of Central and South America. Most can be recognized by the presence of a pair of plate-like scutes on the upper surface of each toe and fingertip. One of the most beautiful is *Dendrobates tinctorius*, which has a shiny black or maroon body with large metallic blue spots. Others are bright green, red, pink or gold with darker spots and stripes.

The poison-arrow frogs include species

Frog Toxins and Poisons

All frogs and toads produce poisons from special glands in their skin. Most are not potent, but a few species, such as the poison-arrow frogs of Central and South America, deploy some of the most poisonous biological toxins known. One of the most lethal is the batrachotoxin in the skin secretions of the Kokoi poison-arrow frog of Colombia. A mere 0.00001g (0.0000004oz) is enough to kill an average-sized man, and the Choco Indians poison the tips of as many as 50 arrows with secretions extracted from one tiny frog. Today they use these arrows for hunting game such as jaguars, deer, monkeys and birds, but in earlier times their blowguns and poison-darts were used with deadly effect against neighboring hostile tribes.

Many poisonous frogs are brightly colored to warn potential predators, and birds which normally eat frogs learn to avoid certain species. When provoked, many leaf frogs quickly extend their legs to reveal bright patches on their sides and along the inside of their thighs. Fire-bellied toads arch their back and twist their legs round so that their bright orange and black undersides can be seen from above. The False-eyed frog of South America has a large and dramatic pair of eye-spots on its rump (see p12). It turns away from an attacker, inflates its lungs, and lifts its backside in the air to display the eyespots. The frog produces an unpleasant secretion from glands around the eye-spots.

The Marine toad can squirt toxic secretions from its parotoid glands (just behind the head) up to 1m (3.3ft) into the eyes or mouth of a predator. Dogs attempting to eat these toads have suffered extreme pain afterwards. Human fatalities in Fiji and the Philippines have occurred when people who habitually ate frogs were not warned of the dangers of eating the Marine toad on its introduction there. Peruvian peasants died just by eating soup prepared from its eggs.

with the most complex social behavior of all amphibians. Adults of most species carry the tadpoles. In the day-active species *Colostethus inguinalis* from Panama and in the Stream frog of Trinidad and Venezuela, both sexes defend territories against frogs of the same and other species. Aggressive behavior includes calling and color changes (in males), postural displays, chases, attacks and wrestling (both sexes). Prolonged fights are most likely to occur between frogs of the same sex, but sometimes males and females wrestle. In the Red-and-blue poison-arrow frog, the male pays daily visits to the eggs he has fertilized, to moisten them with water from his skin. When they hatch, the female nourishes them with unfertilized eggs (see p15).

The **true tree frogs** are much flatter than frogs which live on land. This gives them even distribution of weight over the whole body and enables them to balance and move with great agility on branches and leaves. The circular disks on the tips of their fingers and toes and the loose skin on the belly act as adhesive pads which enable them to climb up smooth surfaces. Some species, eg the Fringe-limbed tree frog of Central America, have extremely large areas of webbing between the toes enabling them to glide from tree to tree with toes spread. The cricket frogs of North America have become terrestrial, and their toe-disks are much smaller than in tree-dwelling species.

The leaf frogs (subfamily Phyllomedusinae) are mostly large, brightly colored animals of lowland rain forest and montane cloud forest in Central and South America. The female lays eggs enveloped by leaves hanging over water and repeatedly empties water from her bladder over them to keep them moist.

Australia and New Guinea have about 150 true tree frog species, some very beautiful, with colors ranging from iridescent gold and sulfur yellow to pink, pale blue and violet. By far the best known of all the Australian frogs is the White's tree frog (10cm—4in long), often found in houses, lavatories, water tanks and drainpipes. It breeds in summer in grassy, rain-filled meadows. The male's voice is a deep "wark-wark-wark."

The **glass frogs** are small, bright green frogs found in rain forests of Central and South America. Most have minute eyes set almost on top of their wide, blunt heads. In some, the skin is almost transparent so that their bones, muscles and organs can be seen through it. They are arboreal, living on the leaves of small trees and shrubs, usually

▲ **Spider-eater.** The warty skin of this Southern toad (*Bufo terrestris*) contains numerous glands that produce a distasteful secretion if it is attacked. The large parotid glands behind the eyes also secrete a toxin; this serves to deter, rather than kill predators.

◄ **Bright skin coloration** of the poison-arrow frogs warns predators that their skin contains lethal toxins. This species, *Dendrobates parvulus*, is found in the Amazon rain forest.

close to running water. Often found resting with their bodies pressed tightly against the surface of leaves, they usually lay their eggs on leaves above water. In at least one species, *Centrolenella valerioi*, the eggs are guarded by the male, who sits close to them on the leaf.

The highly aquatic **pseudid frogs** of South America resemble true frogs but have long, slender toes with an extra bone (phalanx) that gives them more mobility and probably increases swimming efficiency. These frogs use their fingers and toes for stirring up mud to find food on the bottom of shallow lakes. The innermost finger is opposable, a condition not often found in frogs. Reproduction is aquatic, the eggs being laid in a frothy mass on the water's surface. The largest and best-known species is the Paradoxical frog which lives on the island of Trinidad and in parts of the Amazon River. The paradox of this frog (see pp10–11) is that the tadpoles often reach an enormous size, sometimes over 25cm (10in), yet they metamorphose into adults of only 6.5cm (2.5in).

The so-called **true frogs** have the widest range of all the families of frogs—nearly all areas of the world except the polar regions. Their long, muscular legs, usually with webbed hind feet, and their streamlined bodies are ideal for jumping and swimming. The skin is usually smooth and often brown or green in color. Most species are aquatic, but some live in trees and have adhesive disks on their toes for climbing. A few can thrive in brackish waters or warm sulfur springs and others are adapted to terrestrial life and can burrow like spadefoot toads.

Most species lay aquatic eggs and the adults are rarely found far from water. Some breed for several months during the year and the males set up and defend mating territories. However, many from temperate latitudes breed for just a few days very early in the year, soon after the ice has melted from the surface of ponds. In late winter and early spring, males of the European common frog can sometimes be seen swimming about under the ice in amplexus on the backs of females. During the breeding season males of many species develop rough, swollen pads on their fingers for gripping females.

The European common frog and its North American equivalent, the Wood frog, both lay their globular egg masses in communal clusters which may contain hundreds or thousands of separate clutches. Communal spawning may be an adaptation which helps to prevent the eggs freezing during the spring. The small black embryos absorb heat from the sun's rays and the thick jelly mass acts as an insulator. Temperatures within the cluster may be as much as 6°C (11°F) higher than the surrounding water.

One species of torrent frog living in Borneo does not produce calls, but instead signals to females by semaphore-like movements of its hind legs, flashing the brightly colored webbing between its toes. This species lives in rock crevices near noisy waterfalls, where the loud din of the torrent would make vocal signals ineffective. The atypical Mottled burrowing frog of South Africa is squat and stout-bodied with a pointed head and hardened snout for burrowing.

The **Seychelles frogs** are found only on the Seychelles Islands. Best known is the Seychelles frog, which lives in rotting plant matter on the forest floor and feeds on small invertebrates. Eggs are laid in small clumps on moist ground. The female guards her eggs and when they hatch, after two weeks of incubation, the tadpoles wriggle onto her back, where they are protected from dehydration. Already well advanced, with short hind limb rudiments, they respire through their skin and do not have gills or spiracles (tubes leading from the gill chamber). After metamorphosis, the froglets continue to ride on their mother's back for a short time.

The **sedge** and **bush frogs** are mainly small to medium-sized climbers found on reeds, shrubs and trees near water in Africa; a few species live on the ground or are completely aquatic. The ground-dwelling genus *Kassina* runs instead of hopping.

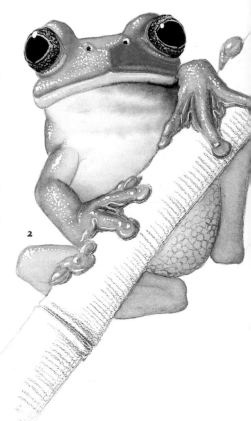

▼▲► **Representative species** of four families of frogs. (1) Male Edible frog (*Rana esculenta*) calling from a pond; this species is a hybrid of the Marsh frog and the Pool frog; Ranidae. (2) Japanese tree frog (*Rhacophorus arboreus*); Rhacophoridae. (3) Male Asiatic painted frog (*Kaloula pulchra*) calling; Microhylidae. (4) Female Seychelles frog (*Sooglossus seychellensis*) carrying tadpoles; Sooglossidae. (5) South African bullfrog (*Pyxicephalus adspersus*) eating a rat; Ranidae.

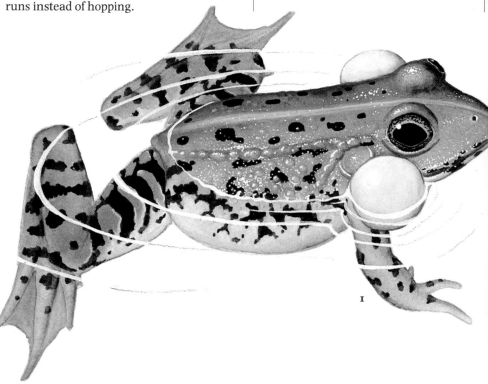

Sedge frogs, comprising over 100 species, display fluctuating skin patterns and brilliant color. In some parts of its range, the Marbled rush frog has black and white stripes with delicate pink tones on its sides and limbs. In other areas it may be black and green, black and yellow, brown and green or brown and yellow. In addition to geographical variation, all these colors are subject to change with temperature, humidity, light intensity and stress (see pp12–13). Most tree-dwellers in the family lay eggs in a gelatinous mass on vegetation over water. To prevent its eggs drying up, the female Golden leaf-folding frog folds leaf edges around the egg mass, and glues them together with sticky secretions from her oviducts.

The bush frogs bury eggs in the ground near water. The tadpoles hatch out during heavy rain and migrate to standing water by wriggling across damp ground. This habit is shared by some terrestrial frogs in the closely related genus *Hylambates*. The tadpoles of one species, *H. natalensis*, are long and eel-like and slither in a long chain to the water after hatching. These tadpoles are capable of very rapid swimming and can jump 7.5cm (3in) out of the water with a jerk of their powerful tail. The female of *H. brevirostris* in equatorial Africa is a mouth-brooder, like the male of Darwin's frog (see p47). She does not feed while the tadpoles are developing.

The small terrestrial frogs in the subfamily Arthroleptinae are found chiefly on the forest floor and in brush country. They have direct development, except in one genus, *Cardioglossa*, which has free-swimming tadpoles. The males of some arthroleptines show a striking sex difference—the 3rd finger is two or three times longer than any other fingers on the hand.

The **Old World tree frogs** are mostly tree-dwellers with adaptations for climbing. They have rather flattened bodies, well-developed toe-disks and loose skin on the belly for adhesion to leaves and branches. Wallace's flying frog of Malaysia and Borneo glides between trees on enormous areas of webbing between its fingers and toes. The Old World tree frogs are typically foam nesters (see p39). In *Chiromantis* species in Africa several males cling to the female and beat the foam, apparently competing to fertilize the eggs as the female deposits them into the nest. Some species lay large-yolked eggs in damp places on land and these develop directly into miniature froglets. The Malaysian hill froglet occurs commonly in montane cloud forest where there is rarely any standing water. It lays its eggs in huge sheets of damp moss hanging from trees.

The **narrow-mouthed frogs**, widely distributed throughout the Old and New World tropics, include terrestrial and arboreal species. Many are small, stout-bodied burrowers with tiny heads and very short legs. Many of the tree-dwellers have disks on their toes to assist climbing. The answering frogs are typical of the subfamily Microhylinae, the most widespread group: during the day they hide in leaf litter or beneath fallen logs and at night they often call from under leaves. Their small size and concealed position makes them very difficult to find, even when they are actively calling. Their calls sound like short buzzes or trills and can be easily mistaken for the chirps of crickets. Some narrow-mouthed frogs lay their eggs in fallen bamboo shoots or between leaves of wild bananas, producing cannibalistic tadpoles specialized for egg-eating. The rain frogs are extremely large, stout-bodied species and only appear above ground during torrential rain. The males have loud, bellowing calls which can be heard from a great distance. AA

THE 20 FAMILIES OF FROGS AND TOADS

Length = length from snout to vent. ✻ CITES-listed Ⓔ Endangered Ⓡ Rare Ⓥ Vulnerable Ⓘ Threatened but status indeterminate Ⓚ Threat suspected but status unknown. Total threatened species = numbers of species endangered, vulnerable, rare or of indeterminate or unknown status. Approximate nonmetric equivalents: 10cm = 4in. 1kg = 2.2lb.

Suborder Archaeobatrachia

Tailed Frog and New Zealand Frogs
Family: Leiopelmatidae
Four species in 2 genera.*

Distribution: W N America (Tailed frog), New Zealand. Length: 2–5cm. Tailed frog aquatic, inhabiting mountain streams; New Zealand frogs montane terrestrial. Color: gray, brown, black, pinkish. Body form: slender; head flattened, slightly broader than long; snout obtusely pointed; fingers long and slender and free of webbing; toes slightly webbed; pupil vertical. Adult male Tailed frog with short tail-like cloacal appendage. Fertilization internal in Tailed frog; tadpoles free-swimming. New Zealand frogs lay eggs on land and provide care for directly developing embryos. Species and genera include: **Hamilton's frog** Ⓡ (*Leiopelma hamiltoni*), **New Zealand frogs** (genus *Leiopelma*), **Tailed frog** (*Ascaphus trueii*). Total threatened species: 3.

* Some authorities place the Tailed frog in its own family, Ascaphidae.

Disk-Tongued Toads
Family: Discoglossidae
Fourteen species in 5 genera.

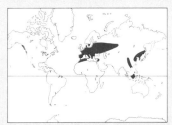

Distribution: Europe, NW Africa, Asia Minor, China, Korea; barbourulas endemic to the Philippines and Borneo. Length: 3–7cm. Fire-bellied toads, painted frogs and barbourulas largely aquatic; midwife toads terrestrial. Color: back green, brown, gray. Fire-bellied toads vividly marked on the underside with red, orange, yellow, white and black. Body form: variable; fire-bellied toads and barbourulas flattened; midwife toads stout, resembling true toads; painted frogs plump and shiny resembling true frogs; key features of the family are breastbone forked behind and disk-shaped tongue. Fire-bellied toads, painted frogs and barbourulas lay

eggs in water and have free-swimming tadpoles. Male midwife toads carry eggs until hatching, when tadpoles deposited in water. Species and genera include: **Common midwife toad** (*Alytes obstetricans*), **barbourulas** (genus *Barbourula*), **fire-bellied toads** (genus *Bombina*), **Iberian midwife toad** (*Alytes cisternasii*), **Israel painted frog** Ⓔ (*Discoglossus nigriventer*). Total threatened species: 1.

Suborder Aglossa

Clawed and Surinam Toads
Family: Pipidae
Twenty-six species in 4 genera.

Distribution: Africa, S C and S America. Length: 4.5–12cm. Adults almost entirely aquatic. Color: gray, brown or green on back; usually paler on lower surface. Body form: broad and flattened; feet large and broad; 3 of hind toes with claws except in some Surinam toads; no tongue; pupil of eye round; no movable eyelids (except *Pseudhymenochirus*); adults of some species retain larval lateral line system. Eggs laid in water, or, in Surinam toads, deposited in skin pits on female's back, development usually involves a free-swimming tadpole stage, but in some Surinam toads tadpoles develop directly into

froglets. Species and genera include: **African clawed toad** (*Xenopus laevis*), **Cape platanna** Ⓥ (*X. gilli*), **clawed toads** (genera *Xenopus, Hymenochirus, Pseudhymenochirus*), **Surinam toad** (*Pipa pipa*). Total threatened species: 1.

Suborder Rhinophrynoidea

Burrowing Toad
Family: Rhinophrynidae
One species: *Rhinophrynus dorsalis*.

Distribution: Costa Rica to Rio Grande Valley of Texas. Length: 6.5cm. Adults terrestrial, burrowing. Color: gray blotched with reddish-orange markings. Body form: egg-shaped; snout pointed; limbs short; feet spade-like; skin smooth; no teeth; pupil vertical. Eggs laid in water; tadpoles free-swimming.

▶ **See-through frog.** The Glass frog (*Centrolenella vireovittata*) from the cloud forests of Central America has a partially transparent body. Glass frogs stick their eggs to leaves overhanging streams and one of the parents, usually the male, guards them until they hatch, when the tadpoles fall into the water below.

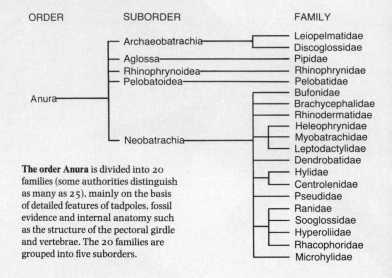

ORDER	SUBORDER	FAMILY
	Archaeobatrachia	Leiopelmatidae
		Discoglossidae
	Aglossa	Pipidae
	Rhinophrynoidea	Rhinophrynidae
	Pelobatoidea	Pelobatidae
Anura		Bufonidae
		Brachycephalidae
		Rhinodermatidae
		Heleophrynidae
		Myobatrachidae
	Neobatrachia	Leptodactylidae
		Dendrobatidae
		Hylidae
		Centrolenidae
		Pseudidae
		Ranidae
		Sooglossidae
		Hyperoliidae
		Rhacophoridae
		Microhylidae

The order Anura is divided into 20 families (some authorities distinguish as many as 25), mainly on the basis of detailed features of tadpoles, fossil evidence and internal anatomy such as the structure of the pectoral girdle and vertebrae. The 20 families are grouped into five suborders.

Suborder Pelobatoidea

Spadefoot Toads, Horned Toads and Parsley Frogs

Family: Pelobatidae
Eighty-eight species in 10 genera.*

Distribution: N America, Europe, NW Africa, Asia Minor, SE Asia, Indonesia, Borneo, Philippines, E Indies. Length: 4–10cm. Adults mainly terrestrial. Color: green, brown, yellow, gray; often marbled in appearance. Body form: plump; limbs short; eyes large with vertical pupil; spadefoot toads with a very prominent sharp-edged "spade" on hind feet; some horned toads with flexible projections of skin resembling horns; parsley frogs small, long-limbed, resembling true frogs. Eggs laid in water; tadpoles free-swimming. Species and genera include: **Eastern** or **Holbrook's spadefoot** (*Scaphiopus holbrookii*), **European common spadefoot** (*Pelobates fuscus*). **Italian spadefoot** E (*P.f. insubricus*), **Malaysian horned toad** (*Megophrys monticola*), **parsley frogs** (genus *Pelodytes*), **Plains spadefoot** (*Scaphiopus bombifrons*), **Western spadefoot** (*S. hammondii*). Total threatened subspecies: 1.

*Some authorities split off parsley frogs into a separate family, Pelodytidae.

Suborder Neobatrachia

True Toads

Family: Bufonidae
Three hundred and thirty-nine species in 25 genera.*

Distribution: worldwide except Antarctica, Greenland, New Guinea, Madagascar, Australia, New Zealand. Length: 2–23cm. Adults terrestrial. Color: brown, green, black, yellow; harlequin frogs sometimes vividly colored. Body form: short and stout; head broad; legs short; skin rough, often covered in "warts"; prominent parotid glands behind head; teeth absent; some harlequin frogs with slender bodies and long legs. Most species with free-swimming tadpoles from eggs laid in water; a few with direct development. Species and genera include: **American toad** (*Bufo americanus*), **European common toad** (*B. bufo*), **Golden toad** ✶ E (*B. periglenes*), **Great Plains toad** (*B. cognatus*), **harlequin frogs** (genus *Atelopus*), **Houston toad** E (*Bufo houstonensis*), **Marine, Giant** or **Cane toad** (*B. marinus*), **Natterjack toad** (*B. calamita*), **Neotropical leaf toad** (*B. typhonius*), **Short-legged toadlet** (*Pelophryne brevipes*), **West African live-bearing toad** ✶ V (*Nectophrynoides occidentalis*), **Yosemite toad** (*Bufo canorus*). Total threatened species: 5. Total threatened subspecies 1.

* The small toads in the genera *Allophryne* and *Atelopus* were formerly assigned to their own families, Allophrynidae and Atelopodidae.

Gold Frog Family

Family: Brachycephalidae
Two species in 2 genera.

Distribution: southeastern Brazil. Length: 2cm. Adults terrestrial, burrowing. Color: Gold frog gold with brown markings on back and head. Body form: slim; limbs slender; snout rounded; Gold frog with bony shield on back fused to vertebrae. Eggs laid in water producing free-swimming tadpoles. Species include: **Gold frog** (*Brachycephalus ephippium*).

Mouth-Brooding Frogs

Family: Rhinodermatidae
Two species in 1 genus.

Distribution: S Chile and S Argentina in Andean foothills. Length: 3cm. Adults mainly terrestrial, living near forest streams. Color: green or brown above, paler below. Body form: slender; pointed extension of skin on snout; digits long, webbed on hind feet but free on forefeet. Eggs laid on land, hatch and complete development in male's vocal sac. Species include: **Darwin's frog** (*Rhinoderma darwinii*).

Ghost Frogs

Family: Heleophrynidae
Four species in 1 genus.

Distribution: S Africa. Length: 6cm. Adults mainly aquatic, some partly arboreal. Color: mottled green, brown with reddish tinge; skin of belly thin and almost transparent. Body form: flattened; limbs long; eyes large and prominent; toe and fingertips expanded; skin with small hooks or spines. Eggs laid on damp ground or in small puddles; tadpoles free-swimming in mountain streams, with large oral suckers for clinging to rocks. Species include: **Table Mountain ghost frog** (*Heleophryne rosei*).

Myobatrachid Frogs

Family: Myobatrachidae
One hundred species in 20 genera.

Distribution: Australia, Tasmania, New Guinea. Length: 2–11.5cm. Adults mostly burrowing or terrestrial, some found in swift streams. Color: very variable; some striking, with yellow, red, blue, black and white markings. Body form: ranging from small toad-like burrowing forms to large, stout-bodied species with powerful limbs, resembling bullfrogs; toes never more than half-webbed; toe disks small or absent. Life history varies from aquatic eggs with free-swimming tadpoles to fully terrestrial with direct development. Some with elaborate forms of parental care. Species and genera include: **Australian shovelfoots** (genus *Notaden*), **Baw-baw frog** R (*Philoria frosti*), **Bibron's toadlet** (*Pseudophryne bibronii*), **Desert shovelfoot** (*Notaden nichollsi*), **Gastric brooding frog** (*Rheobatrachus silus*), **Humming frog** (*Neobatrachus pelobatoides*), **Meeoioing frog** (*N. pictus*), **Pouched frog** (*Assa darlingtoni*), **Shoemaker frog** (*Neobatrachus sutor*), **Spotted grass frog** (*Limnodynastes tasmaniensis*), **Trilling frog** (*Neobatrachus centralis*). Total threatened species: 1.

Leptodactylid Frogs

Family: Leptodactylidae
Seven hundred and twenty-two species in 51 genera.

Distribution: S and C America, N America. Length: 2–30cm. Adults range from completely aquatic to completely terrestrial. Color: very variable; some species vivid red, orange, yellow or purple. Body form: wide-mouthed toads stout-bodied like true toads; *Leptodactylus* resembling large bullfrogs; *Eleutherodactylus* resembling tree frogs. Life history ranges from laying eggs in water, building foam nests on vegetation to laying eggs on land which develop directly into tiny froglets. Species and genera include: **Brazilian horned toad** (*Ceratophrys cornuta*), **False-eyed frog** (*Physalaemus nattereri*), **Lake Titicaca frog** (*Telmatobius culeus*), **Puerto Rican live-bearing frog** R (*Eleutherodactylus jasperi*), **South American bullfrog** (*Leptodactylus pentadactylus*), **White-lipped frog** (*L. albilabris*), **wide-mouthed toads** (genus *Ceratophrys*). Total threatened species: 2.

Poison-Arrow Frogs

Family: Dendrobatidae
One hundred and sixteen species in 4 genera.

Distribution: C and S America from Costa Rica to southern Brazil. Length: 2–5cm. Adults terrestrial or partly arboreal. Color: often very bright red, pink, blue, green, gold, purple with darker markings; some with flash colors around groin. Body form: slim; snout rounded; limbs slender; toe and finger tips expanded into small adhesive disks. Terrestrial, large-yolked eggs often guarded and moistened by male; adults transport tadpoles on their backs to water where they complete development. Species include: **Kokoi poison-arrow frog** (*Phyllobates bicolor*), **Red-and-blue poison-arrow frog** (*Dendrobates pumilio*), **Stream frog** (*Colostethus trinitatus*).

True Tree Frogs
Family: Hylidae
Six hundred and thirty-seven species in 37 genera.*

Distribution: N to S America, W Indies, Eurasia, N Africa, Australia, New Guinea. Adults tree- or ground-dwelling. Length: 1.6–9cm. Color: often green or brown, but some species with vivid markings. Body form: flattened and distinctly slender; legs long; feet often webbed; most species with circular disks on tips of fingers and toes. Most with free-swimming tadpoles from large numbers of eggs laid in open water; some laying eggs on leaves above water; others with direct development. Parental care in some species. Species and genera include: **Australian and New Guinea tree frogs** (genera *Litoria, Nyctimystes*), **Australian water-holding frog** (*Cyclorana platycephala*), **casque-headed tree frogs** (genera *Aparasphenodon, Trachycephalus, Triprion, Pternohyla*), **cricket frogs** (genus *Acris*), **Fringe-limbed tree frog** (*Hyla miliaria*), **leaf frogs** (genus *Phyllomedusa*), **marsupial frogs** (genus *Gastrotheca*), **Northern cricket frog** (*Acris crepitans*), **Spring peeper** (*Hyla crucifer*), **Squirrel tree frog** (*H. squirella*), **White's tree frog** (*Litoria caerulea*). Total threatened species: 1. Total threatened subspecies: 1.

*Some authorities split off the Australian and New Guinea tree frogs into a separate family, Pelodryadidae.

Glass Frogs
Family: Centrolenidae
Sixty-four species in 2 genera.

Distribution: C and N S America, SE Brazil, Paraguay. Length: 2–6cm. Adults arboreal. Color: bright green, nearly transparent skin. Body form: small; head wide and blunt; eyes small and set almost on top of skull; a single bone (tarsus) in ankle and wrist instead of two; adhesive disks on fingers and toes. Most lay eggs on leaves above running water; tadpoles drop into water.

Pseudid Frogs
Family: Pseudidae
Four species in 2 genera.

Distribution: S America. Length: adults 5–8cm, tadpoles up to 25cm. Color: mottled green, brown, yellow and black. Body form: robust and streamlined; snout pointed; eyes and nostrils prominent; hind limbs muscular; fingers and toes long and slender, with additional phalanx bone; skin slippery. Eggs laid in frothy mass in water hatching into free-swimming tadpoles growing to enormous size. Species include: **Paradoxical frog** (*Pseudis paradoxa*).

True Frogs
Family: Ranidae
Six hundred and eleven species in 40 genera.*

Distribution: worldwide except Greenland, Antarctica, Madagascar, New Zealand and most of Australia. Length: 1.5–35cm, most 4–12cm. Goliath frog of W Africa largest frog in world, up to 35.6cm, 3.1kg. Adults mainly aquatic, from rain forest to temperate high altitudes. Color: often green or brown with darker markings. Body form: slender and streamlined; head usually pointed; eyes and eardrum large; legs long with or without webbing between toes. Most lay eggs in water and have free-swimming tadpoles. Species and genera include: **African burrowing frogs** (genus *Hemisus*), **American bullfrog** (*Rana catesbeiana*), **Asian bullfrog** (*R. tigrina*), **Edible frog** (*R. esculenta*), **European common frog** (*R. temporaria*), **Goliath frog** [V] (*Conraua goliath*), **Green frog** (*Rana clamitans*), **Marsh frog** (*R. ridibunda*), **Mottled burrowing frog** (*Hemisus marmoratum*), **Pig frog** (*Rana grylio*), **Pool frog** (*R. lessonae*), **Relict leopard frog** [E] (*R. onca*), **South African bullfrog** (*Pyxicephalus adspersus*), **torrent frogs** (genus *Staurois*), **Wood frog** (*Rana sylvatica*). Total threatened species: 2.

*Some authorities split off *Hemisus* as a separate family, Hemisidae.

Seychelles Frogs
Family: Sooglossidae
Three species in 2 genera.

Distribution: Seychelles. Length: 2–2.5cm. Adults terrestrial. Color: green or brown. Body form: slender; legs long; feet with or without webbing; *Nesomantis* is more toad-like in build than *Sooglossus*. Eggs laid on land, females of *S. sechellensis* carrying tadpoles to water on their backs, others with direct development. Species: **Gardiner's Seychelles frog** [I] (*Sooglossus gardineri*), **Seychelles frog** [I] (*S. sechellensis*), **Thomasset's Seychelles frog** [I] (*Nesomantis thomasseti*).

Sedge and Bush Frogs
Family: Hyperoliidae
Two hundred and ninety-two species in 23 genera.*

Distribution: Africa S of Sahara, Madagascar, Seychelles. Length: 2–8cm. Adults mostly arboreal. Color: many with distinct markings and bright colors—red, yellow, orange, black, white; subject to color change. Body form: many arboreal species resemble true tree frogs: subfamilies Arthroleptinae and Astylosterninae with fingers greatly elongated or curved downwards; aquatic Hairy frog with hair-like filaments on thighs and flanks for underwater respiration. Most arboreal species lay eggs on leaves above water and have free-swimming tadpoles; arthroleptines mostly with direct development. Species and genera include: **bush frogs** (genera *Hylambates, Leptopelis*), **Hairy frog** (*Trichobatrachus robustus*), **Golden leaf-folding frog** (*Afrixalus brachycnemis*), **Marbled rush frog** (*Hyperolius marmoratus*), **sedge frogs** (genus *Hyperolius*), **Seychelle Islands tree frog** [K] (*Tachycnemis seychellensis*). Total threatened species: 1.

*Subfamiles Arthroleptinae and Astylosterninae sometimes placed in separate family (Arthroleptidae).

Old World Tree Frogs
Family Rhacophoridae
One hundred and eighty-four species in 10 genera.

Distribution: Africa, S India, Sri Lanka, China, SE Asia, Indonesia, East Indies, Japan. Length: 2.5–12cm. Adults mostly arboreal. Color: mainly greens and browns, often bright webbing between toes. Body form: from stout with short limbs to slender with long limbs; webbing between fingers and toes; tree-dwelling forms with large disks on toes, resembling true tree frogs. Eggs typically laid in foam nests, tadpoles dropping into water to complete development; some species lay eggs in moist places away from water and have direct development. Species include: **Malaysian hill froglet** (*Philautus vermiculatus*), **Malaysian flying frog** (*Rhacophorus reinwardtii*), **Wallace's flying frog** (*R. nigropalmatus*).

Narrow-Mouthed Frogs
Family: Microhylidae
Two hundred and eighty-one species in 61 genera.*

Distribution: tropical S America, Madagascar, SE Asia, Indonesia, New Guinea, Australia (Queensland only) with extensions into the temperate regions of N and S America, Africa and China. Length: 1–8cm. Adults terrestrial burrowers or tree dwellers. Color: mostly dull browns and grays but some with bright markings on the back. Body form: stout; head small; legs short; mouth narrow and slit-like; usually without webbing between toes with or without disks. Some laying eggs in water, in burrows or in plants of the bromeliad family; some with free-swimming tadpoles, others with direct development. Genera include: **answering frogs** (genus *Microhyla*), **rain frogs** (genera *Breviceps, Kaloula*).

*The African genus *Phrynomerus* is sometimes placed in its own family, Phrynomeridae.

Leaps and Bounds

Why have frogs lost their tails?

Frogs are peculiar—the adults have no tails. The absence of this feature is rare among other animals with backbones because in most the tail plays an important role in locomotion. In fish and otters the undulatory movement of the tail propels the animal forward. In four-legged land animals, the tail is a balancing, occasionally a steering organ.

Although an external tail is absent in adult frogs, it is well developed in tadpoles and is their exclusive means of locomotion. The tadpole consists of a long muscular tail attached to a spheroid package of sense organs and viscera. Undulations of the tail typically propel the tadpole in spurts from one resting place to another.

If a tail is so useful for locomotion, why was it lost in adult frogs? It seems that its loss permitted them to jump easily with synchronous kicks of the hind legs.

The number of frogs that do not jump is a small fraction of the total. Some species walk, at least occasionally, for short distances on all four legs like other vertebrates, moving right forelimb, left hind, left fore, right hind, and so on. A few species are strictly aquatic but their swimming behavior is completely unlike any other vertebrate's, except for humans when they use the breast stroke.

Vertebrates which use their limbs for swimming typically use the same sequence of limb movement as when walking on all fours, thus the hind limbs move alternately. In frogs, however, the hind legs move together just as in jumping, but rather than extending the legs at right angles to the body and throwing the body upward and forward, in swimming the hind legs extend backwards parallel to the frog's body and push it forward. The forelegs are pressed against the side of the body.

As the hind legs push backwards, the large webbed feet are forced open like parachutes by the water pressure. The increased surface area of the hind feet serves to anchor the feet in the water—like a drift anchor on a boat—and the body is pushed forward. When the hind limbs are fully extended, they are flexed; the hind feet fold shut and are feathered forward like oars on a boat. Thus, the swimming movement of frogs is: fast forward as the limbs extend, drift forward as limbs are flexed, fast forward, drift, and so on. Although this may seem a rather inefficient form of swimming, frogs swim quickly.

A less common form of aquatic locomotion is skittering; the frog literally skips or bounces across the surface of the water in a series of rapid jumps. Skittering can begin either on the land or in the water. It requires the frog to maintain a high buoyancy and land flat on the water surface. The hind limbs provide the propulsion as in terrestrial jumping, but the hind feet are held vertically as in swimming in order to push against the water and lift the entire frog up and off the surface. Skittering has been observed in fewer than a dozen species (eg the Northern cricket frog) although it is possibly used by many more species than that limited number.

Among arboreal species, those living in trees or low shrubs, jumping serves mainly for escape and is not the chief means of getting about. Frogs climbing in trees use the same sequence of limb movements as in walking on the ground, but movement is slower and foot placement is more methodical. With each step the frog has to grasp the branch and ascertain that it will support its weight.

Arboreal frogs are generally slender-bodied and slender-limbed, with tips of digits expanded into "suctorial" disks. The actual clinging force of these disks derives from friction and wet adhesion; when there is true suction it is a very minor component of the clinging force. The enlarged toe pads have a specialized outer layer of skin with a fibrous pile-like surface divided by canals into regular blocks. The fibrous piling produces the major clinging force on rough, dry surfaces through friction and the intermeshing of the fibrous piling and the irregularity of the surface. On damp, smooth surfaces, the mucus covering of the toe pads creates adhesion using the force of surface tension.

The combination of friction and wet adhesion enables many tree frog species to cling to steeply inclined surfaces and enables some lightweight species weighing under 10g (0.35oz) to cling and even to walk upside down on smooth surfaces.

A number of unrelated species of tree frogs have heavily webbed feet (fore and hind). One of these frogs is the famed Malaysian flying frog, which does not fly and does not truly glide either. In controlled falling, the frog uses its strongly webbed feet as parachutes, keeping its body rigid and its limbs outstretched.

Burrowing frogs are much less numerous

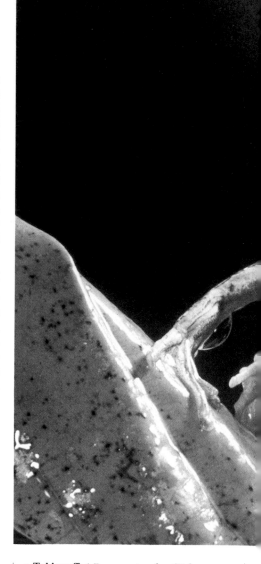

▲ **Taking off.** A European tree frog (*Hyla arborea*) leaps from a leaf by suddenly straightening its powerful hind limbs. Tree frogs jump primarily to escape from enemies, but they sometimes leap and snap at flying insects.

▼ **Jumping sequence.** (1) Forelimbs elevate and aim the forepart of the frog; ankles lift the hind limbs off the ground. (2) Take-off: hind limbs swing open from the hip joint; upper and lower legs extend, propelling the frog forward and upward; ankles and hind feet roll off the ground. (3) The flight path follows a curve of approximately 45°; the eyes are shut and withdrawn downward into the mouth cavity. (4) Landing: forelimbs break the fall, and the chest hits the ground, followed by the rest of the underside; the hind limbs flex and press against the body, ready to leap forward again.

 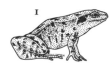  

than tree-dwellers and most burrow backwards. Frogs dig with a sideways shuffle of their hind feet. Limb movement is confined to the lower limb, from the knee to the heel, and the heel bears an enlarged, crescent-shaped metatarsal tubercle. This tubercle serves as a scraper and scoop. In digging, the heel is placed on the ground behind the middle of the body and then is pushed backwards and to the side. This curving sweep of the hind foot displaces soil to the side and the alternate movements of the hind limbs shuffle the frog backwards into the soil.

The presumed advantage of backwards burrowing is that this position permits the frog to survey its surroundings for predators and to jump forward to catch prey. All frogs, whether burrowers or not, possess a bony prehallux (an extra toe-bone in front of the first toe) beneath the metatarsal tubercle. It has even been suggested that backward dig-

ging was a major evolutionary force in the development of the unique body form of frogs; the presence of a tail would be a hindrance to backward digging.

Two opposing schools of thought offer explanations of how the frog's jumping locomotion evolved. The oldest hypothesis is that the synchronized kick of the hind legs was an adaptation for aquatic movement to permit frogs to lunge forward suddenly and quickly in the water, either to catch prey or to escape predators. With the development and refinement of this kicking response, frogs would be preadapted for jumping when they moved onto land.

The opposing hypothesis suggests a terrestrial origin for jumping, as replacement of the tail with the hind legs for aquatic propulsion seems too unlikely. It is suggested that jumping evolved as a rapid means of escape, particularly to allow the animal to

move quickly from a resting site on land to a hiding place in the water.

No matter which view is correct, if in fact either is, both concur that the tail would need to have been short to permit an effective propulsive kick of the hind legs, and that as this type of kicking became more important, the tail's interference with limb movement and its frictional drag would result in a tendency towards its reduction.

The only point which may be made with certainty is that the tail was lost very early in the evolution of the frogs, because all living frogs and most of the fossil species share a strongly modified pelvic girdle and shortened backbone. These modifications (elongated and divergent ilia, reduction and medial compression of pubes and ischia, and fusion of a small set of tail vertebrae into a urostyle) appear to be tightly linked to jumping.   GZ

Frog Chorus

Vocal communication in frogs and toads

In many tropical and semi-tropical areas thousands of males of as many as two dozen species of frogs may call at the same time and place. These "choruses" are among the most impressive of biological phenomena and may be audible from more than 1km (up to 1mi). The main function of vocalization is to attract and stimulate females, and choruses usually occur around bodies of water where eggs will be fertilized and laid.

The female faces a formidable task after she has arrived at a multi-species chorus. She must identify and locate a suitable male of her own species by extracting the proper sound pattern from a background of intense and complex noise. Vision and odor may provide information, but playbacks to females from loudspeakers have shown that the call alone is sufficient for the selection of the correct mate. It follows that each species in a chorus produces calls with distinctive qualities, and with a little practice, humans as well as frogs can determine the composition of the chorus.

Types of Call

Frog calls not only attract females of the same species, but they may also be used in territorial and other disputes between males. Very often the same call is used, so that what was formerly termed the "mating" call is now referred to as the "advertisement" call. It indicates the position and disposition of the male not only to potential mates but also to rivals.

When interacting with another male, a frog may add extra notes to his advertisement call or he may switch to an entirely different kind of call. These other calls have been variously termed "territorial" or "encounter" or "aggressive" calls. They appear to inform a rival of impending attack, or, in the early stages of conflict, they may serve mainly to disrupt the calling pattern of the competitor, making him less likely to attract females. In the species that have been tested, females are attracted to aggressive calls only when no male is making advertisement calls. Indeed, they may leave the vicinity of males that are sparring vocally to mate with a distant male producing advertisement calls.

There are two other kinds of call that are common in the repertoires of many kinds of frogs and toads. "Release" calls, usually given by a male clasped by another male, often have a similar acoustic structure to the aggressive calls described above. Unreceptive females may also give a release call, often similar to but distinguishable from that of the male. A release call is usually sufficient to make the clasping male let go of the unwilling sexual partner.

"Distress" calls differ from other calls, because they are given with the mouth open. They are usually produced when a frog is grasped by a predator, and many sound like screams. Other frogs apparently ignore distress calls, so it is possible that their function is to startle the predator, giving the frog a chance to escape.

While it is well established that calls allow the female to identify males of her own species, some researchers have suggested that the female may also assess calls of individual males in order to choose the fittest one. For example, in most species calls of the lowest frequencies are usually produced by the largest males, and females might gain by mating with these individuals. Large males may be older and their longevity may be due to genetically determined advantages which allow them to obtain food and avoid predators better than small, shorter-lived males.

This is a plausible hypothesis, but in nearly every species in which large males have been found to mate more often than small ones, it has been shown that the large animals gain their advantage by excluding small males from territories in which females lay their eggs or by directly displacing small males from females. There is little evidence that females prefer large males because they produce more attractive calls than small males, and in several species there appears to be no correlation between call pitch and mating success.

The Physiology of Calling

The calls are generated by vibrations of the vocal cords, located in the larynx; most calls are produced when the frog or toad exhales a large volume of air. Notable exceptions are the fire-bellied toads. These frogs produce sounds during inhalation, or during both inhalation and exhalation.

As a frog vocalizes, it inflates one or more vocal sacs. The vocal sac does not amplify (add energy to) the sound produced by the vocal cords but helps to couple these vibrations effectively to the surrounding air, rather like the soundboard of a piano. The sac can also modifiy the frequency spectrum of calls which have harmonics (multiple frequency components) by emphasizing some and filtering out others. Frog calls range in duration from simple, brief clicks of 5–10 milliseconds (eg the Spotted grass frog of Australia) to trills of several minutes as in the Great Plains toad of North America. In this case the long call is sustained by air being shunted back and forth across the

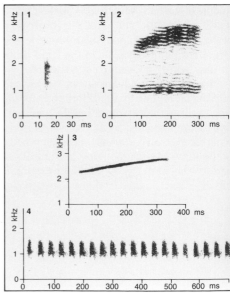

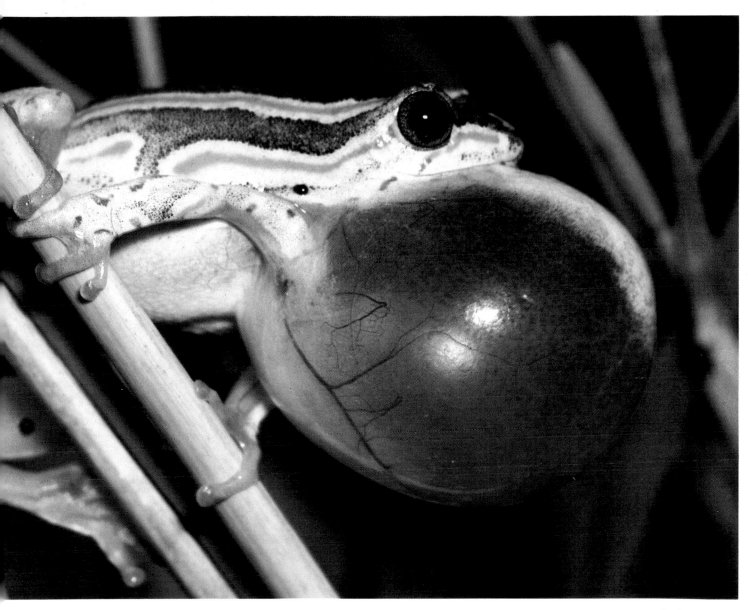

▲ **Fully-inflated vocal sac** of a calling male Marbled rush frog (*Hyperolius marmoratus*) from South Africa.

◄ **Visual interpretations** of frog calls—sonagrams of some types. (1) A short click of the Spotted grass frog (*Lymnodynastes tasmaniensis*). (2) Noisy call of the Squirrel tree frog (*Hyla squirella*). (3) Pure tone whistle of the Spring peeper (*Hyla crucifer*). (4) Long trill of the American toad (*Bufo americanus*), which may last 10 seconds. The vertical axis indicates frequency, or pitch, in kilohertz (kHz) and the horizontal axis time in milliseconds (ms); intensity of black representing loudness.

larynx between the lungs and the vocal sac.

In terms of sound quality, frog calls range from the pure-tone whistles of the Spring peeper to the noisy, duck-like croaks of the Squirrel tree frog. In frogs that produce trills, there are two mechanisms. The air flow from the lungs may be pulsed by rapid contractions of the body wall musculature ("active" pulsing); or the larynx itself may, by a pressure-sensitive mechanism, break a steady flow of air from the lungs into a series of pulses ("passive" pulsing).

Most frogs and toads have conspicuous tympanic membranes (eardrums) on either side of the head, just behind the eyes. Sound waves displace each eardrum directly from the outside and indirectly via the opposite ear and a pathway connecting the two ears internally. Movements of the eardrum are transferred by the middle ear bones to a fluid-filled capsule (otic), which contains two hearing organs, the amphibian and basilar papillae.

The first of these organs is unique to amphibians. Sound waves in the inner ear organs cause the cilia of hair cells to bend, and this in turn results in the generation of nerve impulses that are sent to the brain via the auditory nerve. The frequency of the calls of a particular species roughly matches the frequency sensitivity of one or the other of the two inner ear organs. Indeed, in some species there are two emphasized frequencies in the call, one which best excites the amphibian papilla, the other the basilar papilla. Recognition may, in part, be accomplished by this matching but there are usually also time cues, such as trill rates, that are also important and must be decoded in the female's auditory system.   HCG

REPTILES

CLASS: REPTILIA
Four orders: 48 families: about 905 genera:
6,547 species.

Turtles and Tortoises
Order: Chelonia (Testudines, Testudinata)
Two hundred and forty-four species in 75
genera and 13 families.
Includes: **musk terrapins** (genus *Sternotherus*),
Leatherback sea turtle (*Dermochelys coriacea*).

Lizards
Suborder: Sauria (Lacertilia); order Squamata
Three thousand seven hundred and fifty-one
species in 383 genera and 16 families.
Includes: **geckos** (family Gekkonidae), **Rock
lizard** (*Lacerta saxicola*), **slowworm** (*Anguis
fragilis*), **whiptail lizards** (genus *Cnemidophorus*).

Worm Lizards
Suborder: Amphisbaenia; order Squamata
One hundred and forty species in 21 genera
and 4 families.

Snakes
Suborder: Serpentes (Ophidia); order Squamata
Two thousand three hundred and eighty-nine
species in 417 genera and 11 families.
Includes: **European adder** (*Vipera berus*),
pythons (family Pythonidae), **sidewinder**
(*Crotalus cerastes*).

SNAKES, crocodiles, lizards—all animals that cause revulsion. Often they are thought of as cold, lurking animals, ancient relics of a group that is on its way out, superseded by birds and mammals. Their forerunners, the dinosaurs and other "prehistoric monsters," are the best known of all extinct animals, with a firm place in popular fantasy. They are accused of being cumbersome and stupid.

However, reptiles are in many respects much more successful than is often thought. In some habitats, notably deserts, they are a dominant group; the snakes have a recent evolutionary history of great diversification. Reptiles have one huge advantage over birds and mammals; being less dependent on maintaining a constant body temperature, they can survive on a fraction of the vast food input that birds and mammals require. They are thus able to exploit environments where food supplies are sparse or sporadic.

The reptiles' most obvious feature is their covering of dry, horny scales, which amphibians do not possess. They resemble primitive amphibians and birds in having only a single small bone in the ear, the columella or stapes, to conduct sound vibrations, and they have several bones in each side of the lower jaw. Mammals, on the other hand, have three small auditory bones and a single bone, the mandible, in the lower jaw, which corresponds to the reptilian dentary bone. Unlike birds and mammals, reptiles are mainly dependent upon external sources of heat such as the sun's rays for maintaining their body temperature (see pp70–71).

Reptiles reproduce by laying shelled eggs on land or by bearing their young alive. They do not pass through an aquatic larval stage like most amphibians. Their embryos, like those of birds and mammals, are provided with special membranes, notably the amnion, which are of great importance in terrestrial reproduction (see p65).

Origins and Classification
The reptiles arose from amphibians of some kind, but the details of their early history are not clearly understood and current ideas about them are in a state of flux. Remains of the most primitive known reptiles have been found inside fossil tree stumps of the

◄▼► **Extinct reptiles.** Subclass Diapsida includes the most prominent reptiles, past and present. One important line of diapsids are the archosaurs, which included saurischian dinosaurs such as *Saltoposuchus* (1) and *Cetiosauriscus* (2), ornithischian ("bird-hipped") dinosaurs such as *Corythosaurus* (8) and flying archosaurs such as *Pterodactylus* (9). The lepidosaurs, represented here by *Champsosaurus* (7) were then a less prominent line of diapsids, but include the majority of present-day reptiles: the tuatara, lizards, snakes and worm lizards. The great marine reptiles of the Mesozoic, the ichthyosaurs, such as *Stenopterygius* (4), and plesiosaurs such as *Plesiosaurus* (5), belong to subclass Euryapsida. Subclass Synapsida produced the therapsid reptiles, such as *Thrinaxodon* (3). Subclass Anapsida contains the most primitive reptiles, eg *Bradysaurus* (6).

Approximate lengths of the reptiles are: (1) 1.1m/3.75ft, (2) 13.7m/45ft, (3) 0.5m/1.5ft, (4) 3m/10ft, (5) 3m/10ft, (6) 1.8m/6ft, (7) 0.9m/3ft, (8) 8.2m/27ft, (9) wingspan 0.3m/1ft.

Tuatara
Order Rhynchocephalia
One species: *Sphenodon punctatus*.

Crocodilians
Order: Crocodylia
Twenty-two species in 8 genera and 3 families.
Includes: **American alligator** (*Alligator mississippiensis*), **Nile crocodile** (*Crocodylus niloticus*).

early Upper Carboniferous (about 315 million years ago). They were small terrestrial creatures superficially like lizards; it is likely that they were ancestral to most if not all the principal groups of later reptiles.

However, it would seem that even at this ancient period the reptiles had already split into two main lineages, for there are less numerous remains from the same time of larger reptiles of a different type. These were the earliest members of the mammal-like line which ultimately led to the first tiny mammals at the end of the Triassic period (about 190 million years ago).

The "cheek" or temporal region of the skull behind the orbits (eye sockets) has long been regarded as important in reptilian classification. A key feature distinguishing the various subclasses of reptiles is the number and nature of holes in this region. In the most primitive reptiles it presents an unbroken shell of bone without openings or "apses" (arched recesses). For this reason they are placed in the subclass Anapsida. In reptiles of the mammal-like line, a single opening has appeared with a bar of bone beneath it, a feature which may have been associated with changes in the attachments of the jaw muscles. These mammal-like reptiles belong to the subclass Synapsida.

In Permian times (280–225 million years ago) another group of reptiles appeared, with two temporal openings on each side of the skull, each opening bounded below by a bony bar or "arch." These belong to the subclass Diapsida which contains the majority of reptiles, both living and extinct.

Two main lines of diapsids became numerous and diverse towards the end of the Triassic, when the mammal-like synapsids were disappearing. One line is called the Lepidosauria, not a helpful term since it just means "scaly reptiles." It contains most living reptiles: the tuatara, conventionally placed in the order Rhynchocephalia (although this classification is due for revision), and the three suborders of the order Squamata—the lizards, the snakes, and the worm lizards, a group of worm-like burrowing reptiles.

The tuatara retains the typical skull structure of the early diapsids with two distinct temporal openings. In many ways it can be regarded as a "living fossil." Close relatives occurred in the Triassic. In "typical" lizards the upper temporal opening is surrounded by bone but the bar beneath the lower one has disappeared.

The earliest lizards occurred in the Triassic, but snakes do not appear until the Lower Cretaceous (about 135 million years ago); they are the most recently evolved of all the bigger groups of reptiles, and in terms of numbers of families and species they have been spectacularly successful. They most probably arose from lizards, perhaps from unknown burrowing types which must, however, have been very different from the various kinds of burrowing limbless lizards alive today.

The other principal diapsid line was the Archosauria which became immensely successful during the Jurassic and Cretaceous periods (between about 190 and 65 million years ago). It is these "ruling reptiles" that draw the human imagination to the Jurassic and the Cretaceous, above all other periods in the Age of Reptiles (see pp68–69). The most spectacular archosaurs were the dinosaurs, mostly large or enormous creatures, although a few were little bigger than a pheasant. There were two distinct orders of them, the Saurischia, in which the hip bones were of the typical reptilian pattern, and the Ornithischia, "bird-hipped" forms. The Saurischia contained all the carnivorous bipedal types, culminating in *Tyrannosaurus*, with an overall length of 12m (40ft), and also immense quadrupedal herbivores, the brontosaurs, with tiny heads and long necks and tails. One of these, *Brachiosaurus*, with a length of 23m (75ft) and an estimated weight of 50 tonnes, was one of the heaviest land animals that has ever existed, although incomplete remains of an even larger relative have been reported.

The Ornithischia also contained both bipedal and quadrupedal types, but all were herbivorous. The bipeds include the well-known *Iguanodon* with a spur on its thumb, and the duck-billed dinosaurs, some of which possessed curious crests of disputed function on the tops of their heads. Among the ornithischian quadrupeds were the lumbering *Stegosaurus* with huge plates of bone down its back, and the rhinoceros-like horned dinosaurs such as *Triceratops*. Some

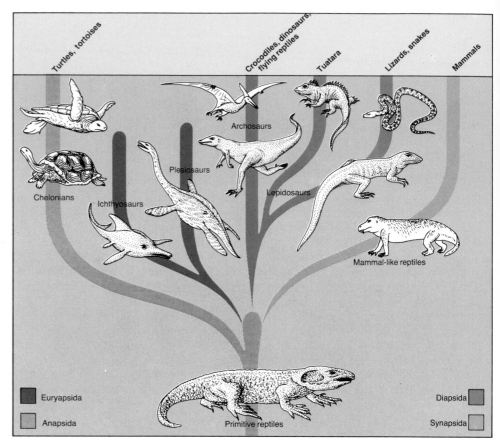

workers believe that the birds were descended from some kind of small primitive dinosaur, and the first known bird, *Archaeopteryx*, might well have been classified as a dinosaur if it were not for its feathers.

Other successful archosaurian groups were the flying reptiles (Pterosauria) and the Crocodylia, which originated like the dinosaurs and most of the other, better-known groups of reptiles in the Triassic. The flying reptiles were similar to birds in certain features, such as the keel on the sternum for the attachment of the flight muscles and the presence of air spaces in many bones to reduce their weight. However, the origin of the two groups seems to have been quite independent and the pterosaurs flew on wings quite unlike those of birds, being membranous and supported by the elongated bones of the fourth finger.

The Crocodylia, beautifully adapted for an amphibious predatory mode of life, are the only surviving archosaurs and their continued existence is threatened by the leather trade. A still unresolved problem of great geological and biological interest is why the crocodiles should have survived the mass extinction of reptiles at the end of the Cretaceous, when the dinosaurs and other spectacular groups became extinct.

There are two further groups of reptiles

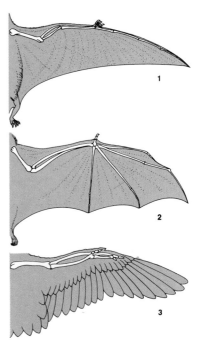

▲ **Wing structure** in (1) pterodactyls, (2) bats and (3) birds. Like a bat's, the pterodactyl wing was a membrane stretched over the bones of elongated fingers, but the longest finger was the fourth rather than the third.

◄ Chart of the evolution of reptiles.

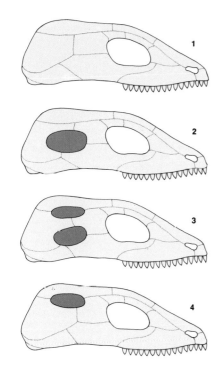

▲ **Reptilian skulls.** The arched recesses (apses) in the temporal region behind the eye sockets distinguish the four subclasses of reptiles. (1) In subclass Anapsida, there are no apses, or if there is a hole in the temporal region, as in many turtles and tortoises, it is anatomically unlike those in other subclasses. (2) In subclass Synapsida, which gave rise to the mammals, there is a single apse with a bar of bone beneath it. (3) In subclass Diapsida, including dinosaurs, pterosaurs and all living reptiles apart from turtles and tortoises, there are two apses. (4) Subclass Euryapsida, marine reptiles of the Mesozoic, has one apse high on the skull.

▼ **Hip joints** of the two lines of dinosaurs. (1) In saurischian dinosaurs the pubis is directed forward. (2) In ornithischian ("bird-hipped") dinosaurs the pubis is parallel to the ischium.

which do not fit easily into either the synapsid or the diapsid pattern. These are the great Jurassic marine reptiles, the fishlike ichthyosaurs, and the plesiosaurs with long necks and chunky bodies. Very little is known of their origins and there is no evidence that they were closely related. However, they both possessed a single temporal opening high up on the side of the skull and are tentatively placed in the subclass Euryapsida.

Finally there is the order Chelonia or Testudines, the tortoises and turtles, in some ways both the oddest and the most familiar of reptiles. They appear almost "fully fashioned" in the Triassic and virtually nothing is known of their origins. Unique features of their anatomy, however, suggest that they branched off from the primitive reptilian stock at a very early stage in evolution. In a few forms, such as the sea turtles, the skull seems to resemble the primitive anapsid pattern, but in many others certain bones appear to have been "eaten away" or emarginated from behind to produce a kind of temporal opening anatomically different from the one in synapsids, diapsids or euryapsids. They are provisionally placed in the subclass Anapsida, together with the most primitive known reptiles.

Skin

The skin is a fascinating organ with many functions. Besides acting as a barrier between the deeper tissues of the animal and the outside world, it can have a role in defense, concealment, mating and locomotion. In reptiles, as in other vertebrates, it consists of two principal layers, the epidermis on the outside and the dermis beneath.

The epidermis is itself subdivided into various layers, the outer one composed of the horny material called keratin. The scales of a reptile are localized thickenings of this keratin layer, connected by hinges of thinner material and often folded back so that they overlap each other. Unlike the scales of fish they are not separate, detachable

structures but parts of a continuous epidermal sheet. Their precise numbers and patterns on different parts of the head and body are of great value in reptilian classification, especially in the distinction between different species.

Periodically the keratinous layer of the epidermis is shed and replaced through the activity of the deeper layers of cells. The keratin may come away piecemeal or in large flakes. In snakes, however, it is often shed as a single slough which is peeled off inside out after the snake has rubbed it through at the snout. In these reptiles the old keratin layer on the surface is not shed until a new one has completely formed beneath it. Then a translucent zone of cleavage appears between the old and new layers so that they can easily become separated.

The brille, the spectacle-like eye-covering of a snake, formed from modified and fused eyelids, becomes blue and opaque some time before the animal is due to shed. Just before this happens, however, it becomes clear again and this clearing seems to coincide with the establishment of the cleavage zone. Skin-shedding in snakes may occur several times a year, being more frequent in young than in old animals. The process is influenced by the activity of the thyroid gland.

The dermis consists mainly of connective tissue and contains many blood vessels and nerves; it does not participate in the skin-shedding process. In some reptiles, including crocodilians and many lizards, it contains plates of bone called osteoderms which lie beneath and reinforce the horny epidermal scales. In the slowworm, and certain other lizards these osteoderms form a flexible bony covering for the body. The huge bony frills and plates of dinosaurs such as *Triceratops* and *Stegosaurus* were structures of this type, and probably had a horny covering which did not become fossilized.

Both epidermis and dermis participate in that remarkable structure, the shell of a turtle (see pp72–74). The horny scutes on the surface are keratinous epidermal formations with a layer of living cells beneath them, while the deeper, thicker shell layer is formed of bony dermal plates.

In reptiles the dermis also contains the majority of pigment cells. Many of these, the melanophores, contain black pigment, but there may also be white, yellow and red pigment cells. The dispersal or concentration of the pigment within the melanophores, and the optical effects of this when seen through the colored cells, are responsible for the

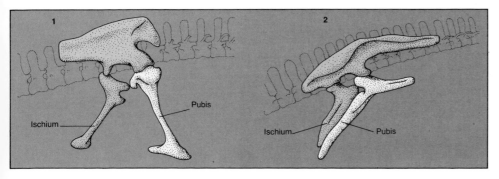

64 REPTILES

changes in color for which chameleons and certain other lizards are noted. Color change in reptiles may be brought about by nervous activity or by the hormonal secretions of glands such as the pituitary, or by a combination of both; in chameleons the action of the nerves seems to be the dominant factor.

The reptilian skin contains comparatively few glands, unlike that of many fish, amphibians and mammals. However, crocodilians possess a pair of glands beneath the throat which produce a musky secretion; this may play some part in sexual behavior. Some freshwater turtles have glands in the chin or the hind-limb pockets; in the musk turtles these produce a powerful smell.

A few otherwise non-poisonous snakes have glands beneath the scales of the neck or back which secrete an irritant material; defense against predators and some role in courtship behavior have been suggested as possible functions. In some geckos of the genus *Diplodactylus* there are a series of large glands beneath the scales of the tail. When the lizard is threatened they squirt out filaments of sticky material which may deter such enemies as large spiders.

Many lizards possess a series of curious gland-like structures on the insides of the thighs and sometimes in front of the cloaca. The function of these has been much debated; they seem to be related to mating since in male lacertid lizards they regress after castration. The most likely suggestion is that their secretions may assist in species or sexual recognition.

The Skeleton

Apart from its diapsid skull, the skeleton of the tuatara probably shows the greatest living resemblance to skeletons of primitive fossil reptiles. The other reptilian groups have departed in varying degrees from this primitive pattern, and such departures are usually in the nature of adaptations to special modes of life.

The loss of the lower temporal bar in lizards has been associated with the development of hinges at various points in the skull, allowing increased mobility of the jaws (kinesis). Jaw mobility has been carried even further in snakes, partly because of the loss of any firm union between the two sides of the lower jaw. This is an adaptation to eating large prey. The reduction or loss of the limbs in some lizards and nearly all snakes and an increase in the number of vertebrae is a dramatic adaptation to a special life-style—one that has been extraordinarily successful, enabling the snake to "outswim

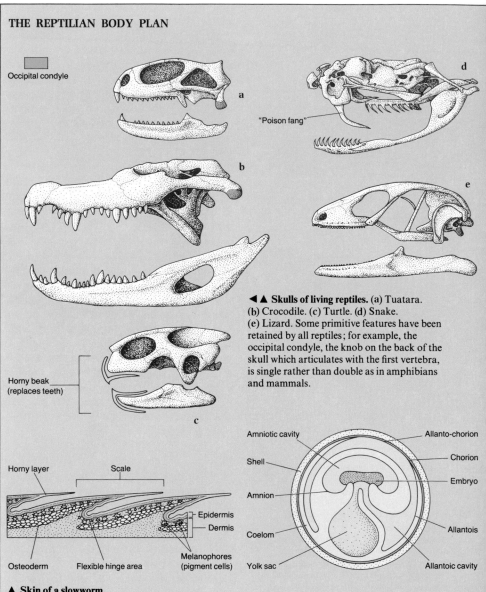

◀▲ **Skulls of living reptiles.** (a) Tuatara. (b) Crocodile. (c) Turtle. (d) Snake. (e) Lizard. Some primitive features have been retained by all reptiles; for example, the occipital condyle, the knob on the back of the skull which articulates with the first vertebra, is single rather than double as in amphibians and mammals.

▲ **Skin of a slowworm.**

▼▶ **Modifications of the skin.** The skin, particularly the epidermis, shows many modifications in reptiles. It may be raised up into tubercles (a), as in the chisel-teeth lizard *Ceratophora stoddarti*, or into defensive spines, as on the tails of certain lizards. It may form crests on the neck, back or tail, often better developed in the male and perhaps assisting in sexual recognition (b), as in *Lyriocephalus scutatus*.

The rattlesnake's rattle (c), composed of interlocking horny segments, is a unique epidermal structure; a new segment is formed at each molt, though the end segments tend to break off when the rattle gets very long.

In most snakes the underbody scales are enlarged to form a series of wide overlapping plates which assist in locomotion, especially in forms such as boas which can crawl stretched out almost straight. The fine bristles on the toe pads of geckos (d), which enable them to climb smooth surfaces, are also modified scales.

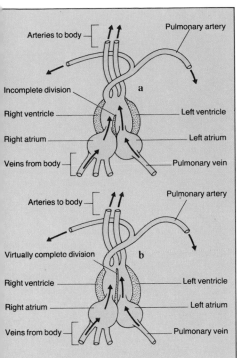

▲ **Reptilian hearts.** In most forms the two sides of the ventricle are not completely separated (a). In crocodilians (b) a separation exists. Even in the unseparated ventricle, there is little mixing of arterial and venous blood.

◀ **Developing egg,** showing layers of membrane between shell and embryo. The partly fused chorion and allantois, on the inner surface of the shell, are richly supplied with blood vessels, enabling the embryo to breathe through pores in the shell. The allantois also acts as a repository for the embryo's waste products. The amnion is a fluid-filled sac around the embryo which prevents it drying out. The yolk-sac contains the embryonic food supply, rich in protein and fats. Eggs of this type, including those of birds, are called cleiodic ("closed-box") eggs, since apart from respiration and some absorbtion of water from the environment they are self-sufficient. Water absorbtion by the eggs of many reptiles, especially the softer-shelled types, is higher than by birds' eggs.

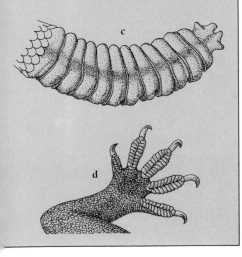

the fish and outclimb the monkey," as Sir Richard Owen wrote with pardonable exaggeration. The remarkable position of the limb girdles of tortoises and turtles, which are situated within rather than outside the ribs, is another striking specialization associated with the incorporation of the ribs into the dermal plates of the shell.

The reptilian skeleton contains a number of bones which are not found in mammals, at least as separate elements. Some of these, such as the parasphenoid and the supratemporal, occur in the skull. There is also a midline bone, the interclavicle, in the shoulder girdle of most reptiles; among mammals it occurs only in the egg-laying monotremes. The tuatara, lizards and turtles have, like birds, a series of small bony plates, the scleral ossicles, in the eye which assist in focusing. In the tuatara, crocodilians and some extinct reptiles, the belly wall is reinforced by a series of abdominal ribs or gastralia. Many lizards have a system of cartilaginous bars called the parasternum in much the same position.

Secondary centers of ossification (bony epiphyses) are lacking in the growing bones of most modern reptiles, although they do occur in many lizards. In mammals such as man the fusion of these with the main part of the bone in early adult life sets a limit to the maximum size attained.

The absence of bony epiphyses is perhaps one of the reasons why certain reptiles such as pythons, crocodiles and giant tortoises may be able to grow throughout much of their lives, albeit at a diminishing rate. If an individual is lucky enough to avoid life's hazards it may eventually become a giant, well above the usual size range of its species. However, many reptiles including the smaller lizards and turtles normally stop growing when they have reached a more or less definite size.

Moreover, reptiles do not lose their teeth when they get old in the way that mammals do; most reptiles have continuous, lifelong tooth replacement, while turtles, which did away with their teeth at an early stage in their history, have evolved a persistently growing horny beak. This removes a constraint on longevity and therefore also on the ultimate potential size attainable by a species.

Reproduction

In most species of reptile the two sexes differ to some extent in adult size, shape or color. The males of many lizards, land tortoises and all crocodilians are bigger than the females, whereas in most snakes and some aquatic turtles it is the females that are bigger.

Differences between the sexes are particularly striking among the agamid and iguanid families, lizards in which the eyes are the predominant sense organs. The males tend to be more brightly colored, especially in the breeding season, and in some species they possess erectile crests and throat fans which play a part in courtship and territorial display.

All reptiles practice internal fertilization, the sperm being introduced directly into the female's cloaca, the common opening which transmits both excretory products and eggs or sperm. In the tuatara fertilization is achieved by cloacal contact, but in all other living reptiles the males have special organs of insemination. In turtles and tortoises and the crocodilians there is a single penis; lizards and snakes have evolved paired organs called hemipenes; only one is used at a time (see pp92, 93). The females of some snakes and some turtles and tortoises have the ability to store sperm in the reproductive tract and instances of isolated females laying fertile eggs after a year or more in captivity have been observed.

Breeding in reptiles is greatly influenced by environmental factors such as temperature and the duration of daylight. Some tropical species may breed at intervals throughout the year, but in the majority, breeding takes place only once, or perhaps twice a year. Indeed, among reptiles which live in relatively severe climates such as the adder in northern Europe an individual female may breed only once every two years, or even less often.

Sexual reproduction is the general rule among vertebrates but it has been discovered that some populations of rock lizards in the Caucasus region of the southwestern USSR consist entirely of females and reproduce by parthenogenesis or "virgin birth." This also happens in certain whiptail lizards in North America. In this method of reproduction, all members of the population are genetically identical, all descended from a single founding female. The low level of genetic variability in such a species both confines it to a limited geographical area and probably limits its future in evolutionary time, because of its reduced ability (compared with a sexual species) to adapt to changing environmental conditions (see p93). Reptiles are the "highest" animal group in which parthenogenesis normally occurs.

Most modern reptiles lay eggs, which, unlike amphibians' eggs, are resistant to

◄ **Hatching from the egg,** a baby Green mamba (*Dendroaspis polylepis*) uses its snout to break the parchment-like covering that has kept it moist during development. The tiny egg tooth, used to slit the eggshell, can be seen on the tip of the snout. It falls off after a few days.

► **Sloughing its skin,** an Ashy gecko (*Sphaerodactylus cinereus*) reveals its new, fully-colored skin beneath the old. This species occurs in Florida and parts of the Caribbean.

▼ **Live-bearer.** A European adder with a newly-born baby. Individual adders, like all vipers, are very variable in appearance, and here the typical zig-zag stripe is more apparent in the baby than its mother.

drying out. Fossilized eggs of dinosaurs and more primitive extinct reptiles have been discovered. These eggs possess a shell which may be pliable or parchment-like in texture, as in many lizards, snakes and aquatic chelonians, or hard and well calcified, as in tortoises, crocodilians and many geckos. Hatching from the egg is facilitated by the presence in young lizards and snakes of a sharp, forward-pointing egg-tooth which is later shed; in the tuatara, tortoises and turtles, crocodilians and birds a horny outgrowth performs the same function.

The replacement of aquatic amphibian eggs by the shelled amniote egg must have played a vital part in liberating the reptiles from their watery ancestral habitat and fitting them to become the first successful vertebrate colonists of the land. The eggs of reptiles are usually laid in holes, among rotting vegetation or buried in the soil. Sea turtles dig nests in sand on beaches and lay large clutches of up to 100 or more eggs. They resort to traditional nesting beaches, and Green turtles may migrate hundreds of kilometers to reach them. Some crocodilians such as the Nile crocodile also dig nests in the sand, but others such as the American alligator construct more elaborate nests out of piled-up vegetation.

The rate of embryonic development is accelerated by warmth. It has been discovered that in certain turtles and tortoises and some crocodilians the sex of the hatchling depends on the prevailing temperature during a critical period of incubation. Thus, in the American alligator temperatures of less than 30°C (86°F) between the 7th and 21st days of incubation produce all females whereas those of more than 34° (93°F) produce all males. It has been suggested that the possible occurrence of a similar method of sex determination in dinosaurs might have contributed to their extinction. If temperatures increased or decreased markedly at the end of the Cretaceous, a unisex population might have resulted. But why were the crocodiles apparently not affected?

The majority of reptiles abandon their eggs after laying but in certain lizards, for example in some skinks, and also in a few snakes such as cobras, the female remains with her eggs and may try to drive intruders from the nest. Attendance by the male has also been reported in cobras. Female pythons remain coiled round their eggs for up to several weeks and in some species the

egg temperature may be actively raised; this incubation may be assisted by muscular contractions of the mother's body (see p116). During recent years remarkably elaborate forms of parental care have been observed in crocodilians (see p140).

A very substantial number of lizards and snakes have forsaken egg-laying and gone over to live-bearing, the young escaping from their membranes at or shortly after birth. In such reptiles the eggshell is lost or reduced, and in many species a kind of placenta is developed from the fused chorion and allantois and from the yolk sac. This allows exchange of some waste products and nutritional substances, as well as water and gases, between the embryo and the mother. Most viviparous species are "ovoviviparous"—the yolk remains large and is still the principal source of embryonic food—but in a few with particularly well-developed placentae, the yolk is reduced.

Most sea snakes have become viviparous, and therefore do not have to come on land to lay their eggs, as the turtles have to do. This method of reproduction is also prevalent in reptiles which live under very severe climatic conditions, as in high latitudes or altitudes. It is found in three out of the six species of British reptiles. Under such conditions viviparity seems to be advantageous in enabling the mother to act as a mobile incubator, able to seek out sources of warmth which are optimal for the development of her embryos.   AAB

Dinosaurs and other "Prehistoric Monsters"

The age of reptiles

Between 280 and 65 million years ago, a multitude of reptiles occupied ecological niches comparable to those filled by mammals and birds today. Their remains exhibit an astonishing, often bizarre, variety of form and habit. This "Age of Reptiles" opened in the Permian (280–225 million years ago), when early reptiles gained ascendancy over the amphibians, and it lasted throughout the Mesozoic (225–65 million years ago). Pelycosaurs, then therapsids, were the dominant reptiles until the thecodonts, ancestral order of the subclass Archosauria, underwent a remarkable evolutionary explosion in the late Triassic (ending 190 million years ago). Thecodonts spawned the crocodilians, the pterosaurs (flying reptiles) and the dinosaurs that were to dominate the greater part of the Mesozoic era.

When dinosaur remains were first recognized in the 1820s, these animals were viewed as enormous herbivores, which, like modern reptiles, were "cold-blooded" and moved with a sprawling gait. Today's definition of a dinosaur includes some small creatures and many carnivores. One school maintains that some at least were "warm-blooded" endotherms. Another, much more accepted, modern view is that dinosaurs did not sprawl. Changes in the limbs and girdles allowed some of their thecodontian ancestors to develop a "semi-improved" stance and gait. The dinosaurs themselves reached the "fully improved" stage, with limbs supporting the body from underneath.

Some became bipeds, running and walking on their hind legs.

The increased agility thus achieved and an increasing size allowed the archosaurs to succeed at the expense of the therapsids in the middle to late Triassic. The earliest archosaurs were all carnivorous. As the first of them reached the dinosaurian level of evolution, the carnivores among the therapsids almost disappeared under the pressure of competition. A few survived and in the late Triassic evolved into the first tiny mammals. Next, selective pressure among the dinosaurian carnivores compelled some to turn to a vegetarian diet, resulting in the demise of the therapsid herbivores.

Most authorities believe that "fully improved" locomotion evolved independently in three different lines of dinosaurs: the theropods, sauropodomorphs and ornithischians. These groups are sometimes regarded as three separate orders, but it is more customary to classify the theropods and sauropodomorphs together as a single order, the Saurischia. The three groups of dinosaurs remained terrestrial. Flying pterosaurs comprise a separate order of the Archosauria and the aquatic ichthyosaurs and plesiosaurs, prominent in the Jurassic

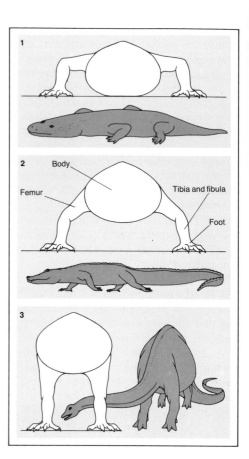

(190–136 million years ago) are even more distantly related, belonging to the subclass Euryapsida. Some dinosaurs may have ventured occasionally into lakes and rivers, but this tendency was not great.

The smallest dinosaur, *Mussaurus*, was no bigger than a thrush; the largest complete skeleton known is of *Brachiosaurus*; it stands 12.6m (42ft) high and the weight of the animal is estimated at 80 tonnes. Some fragmentary remains indicate that there were considerably larger creatures. There were hunting dinosaurs and scavengers, egg-eaters, browsers and fruit-eaters. Some had armored skin, others enormously thickened skulls, horns on the face, crests on the head, bony frills protecting the neck, huge plates along the back, or spikes or a club on the tail. For the most part, each form flourished for only a short time, so that late Cretaceous dinosaurs were very different from their Triassic ancestors.

At the end of the Cretaceous (about 65 million years ago) the dinosaurs became extinct—as did many other groups of organisms. There is much controversy over these extinctions: were they simultaneous world-wide, or did their timing vary from place to place? Were they gradual, or sudden? Were they a normal evolutionary phenomenon, differing only in scale from what is happening all the time, or were they due to some unique catastrophe such as an asteroid hitting the planet, causing major climatic changes? Some 90 different causes have

been suggested, but none gives a satisfactory explanation for the extinctions while still allowing for the survival, apparently unaffected, of dozens of other groups living in the same habitats.

When the dinosaurs were gone, the tiny mammals which had scurried at their feet were able to evolve new forms to occupy the major land-animal niches; and so, ironically, the dinosaurs were superseded by descendants of the therapsid reptiles that they had displaced in their own rise to dominance. However, the dinosaurs' own descendants may also be alive and flourishing. *Archaeopteryx*, the oldest known bird (dating from the late Jurassic), may be nothing more than a small theropod dinosaur with feathers and some flying capability. AJC

◀ **Limb posture** in extinct and living reptiles. (1) Sprawling stance of early reptiles and living lizards. (2) "Semi-improved" stance of early thecodonts and living crocodilians. (3) "Fully improved" stance of dinosaurs, which evolved independently in mammals.

◀▼ **Representative species** of dinosaurs (approximate lengths are given in brackets). (1) *Massospondylus* (3.7m/12ft). (2) *Pachyrhinosaurus* (4.6m/15ft). (3) *Triceratops* ((6.1m/20ft). (4) *Struthiomimus* (2.4m/8ft). (5) *Psittacosaurus* (1.8m/6ft). (6) *Stegosaurus* (5.5m/18ft). (7) *Scolosaurus* (5.5m/18ft). (8) *Tyrannosaurus* (9.1m/30ft).

Temperature Control by Sun and Shade
Ectothermy in reptiles

Early on a sunny day, lizards can be seen emerging from their retreats, climbing onto rocks and basking in the warm sun. Soon they will start moving in search of a meal or a mate, but before long they shuttle back to the shade. They typically bask, then forage, then pause in the shade, then resume basking, and forage again. As the day becomes warmer, they spend less time basking and more in shade.

Not all reptiles behave like this. Some lowland tropical reptiles, whose environments are almost always warm and constant, never bask. Geckos and many snakes are active in the relatively uniform microclimates of the night; some may seek out warm surfaces such as roads, but opportunities are limited.

However, for most reptiles the world is a mosaic of distinctly warm and cold spots. By shuttling between locations of higher and lower environmental temperature, they can regulate their body temperature, even influencing rates of heat gained in basking by making subtle changes in posture or orientation to alter the surface area exposed to the sun. The pattern of regulation varies with the seasons. During cool months, reptiles become active only at midday when environmental temperatures are warm. During summer months they retreat underground at midday to avoid overheating. Remarkably, in some reptiles this behavioral thermoregulation keeps body temperatures at higher and only slightly more variable levels than physiological thermoregulation does in some mammals and birds. Most importantly, the animal's core temperature, especially that of the brain, is kept at levels permitting normal functioning.

Birds and mammals also use behavior to help maintain high body temperatures, but most of their body heat comes from their high metabolic rates. Feathers or fur are good insulation and minimize the loss of this body heat to the environment. Although reptiles do produce some metabolic heat, metabolic control of body temperatures is ineffective for them because their metabolic rates are very low and their scales are an ineffective barrier against heat loss.

However, reptiles may enhance behavioral temperature regulation with certain physiological adjustments. Early in the day, hormones cause a lizard to darken by dispersing melanin pigments in its skin: dark skin readily absorbs radiant energy from the sun and promotes rapid heating. Control of body temperature is possible because part of the brain (the hypothalamus) works like a thermostat. Nerve signals from the hypothalamus cause a reptile to seek either heat or cold, depending on whether the hypothalamus is cooler or warmer than the preferred temperature range.

Temperature regulation promotes the growth, reproduction, and survival of reptiles by controlling the rates of physiological processes. An increase of 10 Celsius degrees (18 Fahrenheit degrees) generally doubles or triples these rates. High temperatures are necessary for rapid digestion, and a captive snake denied access to heat may die because the food in its stomach is too cold and rots.

Reptiles active in poor weather may have low body temperatures and may be slow and thus vulnerable to predators. Some species compensate by becoming very wary. Some others, which flee from predators when warm, become very aggressive, switching from "flight to fight," apparently because they are too sluggish to outrun predators.

Lizards prefer the highest temperatures, some being active at temperatures averaging 42°C (107°F), and the physiology of any day-active desert reptile usually functions best at high temperatures. The tuatara has

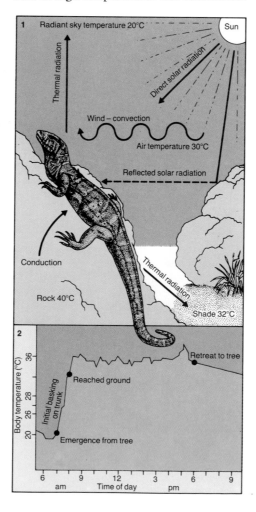

◀ **Heat flows from warm to cold objects.**
(1) Diagram showing the major avenues of heat exchange between reptiles and the physical environment. In regulating their body temperature, reptiles take advantage of the fact that their environment is thermally diverse.
(2) The body temperature of a lizard during the day is relatively high and constant, but it may fall when the lizard is in its retreat at night. These continuous records of body temperature were gathered by a small, temperature-sensitive radiotransmitter swallowed by the lizard. The pulse rate of signals from the transmitter increases with the temperature.

▶ **Darkening of the skin** in response to light. ABOVE A chameleon is partly shaded by a leaf. BELOW The pattern of the leaf momentarily remains as paler skin when the chameleon moves into the full light of the sun.

▼ **Incubating snake** – a python coiled around its eggs to keep them at the correct temperature.

the lowest temperatures when active: 6–16°C (43–61°F). The thermal preferences of individuals also vary. To speed their digestion, snakes often select higher temperatures after feeding. Lizards with bacterial infections maintain above-normal body temperatures, a "behavioral fever."

The discovery of temperature regulation in reptiles has brought about changes in terminology. Reptiles had long been described as "cold-blooded" or "poikilothermic" animals whose body temperatures were invariably lower and more variable than those of the "warm-blooded" or "homeothermic" birds and mammals. The thermoregulatory abilities of reptiles having demonstrated the inappropriateness of these expressions, biologists now distinguish between "endotherms," whose primary source of body heat is internal (birds and mammals), and "ectotherms," whose primary source is external.

Each group has distinct advantages and disadvantages. Ectotherms exploit solar heating, which is economical but effective only when the sun is shining. Endotherms use metabolic "furnaces" effective even in poor weather or at night but requiring considerable fuel: endotherms need 30–50 times more food than reptiles of comparable size. Hence reptiles can even survive in extreme deserts, where birds and mammals have difficulty obtaining enough food. The long success of reptiles must be due in part to their thermoregulatory abilities and to their economical life-style.   RBH

▲ **Basking monitor.** The Lace monitor (*Varanus varius*) is a lizard of Australia.

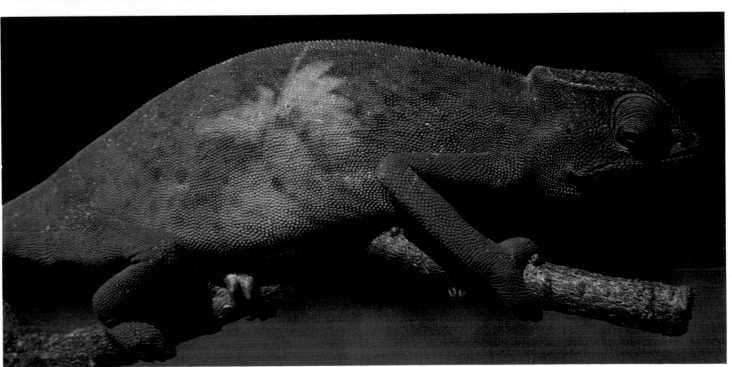

TURTLES AND TORTOISES

Order: Chelonia (Testudines, Testudinata)
Two hundred and forty-four species in 75 genera and 13 families.
Distribution: temperate and tropical regions, on all continents except Antarctica and in all oceans.

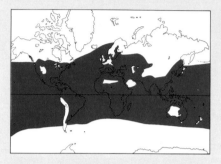

Habitat: marine, freshwater aquatic and semiaquatic, terrestrial.

Size: maximum straight-line shell length 11–185cm (4–73in).

Color: highly variable, ranging from dull, dark and cryptic in bottom-dwellers to brightly patterned conspicuous forms. Browns, olives and shades of gray or black predominate on upper surfaces, with yellows, red and oranges common for pattern markings. Yellows, with brown, black and white predominate on undersurfaces.

Reproduction: fertilization internal; all lay eggs on land; parental care in one species.

Longevity: occasionally living more than 100 years in captivity (best documented record more than 152 years); some American box turtles thought to survive up to 120 years in wild; aquatic species probably shorter-lived.

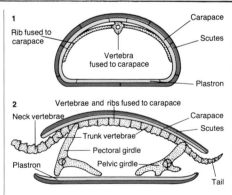

▲ Structure of the chelonian shell.
(1) Transverse section. (2) Longitudinal section, showing the arrangement of pectoral and pelvic girdles.

► Aggressive and short-tempered, the Snapping turtle of eastern North America commands respect from all who know it. Reaching 47cm (18in) in length, it includes turtles in a varied diet.

OVER 200 million years ago, before there were mammals, birds, lizards, snakes or crocodiles, turtles with fully formed shells abruptly appear in the fossil record as contemporaries of the earliest dinosaurs. Unlike modern species, they had teeth and could not withdraw their heads, but they were unmistakeably turtles. The character positively identifying them is their shell.

The Turtle's Shell

No other vertebrate has evolved an armor quite like the turtle's shell. Comprised of some 59–61 bones, a turtle shell consists of two parts: a "carapace" covering the animal's back and a "plastron" covering its belly. These are connected on each side by a bony bridge formed by extensions at the sides of the plastron.

The carapace is formed from bones originating in the dermal layer of the skin. They are fused with one another and with the animal's ribs and vertebrae. Large scales or scutes, derived from the epidermal layer of the skin, cover and strengthen the bony constituents of the shell. The plastron is derived from certain bones of the shoulder girdle (the clavicle and interclavicle) and the gastralia (abdominal ribs like those found in crocodilians today). The remaining portion of the shoulder girdle has shifted inside the turtle's ribs, a unique feature found in no other vertebrate present or past.

So successful was this protective armor that it became the cornerstone of turtle architecture. Other adaptations have been built around it, and it accounts both for the longevity of the line and its limited diversity.

Because of the shell, running, jumping and flying turtles were not viable evolutionary options, but moderate adaptive radiation has occurred within the group. Beginning as semiaquatic marsh dwellers, some turtles evolved to become totally terrestrial, inhabiting forests, grasslands and deserts. Others became more thoroughly aquatic, invading lakes, rivers, estuaries and the sea.

Ironically, the massive shell which led to their initial success has become much reduced in most modern lines. The larger tortoises have retained an extensive shell while greatly reducing its weight through marked thinning of the shell bones. Strength is provided by the durable light-weight scutes and by the shape of the shell rather than by heavy bone. In highly aquatic forms such as softshells and sea turtles, the bones of the shell have decreased in size, leaving large spaces (fontanelles) between them. The most extreme case is the Leatherback sea turtle which as an adult lacks epidermal scutes and has only small bony platelets embedded in its leathery skin. The chief advantages of shell reduction seem to have been a lower energy cost for locomotion and greater buoyancy in the aquatic forms.

Different life-styles and ecologies have led to other alterations in shell structure. Land turtles typically have high-vaulted shells as a defense against their predators' crushing jaws. Water turtles have lower, more streamlined shells that offer less water resistance during swimming. Extreme flattening is found among the softshells, helping them to hide beneath sand and mud on the bottom of their watery habitat. Exceptions exist in both categories, however. The shell of the African Pancake tortoise is not domed, but extremely flattened, allowing it to squeeze into narrow crevices within its rocky habitat. With force generated by its legs and the natural elasticity of the shell bones, the tortoise becomes extremely difficult to extract once it has become wedged. On the other hand, aquatic species such as the Asian River terrapin and the Florida redbelly turtle, which cohabit with large voracious crocodilians, have forfeited some streamlining and evolved high-vaulted, buttressed shells for protection.

The protective importance of the bony shell improves with age. The small, soft-boned young of certain species have evolved prominent epidermal spines, most commonly around the edge of the shell, to discourage predators. The extreme of this adaptation is found in the Spiny forest turtle of southeast Asia. Nearly circular in outline with each marginal scute attenuated into a spine, juveniles of this species resemble sharply-toothed cogwheels. The shells of the matamata and the Alligator snapping turtle are disguised with bumps and ridges giving them a nonturtle-like appearance.

A number of turtles have evolved nonrigid shells with varying degrees of movement between bones (kinesis). A common modification is the hinged plastron. Various turtles including Indian flapshells, American and African mud turtles, Asian and American box turtles and Madagascan and Egyptian tortoises have evolved one or two plastral hinges. African hinge-backed tortoises have a hinge on the carapace rather than on the plastron. Hinges give these turtles the capability of tightly closing the shell with the vulnerable parts within. While this no doubt provides protection from predators, protection against loss of moisture is probably an equally important function: few species with hinges are fully aquatic.

A lesser degree of movement is found among certain pond and river turtles. Some such as the Asian leaf turtle, the Malayan flat-shelled turtle and neotropical wood turtles have partial hinging of the plastron and connections of ligament rather than bony connections between the plastron and carapace. Their plastrons are somewhat movable but cannot close the carapace. This flexibility appears necessary to allow the turtles to lay their exceptionally large, brittle-shelled eggs, which could not otherwise fit through the shell opening. In the Cane turtle, Spiny turtle and Tricarinate hill turtle only mature females develop the kinetic plastron.

Certain large-headed, aggressive turtles, such as snapping turtles and Mexican musk turtles, also have movable plastrons due to a reduction in the bones and a ligamentous connection to the carapace. In these species the flexibility of the plastron allows the turtle to retract its large head within the shell with jaws agape, thus providing a formidable and nearly impregnable defense.

Growth

Most turtles and tortoises attain a maximum size of at least 13cm (5in) in shell length. The Speckled cape tortoise, Flattened musk turtle and Bog turtle with maximum shell lengths of less than 12cm (4.7in) are among the world's smallest turtles. The giant of living turtles is the Leatherback which attains a shell length of more than 183cm (72in) and may weigh up to 683kg (1,503lb). Other impressively large species are the Alligator snapping turtle at 72cm (28in) and 91kg (200lb), Narrow-headed softshell at 115cm (45in) and 120kg (264lb), South American river turtle at 90cm (35.5in) and 90kg (198lb) and Aldabra giant tortoise at 140cm (55in) and 254kg (559lb).

Growth rates of turtles vary considerably even within members of the same clutch. Habitat, temperature, rainfall, sunshine, food type and availability and sex have been associated with growth rate in turtles. Generally, a species grows rapidly to sexual maturity; then the rate slows markedly. In later years small species may stop growing completely but larger turtles can grow throughout life.

Growth can be more conveniently studied in turtles than in most reptiles because many species carry growth records along with them on their horny scutes. Each time a turtle stops growing, such as during the winter or dry season, a growth-ring depression forms on each scute, much like an annual ring on a tree trunk. In turtles which do not shed the scutes (most terrestrial and semiaquatic species), a permanent record accumulates, which researchers can use to calculate growth rate and age, provided the turtle is still growing. Many aquatic species regularly shed their scutes, however, and within a few years the impressions of the earlier growth rings fade, then disappear, making age estimates unreliable. The technique also works better where the growth season is well defined by the onset of winter. Tropical turtles with a year-round growing season may still form growth rings on their scutes but these do not necessarily represent the end of a year's growth.

Locomotion

Turtles are reputedly slow-moving animals. Certainly most tortoises, with their mobility greatly restricted by a large cumbersome

Longevity in Turtles

Some turtles have been known to live well over one century, and they may be among the longest-lived vertebrates. The most exceptional ages are recorded for pet terrestrial forms, but reliable records about pets which outlive their original owners are difficult to obtain.

One somewhat questionable record concerns a Radiated tortoise reputed to have been given to the King of Tonga by Captain Cook in either 1773 or 1777. The tortoise was considered to be an important gift and Tongan rulers accorded high status and privileges to it. After surviving two forest fires, being run over by a cart and being kicked by a horse, the tortoise reportedly died in 1966 after a minimum of 189 years in captivity. Unfortunately there appears to be no record of this gift in Captain Cook's journals.

The so-called "Marion's" tortoise is better documented. Five tortoises collected by the French explorer Marion de Fresne in 1776 from the Seychelles were taken to Mauritius. When the British captured Mauritius in 1810 they inherited the tortoises along with the island. The tortoises were kept on the grounds of the Royal Artillery Barracks at Port Louis, the island's capital. The last of the five survived until 1918 when, after 152 years of captivity and owing to blindness, it fell into a gun emplacement and died. The tortoise was presumably an adult when captured and could have been nearing 200 years old when it died.

The Spur-thighed tortoise (a common pet in Europe) occasionally survives over a century. In North America, Eastern box turtles are often found with initials and dates carved in their shells. Researchers have determined that people with initials found on some shells actually lived within the turtles' ranges at the date of carving. It appears likely that some box turtles survive over a 100 years in the wild.

Estimates of the longevity of aquatic turtles in the wild have ranged from 40 to 75 years but reliable documentation exists only for those near the lower end of the range (eg painted turtles). Captive European pond turtles have survived for 70 years, wood turtles and Alligator snapping turtles for 60 years and a number of other captive species have approached 40 (eg Australian Snake-necked turtles, West African mud turtles and spotted turtles). A Loggerhead sea turtle reached 33 years in captivity. Mature female Green turtles have returned to the same nesting beach for at least 20 years.

▲ **Food for Darwinian thought.** The Galapagos giant tortoise is a leisurely browser reaching shell lengths of 1.2m (4ft). Several races live in geographic isolation from each other on different members of the Galapagos island group in Equador. The correlation between their isolation and their divergence in size and shape helped to stimulate Charles Darwin's formation of ideas about evolution. Today three races are probably extinct, and the rest are endangered. In some populations reproduction is impossible without the aid of conservation authorities: naturally produced eggs and young are eaten by introduced rats, dogs and pigs, or trampled by grazing donkeys.

shell, are slow. The Desert tortoise moves at speeds of 0.22–0.48km/hour (0.13–0.3 mph). Charles Darwin clocked a Galapagos giant tortoise at 6.4km (4mi) per day. However, sea turtles with swimming speeds in excess of 30km/hour (18.6mph) can move as swiftly through water as humans can run on land.

The limbs of a turtle are good indicators of their habitat and means of locomotion. Tortoises, the most terrestrially adapted group, have elephantine feet in which the toes are very short and lack all traces of webbing. In the Gopher tortoise, an accomplished burrower, the front limbs are much flattened and serve as digging scoops.

The feet of aquatic turtles differ by having longer toes joined together by a fleshy or membranous web providing the feet with additional thrust through water. Aquatic turtles move either by bottom walking or by swimming. Bottom walkers move over the bottom in much the same manner that they walk on land. The matamata, Malayan box turtle, snapping turtles and mud turtles use bottom walking as their primary mode of locomotion. Swimming species such as the Smooth softshell, the River terrapin and the Central American river turtle may bottom walk but usually paddle through the water using all four limbs in an alternating sequence. Much of the power stroke is accomplished by simultaneous retraction of the opposing front and hind foot. The stroke provides thrust while maintaining the animal's direction of travel. Sea turtles and the Pig-nosed softshell are the most specialized swimmers. Their forelimbs, modified into flipper-shaped blades, move synchronously and gracefully in what might be best termed aquatic flying. The hind feet provide little propulsion and serve chiefly as rudders.

Respiration
Descendants of terrestrial ancestors, turtles not surprisingly respire with lungs. However, due to their rigid shell, their breathing differs from that of other vertebrates. Pressure changes within the lungs of most turtles are created by muscles that expand, then retract within the front- and hind-limb pockets. Expiration is aided by abdominal muscles which compress the lungs by forcing the internal organs against them. Movements of the limbs and girdles augment these actions.

Lungs are not the only organs of respiration in turtles. Aquatic species can also respire through their skin, the lining of the throat and through thin-walled sacks, or

bursae, in the cloaca. The degree to which these accessory devices are used varies with the species. In African softshells which lack cloacal bursae, 70 per cent of the submerged oxygen intake is through the skin and 30 percent is through the lining of the throat. Because of their dependency upon underwater respiration, softshells tend to be more sensitive to rotenone (a selective poison for gill breathing vertebrates) than are cohabiting species of pond turtles. Cloacal bursae are common to most other aquatic species including pond, snapping and side-necked turtles. These structures are particularly well developed in Fitzroy's tortoise. This Australian side-necked turtle, which lives in well-oxygenated streams, continually maintains a widely gaping cloacal orifice and rarely surfaces.

Turtles are exceptionally tolerant of low oxygen levels, and individuals have survived for up to 20 hours in an atmosphere of pure nitrogen. How long a turtle can stay submerged depends upon the species, the temperature and the amount of oxygen dissolved in the water. Sliders can survive submerged in water saturated with oxygen no more than 28 hours while Loggerhead musk turtles seem capable of surviving indefinitely under similar conditions. Species that overwinter underwater in a torpid state can survive for weeks without surfacing.

Reproduction
Sexing turtles is often difficult. Males usually have longer, thicker tails with the vent somewhat farther back than in females. In many aquatic swimming species, the males are considerably the smaller sex, but males in terrestrial and semiaquatic forms tend to be as large as or larger than females. To accommodate the female's high-vaulted shell during copulation, the male's plastron is often concave. Elongated foreclaws, attenuated snouts or a spiny-tipped tail distinguish males of certain species.

Coloration can be used for sexing some species but, in the majority, the sexes are similarly colored. Even in sexually dichromatic species, the differences are often subtle. The male Eastern box turtle has red eyes, the female brown eyes. The female Spotted turtle has a yellow chin and orange eyes; the male has a tan chin and brown eyes. Certain tropical Asian river turtles are exceptional, however, in that the males exhibit spectacular seasonal breeding coloration in contrast to the drab females.

All species lay eggs on land. Nesting in most is annual and seasonal although

individual females may not reproduce every year. The Green turtle nests on average every third year. Courtship and nesting usually occur in the spring in temperate zone turtles; in tropical species commonly in either the wet or the dry season. A few rainforest species reportedly lay year-round (eg the Twist-necked turtle). Females of some species can store sperm (eg the Diamond-backed terrapin and Eastern box turtle) and do not need to mate annually. The majority of turtles nest in the vicinity of their foraging areas. However, some sea and river turtles make extensive migrations in order to nest. Green turtles inhabiting the Brazilian coast of South America may migrate over 4,500km (2,800mi) to nest on Ascension Island.

Certain migrating species nest in large numbers over a short period of time. The most spectactular is the mass nesting ("arribada") of the ridley sea turtles. One of the largest arribadas occurs in Orissa, India, where up to 200,000 Pacific ridleys nest on 5km (3mi) of beach over a period of one or two days. A few freshwater turtles such as the South American river turtle and the River terrapin of southeast Asia, similarly nest en masse. An advantage of mass nesting is that predators become overwhelmed by the volume of the reproductive output, with many nests escaping detection.

In many aquatic swimming species (some pond and river turtles, side-necked turtles and sea turtles) males are usually smaller than females and have elaborate courtship behavior. In semiaquatic bottom-walking species (eg mud turtles, snapping turtles) where males are equal to or larger than females, courtship displays are minimal and males often simply overpower females. Among male tortoises, combat for territories and mates is common. Again males equal or exceed females in size, and courtship displays are relatively simple.

In temperate zone pond and river turtles (the Painted turtle, the slider and the map turtles) males employ elongated claws on the forefeet in their courtship displays. While swimming backward in front of the female (or in some species just above), the male fans his claws across the female's snout and chin. When receptive, the female sinks to the bottom. The male then mounts

from the back and, using the foreclaws to grip the anterior edge of the shell, forces his tail beneath that of the female, bringing their vents together. Intromission is achieved by the male's single penis. Copulation may require an hour or more during which time the participants occasionally surface for air.

Courtship in tortoises typically consists of some head-bobbing, the male butting and biting the female to immobilize her, and finally mounting her shell from the rear. The courtship and mounting of some giant tortoises is accompanied by bellowing that could make elephants envious.

In order to achieve intromission, males may have to incline their body towards the vertical, the extreme being seen in American box turtles which lean back somewhat beyond the vertical.

The eggs may be laid beneath decaying vegetation and litter (eg the Spot-legged turtle and the stinkpots), in nests of other animals (eg the Florida redbelly turtle), in specially dug burrows (Yellow mud turtle), but usually in carefully constructed flask-shaped nests excavated with the turtle's hind feet. Some species quickly cover the eggs and leave the area (eg most softshells and the Painted terrapin). Others spend considerable time concealing the nest. Leatherbacks may spend an hour or more traveling over the site kicking sand in all directions before returning to the sea. The River terrapin often digs a false nest some distance from the first and in certain areas divides the clutch into 2 or 3 nests to confound predators. Parental care is rare in reptiles and largely lacking among turtles, but the Burmese brown tortoise, which fashions a mound nest of leaf litter, will defend eggs from predation for several days following laying.

Fecundity correlates generally with body size. Smaller species lay 1–4 eggs per clutch whereas large sea turtles regularly lay over a hundred eggs at a time. The majority of species lay twice or even more often each nesting season. The Green turtle is the most prolific reptile known. In Sarawak it annually lays up to 11 clutches of over 100 each at 10.5 day intervals.

Turtle eggs are of two shapes. Pond turtles and American mud turtles lay elongated

▲▼ Courtship in turtles and tortoises. (1) Male Gopher tortoise head bobs and circles female, then bites her on the shell and limbs. (2) Mating positions in Eastern box turtles: (a) male biting female's head, (b) gripping her shell with his hind feet. (3) Head-bobbing at surface (a) and head-stroking beneath the surface (b) during courtship of the side-necked turtle *Emydura macquarii*.

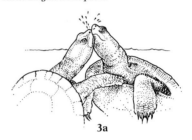

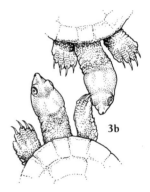

► **Nesting in sand.** All marine turtles lay their eggs on land, where their movements are clumsy and awkward. The female Loggerhead turtle excavates a flask-shaped hole on the beach, where she deposits her eggs.

▼ **Running the gauntlet** of predators, mostly birds, hatchlings of the flatback (*Chelonia depressa*) make their way as quickly as they can to the safety of the sea.

temperate pond and river turtles, snapping turtles, sea turtles, and Afro-American side-necked turtles tend to have eggs with flexible shells (indentable by thumb pressure), while the eggshells of tropical pond and river turtles, American mud turtles, softshells and Austro-American side-necked turtles are more inflexible and often brittle.

Eggs with brittle shells tend to be more independent of the environment, losing and absorbing water slowly compared to eggs with flexible shells. However, those with flexible shells develop faster. Species that do not dig nests or which nest in particularly dry or moist soils tend to lay eggs with brittle shells. Conversely, those nesting on beaches prone to flooding, or in areas with limited growing seasons, where rapid egg development is important, are more likely to lay eggs with flexible shells.

Egg size tends to increase with body size but there are exceptions. The enormous Leatherback sea turtle and the Galapagos giant tortoise lay the largest spherical eggs, with diameters of 5–6cm (2–2.4in). However, the largest elongated eggs occur in tropical pond turtles, many only small to moderate-sized. The Malaysian giant turtle, largest of the pond and river turtles, with a shell length of 80cm (31.5in), lays eggs from 3.7–4.4 × 7.1–8.1cm (1.5–1.7 × 2.8–3.2in). However, the Black wood turtle, with much less than half the maximum shell length (32.5cm–12.8in), lays only slightly smaller eggs (3.4–3.9 × 5.8–7.6cm—1.3–1.5 × 2.3–3in).

Incubation typically requires approximately two months in temperate species but among tropical turtles periods of four months to over one year are not unusual. It seems that longer-incubating eggs often undergo periods of arrested development and even within the same clutch incubation times can vary widely.

Temperature during incubation not only determines speed of development but in some groups (eg pond and river turtles, snapping turtles, sea turtles) the sex of the hatchlings as well. The eggs of the Loggerhead sea turtle produce close to a 1:1 sex ratio when incubated at 30°C (86°F) but only females at 32°C (89.6°F) and only males at 28°C (82.4°F). Snapping turtle eggs produce more females at high incubation temperatures and more males at lower temperatures but at still lower temperatures females predominate once again.

Following hatching, young turtles must often wait before emerging. The Painted turtle and snapping turtles overwinter in their nests in northern United States. Hatchlings

eggs whereas softshells, snapping turtles and sea turtles lay more spherical ones. Members of other diverse groups such as tortoises and side-necked turtles have members laying eggs of both shapes. Turtles laying the largest clutches (50 eggs or more) have spherical eggs, suggesting that this shape is more efficient for packing large numbers within a confined space. The spherical shape has the lowest possible surface-to-volume ratio. It is also less subject to dehydration. Possibly this explains why many tortoises lay such eggs.

The egg shell also varies. Although some exceptions and intermediate types exist, of sliders in Central America and the Australian Giant snake-necked turtle cannot escape their nests until rain softens the mud plug at the entrance. One report claims that living Giant snake-necked young were entrapped in their nest for 664 days during an Australian drought.

Feeding Behavior

Relatively few turtles have the speed and agility to catch fast-moving prey. Hence most feed either on vegetation or on more sedentary animals (eg mollusks, worms and insect larvae). Windfalls such as a dead animal or ripening fruit on a riverside tree, however, are rapidly exploited and often attract large numbers of turtles.

Diets of omnivorous species often change with age. Typically, juveniles tend to be highly insectivorous while adults are more herbivorous (eg the slider and the Painted turtle), or exploit a more specialized diet such as mollusks (eg the Razorback musk turtle). In species where the sexes differ greatly in size, diets of males and females may also differ. Females of Barbour's map turtle are chiefly mollusk-eaters whereas the smaller males mostly consume arthropods.

For the most part, turtles feed in a simple and straightforward fashion. However, a few have special techniques and strategies to obtain their food, such as ambush, gape and suck, and luring (fishing) methods. Turtles which use ambush lie in wait rather than pursue their prey. However, many species employ both strategies. Commonly, ambush feeders have cryptic coloration and/or cryptic shapes along with long, muscular necks which can strike out for prey at some distance. The Snapping turtle, with its long, tubercle-covered neck, muck-colored skin and algae-festooned shell, illustrates these characteristics well. The Narrow-headed softshell of southern Asia is an ambush feeder which appears to be brightly patterned. However, when it is lying on the bottom of its riverine habitat, partially covered, the turtle's dark stripes and patches blend well with shadows cast on the uneven river bed.

Most aquatic species use the gape and suck technique to some degree. By quickly opening the mouth and simultaneously expanding the throat, a low pressure is created which can pull small food items into the gullet along with a rush of water which is later expelled.

The most adept practitioner of this technique and also an ambush feeder, the bizarre matamata, is extremely well camouflaged. The shell is ridged, lumpy, flattened and usually covered with algae. The unusually broad head and long, muscular neck are adorned with an array of irregular flaps and projections. The tiny beady eyes are far forward and flank an attenuated snorkel-like snout. The mouth is

▲ ▶ ▼ **Representative species of turtles and tortoises.** (1) Big-headed turtle (*Platysternon megacephalum*) making visit to land; Platysternidae. (2) Gopher tortoises (*Gopherus polyphemus*) mating; Testudinidae. (3) Yellow mud turtle (*Kinosternon flavescens*); Kinosternidae. (4) Yellow-spotted Amazon turtle (*Podocnemis unifilis*); Pelomedusidae. (5) Green turtle (*Chelonia mydas*) grazing; Cheloniidae. (6) Central American river turtle (*Dermatemys mawei*); Dermatemydidae.

preposterously wide and the jaws lack the horny covering of other turtles. The matamata waits passively on the bottom of its aquatic haunts for fish to approach. Experiments have shown that certain of the turtle's skin flaps on the chin and neck are more than just camouflage. Rich in nerve endings, they respond to slight disturbances in the water, alerting the turtle to the approach of prey even in murky waters. It has also been suggested that passive movements of the skin flaps by water currents might serve as a lure to attract fish. Once a fish comes in range, the turtle rapidly strikes while expanding its widely distensible mouth and throat, thus pulling in the day's dinner. Matamatas have also been observed actively herding fish into shallow water where they could be more easily captured.

Only slightly less cryptic in appearance and occupying a similar niche, the Alligator snapping turtle of the United States uses a lure to attract fish. The Alligator snapper has a small worm-like projection on its tongue which becomes bright pink when filled with blood. By moving underlying mucles, the lure can be made to wriggle. When fishing, the snapper sits quietly on the bottom with jaws agape, moving the lure. A fish swimming between the sharp horny jaws to investigate rarely escapes the swift snapping response. If the prey is small enough, it is swallowed whole or, if too large, the turtle uses its jaws to hold the fish while the forefeet are used alternately to tear it apart. The lure darkens with age and may be of less importance to adults.

An additional feeding adaptation worthy

of mention is the broad alveolar shelf, or secondary palate, in the upper jaw of certain turtles. Species which eat snails and clams (eg map turtles, the Malaysian snail-eating turtles) use this shelf for crushing the calcareous shells of their prey. A similar shelf is also present in certain herbivorous species (eg the American Redbelly turtle, the River terrapin, roofed turtles). These turtles have one or two serrated ridges on the shelf and serrated edges on their jaws which are used for cutting and crushing stems and fruits.

Social Behavior

There is little evidence to indicate that turtles defend territories. Many appear to have definite home ranges and some species, particularly terrestrial and semiaquatic ones with overlapping ranges, may develop dominance relationships. The Galapagos giant tortoise establishes dominance hierarchies based on the height to which each animal can extend its head. Geographic races on certain islands have evolved a narrow saddle-backed shell with

a high anterior notch which allows for greater vertical extension of the head and neck. In captive groups of Galapagos giant tortoises, saddle-backs typically establish dominance over races from other islands which have more restrictive, dome-shaped shells.

Although not highly social, aquatic turtles also aggregate and interact for purposes other than mating and egg laying. Some species congregate to overwinter (eg Green and Loggerhead sea turtles). Other species (the Painted turtle, the Indian tent turtle) may congregate on exposed sites for basking. Whether they are being gregarious or simply selecting the most favorable site is debatable.

Juvenile sliders in the New World tropics seek out fellow members of their species for mutual cleaning behavior. One turtle uses its jaws to pull algae (and pieces of scute) from another's shell positioned at right angles to it. Then the positions are reversed and the other reciprocates. Similar behavior has been observed in roofed turtles and South American river turtles in captivity. A similar behavior is found in African Helmeted turtles which reportedly clean ectoparasites from rhinoceroses that enter their water holes.

Turtles and Man

Populations of many turtles and tortoises are declining today. Overexploitation and habitat destruction are among the chief causes. Most seriously affected are the tortoises, large river turtles and sea turtles. Species in these categories, because of their accessibility, large size, and/or prolificacy, have been utilized heavily as a protein resource throughout developing countries in tropical and subtropical regions of the world.

The developed nations have placed additional pressure on declining populations by providing markets for luxury items such as tortoise shell jewelry from the Hawksbill sea turtle, leather goods from the Pacific ridley, and pets (tortoises and any unusual species).

River and sea turtles are particularly vulnerable to overexploitation due to their stereotyped nesting behavior, their regular seasonal appearance in large numbers on traditional beaches, which allows predators, including humans, to harvest large numbers of eggs and females over relatively short periods. The passive defensive strategies of slow, lumbering tortoises make them susceptible to human predation at all times.

EOM

◄▲▼ **Representative species of turtles.**
(1) Spring softshell (*Trionyx spiniferus*) snorkeling; Trionychidae. (2) Red-eared turtle (*Chrysemys scripta elegans*) courting; Emydidae. (3) Leatherback sea turtle (*Dermochelys coriacea*) feeding on jellyfish; Dermochelyidae. (4) Pig-nosed softshell turtle (*Carettochelys insculpta*) swimming; Carettochelyidae. (5) Chiapas cross-breasted turtle (*Staurotypus salvinii*), Staurotypidae. (6) Matamata (*Chelus fimbriatus*); Chelidae. (7) Alligator snapping turtle (*Macroclemys temminckii*) fishing; Chelydridae.

THE 13 FAMILIES OF TURTLES AND TORTOISES

Abbreviations: Length = maximum straight-line shell length. wt = weight. Approximate nonmetric equivalents: 10cm = 4in. 1kg = 2.2lb.
⬚ CITES-listed Ⓔ Endangered Ⓘ Threatened but status indeterminate Ⓚ Threat suspected but status unknown Ⓡ Rare Ⓥ Vulnerable.
Total threatened species = number endangered, vulnerable, rare or threatened or with status indeterminate or unknown.

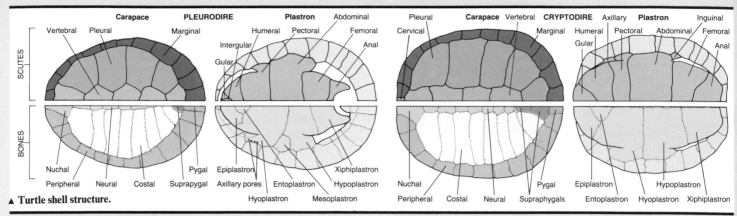

▲ **Turtle shell structure.**

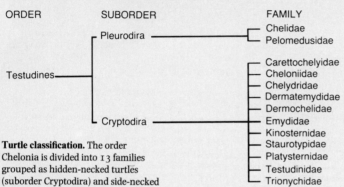

Turtle classification. The order Chelonia is divided into 13 families grouped as hidden-necked turtles (suborder Cryptodira) and side-necked turtles (suborder Pleurodira). Hidden-necked turtles retract their heads into the shell by bending the neck into a vertical S-shaped curve. They have 11–12 plastral scutes and 8–9 plastral bones. Side-necked turtles retract their heads under the lip of the shell by bending the neck to the side. They have 13 plastral scutes and 9–11 plastral bones, and the pelvis is fused to the shell.

Suborder Cryptodira

Pig-Nosed Softshell Turtle Ⓚ
Pig-nosed softshell turtle or New Guinea plateless turtle
Family: Carettochelyidae
One species, *Carettochelys insculpta*.

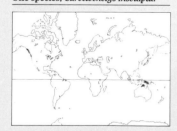

Distribution: S New Guinea, N Australia. Habitat: rivers, lakes, lagoons. Length: 55cm or more. Color: unpatterned gray, gray-olive or gray-brown above; white, yellowish or cream below; pale streak or white blotch between eyes. Body form: shell covered with soft, pitted skin; limbs paddle-shaped; snout a fleshy, pig-like proboscis. Eggs: spherical, brittle; about 4cm in diameter; clutches of 15–20. Nest: shallow, dug in high sand bank in dry season (Sept-Nov in New Guinea). Diet: crustaceans, insects, mollusks, fish, aquatic plants, fruits of riverside trees.

Snapping Turtles
Family: Chelydridae
Two species in 2 genera.

Distribution: from Canada to northwestern S America. Habitat: freshwater bottoms. Length: from 47cm in Snapping turtle to 66cm in Alligator snapping turtle. wt: 16–91kg. Color: drab, with gray, black or brown top. Body form: head large, with strong, hooked jaw; tail long; plastron reduced, cross-shaped; abdominal scutes widely separated, chiefly confined to bridge; 24 marginal scutes. Eggs: spherical, 2.3–3.3cm, clutches of 20–30 (maximum 80) in Snapping turtle; 3–5cm, 30–40 (maximum 50) in Alligator snapper. Diet: carrion, insects, fish, turtles, mollusks, plant food. Species: **Alligator snapping turtle** (*Macroclemys temminckii*), **Snapping turtle** (*Chelydra serpentina*).

Central American River Turtle ⬚ Ⓥ
Family: Dermatemydidae
One species, *Dermatemys mawei*.

Distribution: from Vera Cruz, Mexico, S to Honduras. Habitat: rivers and lakes. Length: up to 65cm. Color: unpatterned dark gray to gray-brown above; head olive-gray in females, with yellowish to reddish-brown back of head in males. Body form: shell well developed, streamlined, covered with thin scutes fusing with age to obliterate seams; 24 marginal, 4–5 inframarginal scutes; head relatively small, with moderately upturned, tubular snout. Eggs: oblong, 6.4 × 3.2cm; clutches of up to 20. Diet: juveniles omnivorous, adults chiefly herbivorous, feeding on fruits, fallen leaves and aquatic plants.

Sea Turtles
Family: Cheloniidae
Six species in 4 genera.

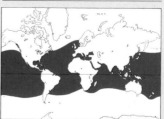

Distribution: circumtropical, extending into subtropical and temperate oceans. Length: from 75cm in the Atlantic ridley to 213cm in Loggerhead sea turtle. wt: up to 450kg in Loggerhead. Body form: shell low, streamlined, scute-covered; limbs paddle- or flipper-like; skull completely roofed, cannot be retracted within shell. Eggs: spherical; 80–200, laid in multiple clutches at intervals of 10–30 days. Both sexes migrate between feeding and nesting areas, female reproducing on 1–3 year cycle. Diet: chiefly carnivorous (except adult Green turtle, which grazes on sea grasses), including sponges, jellyfish, mussels, crabs, barnacles, sea urchins and fish. Species include: **Atlantic** or **Kemp's ridley** ⬚ Ⓔ (*Lepidochelys kempi*), **Green turtle** ⬚ Ⓔ (*Chelonia mydas*), **Hawksbill turtle** ⬚ Ⓔ (*Eretmochelys imbricata*), **Loggerhead sea turtle** ⬚ Ⓥ (*Caretta caretta*), **Pacific** or **Olive ridley** ⬚ Ⓔ (*Lepidochelys olivacea*). Total threatened species: 5.

Leatherback Sea Turtle ⬚ Ⓔ
Family: Dermochelyidae
One species, *Dermochelys coriacea*.

Distribution: tropical waters, with periodic occurrences in temperate and subarctic seas. Largest living turtle: length 185cm, wt 680kg. Color: black. Body form: adult shell without scutes, covered with oily skin, reduced to mosaic of small bony platelets embedded in the skin—carapace with 7 prominent ridges, plastron with 5; forelimbs modified into broad flippers. Can maintain body temperature to several degrees above surrounding water even in Subarctic. Eggs: spherical, 5–6cm; several clutches of 50–170 laid at intervals of about 10 days on tropical beaches. Diet: jellyfish, crustacea and mollusks.

Pond and River Turtles

Family: Emydidae
Eighty-five species in 31 genera and 2 subfamilies.

Distribution: subfamily Batagurinae chiefly tropical to subtropical Asia, with striped-necked turtles reaching N Africa and S Europe, and neotropical wood turtles endemic to tropical America; subfamily Emydinae chiefly in temperate N America, with European pond turtle over most of Europe, W Asia and NW Africa, and slider from Michigan in USA to Argentina. Habitat: fully aquatic species in estuaries and coastal waters or freshwater rivers and lakes; semiaquatic species in forested ponds and streams, marshes and bogs; also fully terrestrial species. Length: from 11.4cm in Bog turtle to 80cm in Malaysian giant turtle. wt: up to 50kg in Malaysian giant turtle. Color: variable; browns, olives and shades of gray and black above, often marked with yellow, orange, red or white; yellow, white, brown and black most common below; striped and spotted patterns common on soft parts. Body form: shell well developed, with 24 marginal and 12 plastral scutes, pectorals and abdominals meeting marginals; feet usually with some webbing between toes. Eggs: elongated, 3–8cm; leathery to brittle shells; usually 2 or more clutches per year of 1–2 eggs, in small species, to 30 or more in large riverine forms. Diet: chiefly omnivorous, including insects, mollusks, aquatic vertebrates, and plants. Species and genera include: **Asian leaf turtle** (*Cyclemys dentata*), **Barbour's map turtle** (*Graptemys barbouri*), **Black marsh turtle** (*Siebenrockiella crassicollis*), **Black wood turtle** (*Rhinoclemmys funerea*), **Bog turtle** ⊡ ⊡ (*Clemmys muhlenbergii*), **box turtles** (genus *Terrapene*), **Cane turtle** (*Geoemyda silvatica*), **slider** (*Pseudemys scripta*), **Diamondback terrapin** (*Malaclemys terrapin*), **Eastern box turtle** (*Terrapene carolina*), **European pond turtle** (*Emys orbicularis*), **Florida redbelly turtle** (*Pseudemys nelsoni*), **Indian tent turtle** (*Kachuga tentoria*), **Malayan box turtle** (*Cuora amboinensis*), **Malayan flat-shelled turtle** (*Notochelys platynota*), **Malaysian giant turtle** (*Orlitia borneensis*), **Malaysian snail-eating turtle** (*Malayemys subtrijuga*), **map turtles** (genus *Graptemys*), **neotropical wood turtles** (genus *Rhinoclemmys*), **Painted roof turtle** (*Kachuga kachuga*), **Painted terrapin** ⊡ (*Callagur borneensis*), **Painted turtle** (*Chrysemys picta*), **Redbelly turtle** (*Pseudemys rubriventris*), **River terrapin** ⊡ ⊡ (*Batagur baska*), **roofed turtles** (genus *Kachuga*), **Spiny turtle** (*Heosemys spinosa*), **Spot-legged turtle** (*Rhinoclemmys punctularia*), **Spotted turtle** (*Clemmys guttata*), **stripe-necked turtles** (genus *Mauremys*), **Tricarinate hill turtle** (*Melanochelys tricarinata*). Total threatened species: 6. Total threatened subspecies: 2.

American Mud and Musk Turtles

Family: Kinosternidae
Twenty species in 2 genera.

Distribution: E Canada to Argentina. Habitat: permanent or semipermanent water. Length: from 11cm in Flattened musk turtle to 27cm in Scorpion mud turtle. Color: predominantly drab brown, olive and black above, with white, yellow, red or orange markings on some species; plastron yellow to brown or black. Body form: carapace with 22 marginal scutes and cervical scute; hinged plastron lacking entoplastron; small fleshy barbels on chin; scent glands producing malodorous secretions on skin near bridge; musk turtles with soft, uncornified areas of scute centered around middle of plastron, squarish pectoral scutes and single plastral hinge at rear; mud turtles with completely cornified plastral scutes, triangular pectoral scutes and plastron hinged front and back. Eggs: elongated, with brittle shells; multiple clutches of 1–6 laid in well-formed nests excavated with fore- or hind feet or in litter or rotting wood or simply abandoned. Diet: omnivorous, including mollusks, arthropods, annelids, fish and aquatic plants. Species and genera include: **Flattened musk turtle** (*Sternotherus depressus*), **Razorback** or **Keel-backed musk turtle** (*S. carinatus*), **Illinois mud turtle** ⊡ (*Kinosternon flavescens spooneri*), **Loggerhead musk turtle** (*Sternotherus minor*), **Scorpion mud turtle** (*Kinosternon scorpioides*), **Stinkpot** (*Sternotherus odoratus*), **Yellow mud turtle** (*Kinosternon flavescens*). Total threatened species: 3. Total threatened subspecies: 2.

Mexican Musk Turtles

Family: Staurotypidae
Three species in 2 genera*

Distribution: S Mexico to Honduras. Habitat: fresh water. Length: up to 38cm. Color: carapace brown to yellow-olive; plastron yellow or white, sometimes marked with black; head black or brown with white or yellow-orange spotting in cross-breasted turtles. Body form: head large; carapace 3-keeled; plastron reduced, cross-shaped, with entoplastron. Eggs: elongated (3.2–4 × 1.8–2.5cm), with brittle shells; clutches of 2–10; incubation 80–200 days. Diet: chiefly carnivorous. Species: **Chiapas cross-breasted turtle** (*Staurotypus salvinii*), **Mexican cross-breasted turtle** (*S. triporcatus*), **Narrow-bridged musk turtle** (*Claudius angustatus*).

*Sometimes included as subfamily in family Kinosternidae

Tortoises

Family: Testudinidae
Forty-one species in 10 genera.

Distribution: chiefly tropical and subtropical, on all major land masses except Australia and Antarctica. Habitat: terrestrial. Length: from 10cm in Speckled Cape tortoise to 140cm in Aldabra giant tortoise. wt: up to 254kg in Aldabra giant tortoise. Color: predominantly shades of brown, olive, yellow and black above; predominantly yellow, brown and black below; scutes plain or commonly patterned with bright rays or concentric rings; head and neck rarely striped or spotted. Body form: hind legs columnar, elephantine; forelimbs somewhat flattened, armored with large, bony-cored scales; short, unwebbed toes each with no more than 2 phalanges; most with high-arched or domed shells. Eggs: elongated to spherical, 3–6cm greatest diameter; leathery to brittle shells; 1–50 per clutch, multiple clutches known in some species. Diet: chiefly herbivorous, a few forms omnivorous. Species and genera include: **Aldabra giant tortoise** ⊡ ⊟ (*Geochelone gigantea*), **Bolson tortoise** ⊡ ⊟ (*Gopherus flavomarginatus*), **Burmese brown tortoise** ⊡ ⊟ (*Geochelone emys*), **Desert tortoise** ⊡ ⊟ (*Gopherus agassizi*), **Egyptian tortoise** ⊡ ⊟ (*Testudo kleinmanni*), **Galapagos giant tortoise** ⊡ ⊟ (*Geochelone elephantopus*), **Gopher tortoise** ⊡ ⊟ (*Gopherus polyphemus*), **hinge-backed tortoises** ⊡ (genus *Kinixys*), **Indian star tortoise** ⊡ (*Geochelone elegans*), **Madagascan spider tortoise** ⊡ ⊟ (*Pyxis arachnoides*), **Madagascan spurred tortoise** or **angonoka** ⊡ ⊟ (*G. yniphora*), **Pancake tortoise** ⊡ ⊟ (*Malacochersus tornieri*), **Radiated tortoise** ⊡ ⊟ (*Geochelone radiata*), **Speckled Cape tortoise** ⊡ (*Homopus signatus*). Total threatened species: 21. Total threatened subspecies: 1.

Softshell Turtles

Family: Trionychidae
Twenty-two species in 6 genera in 2 subgroups—flapshells and typical softshells.

Distribution: widespread in temperate to tropical N America, Africa, Asia and Indo-Australian Archipelago. Habitat: fresh water, but Giant softshell commonly enters estuaries and has occasionally been found at sea. Length: from 30cm in Indian flapshell to 115cm in Narrow-headed softshell. Color: predominantly shades of brown, olive or gray above; some with white, black, yellow, red or orange markings; white, yellow or gray most common below. Body form: characterized by flattened, reduced shell lacking peripheral bones (except in Indian flapshells) and covered by a leathery skin instead of scutes; elongated, retractable neck; limbs somewhat paddle-like with 3 claws per foot; snout an elongated proboscis; plastron reduced, typically with large spaces (fontanelles) between bones, and with ligamentous or cartilaginous rather than bony connection to carapace; flapshell subgroup named for a pair of fleshy cutaneous flaps on rear of plastron covering hind limbs when withdrawn. Eggs: spherical, hard- to brittle-shelled; 2.5–3.5cm in diameter; clutches of 4–100, multiple clutches common. Diet: chiefly carnivorous, some omnivorous; insects, crustaceans and fish

commonly eaten. Species and genera include: **Central African flapshells** (genus *Cycloderma*), **Dark softshell** R (*Trionyx nigricans*), **Giant softshell** (*Pelochelys bibroni*), **Indian flapshell** (*Lissemys punctata*), **Narrow-headed softshell** (*Chitra indica*), **Smooth softshell** (*Trionyx muticus*), **sub-Saharan flapshells** (genus *Cyclanorbis*). Total threatened species: 1.

Big-Headed Turtle

Family: Platysternidae
One species, *Platysternon megacephalum*.*

Distribution: S China, Indochina, Thailand, S Burma. Habitat: cool mountain streams. Length: 20cm. Color: carapace olive-brown; plastron cream, yellow or orangish with or without dark markings; head brown above, sometimes with orange spotting or pale stripe behind eyes. Body form: distinguished by long muscular tail, powerful hooked jaws and large, completely roofed skull that cannot be retracted into the flattened shell. Eggs: elongated (3.7 × 2.2cm); clutches of 1–2. Active at night, with exceptional climbing ability.
*Sometimes included as subfamily in family Chelydridae.

Suborder Pleurodira

Austro-American Side-Necked Turtles

Family: Chelidae
Thirty-seven species in 9 genera.

Distribution: tropical to temperate S America, Australia, New Guinea. Habitat: family includes aquatic and semiaquatic species. Length: from 14cm in Western swamp turtle to

◀ **Fortress shell** of the Florida redbelly turtle is untypical of aquatic species. It is a defense against the crushing jaws of alligators.

48cm in Giant snake-necked turtle. Color: variable; predominantly brown, olive and black above, with yellow, red and orange markings in some species; plastron commonly yellow or white, sometimes red or orange, often with dark markings. Body form: distinguished by biconvex 5th and 8th cervical vertebrae; shell without mesoplastral bones; cervical scute present; intergular scute seldom contacting plastral rim; skull and mandible without quadratojugal and splenial bones. Eggs: elongated to spherical, 3–6cm in greatest diameter; clutches of 1–25; 2 or more clutches in some species. Diet: family includes omnivorous and carnivorous species. Species include: **Fitzroy's turtle** (*Rheodytes leukops*), **Giant snake-necked turtle** (*Chelodina expansa*), **matamata** (*Chelus fimbriatus*), **Twist-neck turtle** (*Platemys platycephala*), **Western swamp turtle** ▪ E (*Pseudemydura umbrina*). Total threatened species: 6.

Afro-American Side-Necked Turtles

Family: Pelomedusidae
Twenty-four species in 5 genera.

Distribution: tropical S America, Africa S of Sahara, Madagascar, Seychelles, Mauritius. Habitat: family includes aquatic and semiaquatic species. Length: from 12cm in African dwarf mud turtle to 90cm in South American river turtle. Color: brown, olive or black above; head commonly with yellow, orange or red markings; plastron commonly yellow, gray or brown. Body form: shell with mesoplastral bones; cervical scute absent; intergular scute touches back rim of plastron; second cervical vertebrae biconvex; quadratojugal bone in skull and splenial bone in mandible. Eggs: with leathery shells, spherical to elongated. Diet: herbivorous to omnivorous. Species include: **African dwarf mud turtle** (*Pelusios nanus*), **Helmeted turtle** (*Pelomedusa subrufa*), **South American river turtle** ▪ E (*Podocnemis expansa*), **West African mud turtle** (*Pelusios castaneus*). Total threatened species: 6.

LIZARDS

Suborder: Sauria (Lacertilia)
Three thousand seven hundred and fifty-one
species in 383 genera and 16 families.
Distribution: in the New World from S Canada
to Tierra del Fuego, in the Old World from
N Norway to Stewart Island, New Zealand; also
islands in the Atlantic, Pacific and Indian
Oceans.

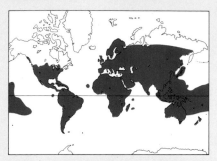

Habitat: terrestrial, tree-dwelling, burrowing or
semiaquatic.

Size: snout-to-vent length 1.5–145cm (0.6–
57in), but most are 6–20cm (2.5–8in).

Color: highly variable including green, brown,
black and some brightly colored species.

Reproduction: fertilization internal. Most lay
eggs, on land, but in some the eggs develop to
an advanced stage inside female. A true
placenta is present in a few species.

Longevity: 50 years or more in captivity in
some species.

▲ **Out of its element,** a Common chameleon
(*Chamaeleo dilepis*) crosses a hot road, a
grasshopper hitching a ride. Chameleon feet,
with two pairs of toes opposing each other to
form a pincer that grips twigs, are adapted for
life in trees, not for walking on flat surfaces.

▶ **Tongue display** of the Australian Blue-
tongued skink (*Tiliqua scincoides*). The purpose
of this behavior has not been determined but it
is probably a defensive strategy to frighten
predatory birds and mammals.

LIZARDS are perhaps the most familiar of the reptiles. They were once thought to be so typical of their order that when naturalists discovered the remains of giant reptiles of the Mezozoic era, it was assumed that these beasts must have been great lizards, and they were thus given the name "dinosaur." In fact, lizards differ dramatically from dinosaurs, and from other reptiles, in the nature of their skeletons.

The familiarity of lizards stems partly from their great diversity and wide distribution. Although most are tropical, many occur in temperate climates. In the New World, they are found as far north as southern Canada, and as far south as Tierra del Fuego, at the tip of Argentina. In the Old World, one species, the Viviparous lizard, occurs above the Arctic Circle in Norway. Others are found as far south as Stewart Island, New Zealand. Species occur from sea level up to 5,000m (16,500ft).

In addition, most lizards are, like us, dwellers on the land and active by day. Even nocturnal geckos are a familiar part of many people's lives: in tropical countries certain of these insect-eaters, with their intent, bulging eyes, are common and welcome members of the household. Brook's half-toed gecko of West Africa, for example, advertises through its transparent belly how many captured flies have earned it the right to scurry, on its faultlessly gripping toes, up and down household walls and windows and even upside down across the ceilings.

One of the most distinctive features of lizards is their horny skin folded into scales. Scales vary greatly in appearance from small and granular to large and plate-like; they touch one another (juxtaposed) or overlap (imbricate), and are smooth or possess one or more ridges (keels).

This covering of scales reduces water loss and may facilitate the uptake of solar energy. It is thick and tough in most species and not easily torn. Certain scales have been modified into sharp spines which can dissuade attackers. Some are fortified with internal bony plates called osteoderms.

A curious feature of lizards is their development of the pineal body. Speculation led the 17th-century French philosopher Descartes to assert that the pineal body in the human brain is the point at which mind and body interact. He thought that the pineal was an eye for the immortal soul, communicating to it the sensory intake of the material body. In lizards, at least, it seems that this part of the brain is indeed connected to a sort of "third eye," but it connects the animal only with the physical world. A cranial bone is perforated at this point to allow an extension of nervous tissue from the brain to a light-sensitive transparent disk on top of the head. Research suggests that the pineal may be involved in regulating the animal's "biological clock," influenced by the recurring pattern of day and night.

The bones of the skull are usually rather loosely attached to one another, and the cranial vault of most lizards is open towards the snout. The two halves of the lizard's lower jaw are firmly united at the front in adults, which restricts the gape and limits the size of food items that can be swallowed to something less than a head's width in diameter. The tongue is well developed in all lizards and attached at the back of the oral cavity (see box). There are invariably teeth bordering the oral cavity and there may be additional teeth on the palate. Lizard teeth are usually pleurodont: they have elongated roots that are weakly attached to the inside margins of the jaws, and the bases of the roots are not coextensive with the jaw. A few groups have acrodont teeth; these are usually short and very firmly attached to the jaws by either their bases, sides or both. In most species the teeth are replaced frequently.

The external ear opening is usually visible, and there is a movable eyelid in most species. Typically, lizards have well-developed paired lungs, a urinary bladder and the subclavian artery arising from the systemic artery. The paired kidneys are usually symmetrical in general appearance and lie in the rear part of the body cavity, beyond the level of the cloacal region. The anal opening is a transverse slit. Male lizards have paired intromittent organs, called hemipenes (singular, hemipenis–see p92).

Locomotion

The familiar scurrying of lizards is not possible for some, for in many burrowers and some surface dwellers the limbs are reduced or absent. Female blind lizards, some anguids and some girdle-tailed lizards are completely legless, with only traces remaining of the internal bony girdles associated with the limbs. In snake lizards and male blind lizards there are no forelimbs, only vestigial hind limbs. Limb reduction is a special advantage in habitats that have narrow openings, such as dense vegetation and broken earth and rock. In these species, movement is achieved by snake-like sideways undulation, with the vestigial limbs being held close to the body.

Most species, however, have four legs

The Versatile Lizard Tongue

All lizards possess a well-developed tongue which can be extended. Many species constantly "sense" the world around them with this organ, sampling molecules from the environment and retrieving them into the mouth as chemical information on food, mates, territories and predators.

The site of chemical sensation is called the vomeronasal, or Jacobson's, organ. It occurs in a variety of vertebrates including amphibians, lizards, snakes, bison and members of the cat family. In lizards it consists of small paired cavities lined with sensory cells located within the roof of the mouth near the snout (1). The molecules gathered on the lizard's tongue are transported to narrow ducts leading to these cells, and the information recorded is sent to the brain by way of the vomeronasal nerve. This type of

chemosensation is different from smell and taste, of which lizards are also capable.

Lizards with long, forked tongues, such as the beaded lizards, whiptails and monitors (2), have better developed Jacobson's organs than do their short, broad-tongued relatives such as the Common bloodsucker (3), which flick their tongues less often.

The tongue has other functions. In many species of geckos, eg the Green tree gecko, it is frequently used to clean the spectacles of the lidless eyes, and in the Great Plains skink the mother regularly licks her eggs. In several species of Australian blue-tongued skinks, the brightly colored tongue is probably used to frighten predatory birds and mammals. The extraordinarily long, sticky and highly extensible tongues of chameleons are used to capture distant insects.

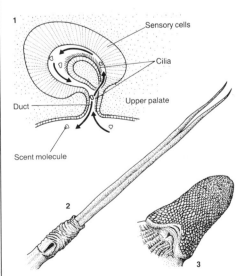

1

Sensory cells

Cilia

Duct

Upper palate

Scent molecule

2

3

with five toes each. These exhibit the most typical pattern of lizard locomotion, a sprawling, undulating body slung between limbs moving in a symmetrical gait on either side. The body can be cylindrical, depressed (flattened against the ground) or compressed (flattened vertically). The legs can be short or long, stout or slender. Burrowing lizards tend to be cylindrical, whereas crevice dwellers are usually depressed. A compressed body form is typical of aquatic and arboreal species. Stout, long-legged species—eg Gould's monitor of Australia—are usually runners that live in open grasslands and deserts. Arboreal species, eg the anoles and iguanas, usually have long, slender legs, useful in jumping between perches, or stretching from one branch to another. Other factors, such as digging and fighting, have probably also been important in limb evolution.

The Bornean earless lizard is in a family by itself (the Lanthanotidae), and, in terms of its locomotion, is unique. It is a good swimmer, propelling itself with small forelimbs and snake-like sideways undulations of the body, moving on land in a similar fashion (see p106). A less extreme swimming adaptation can be seen in the webbed feet of the Marine iguana. The Leafy plumbtree basilisk has a fold of skin along the side of the toes which appears to help it to run

▶ **"Depressed" body form** of the Flat lizard (*Platysaurus intermedius*) of South Africa enables it to hide in the narrowest of cracks, where its enemies cannot reach it. Lizards which are flattened vertically (eg chameleons) have a "compressed" body form.

▶ **Snake-like predator.** BELOW Despite its shape, the Legless snake lizard (*Lialis burtonis*) of Australia and New Guinea is closely related to the geckos. It feeds on other lizards.

▼ **Triple tail.** After shedding its original tail, this Australian marbled gecko has grown three new ones in its place.

The Expendable Tail

Confronted by a snake or other predator, a lizard will sometimes voluntarily shed (autotomize) its tail in one or more pieces. Prior to autotomization, some lizards, such as the Texas banded gecko, slowly undulate the vertically erect tail from side-to-side. This movement is believed to cause the predator to shift the focus of its attack from the more vulnerable head and trunk. The shed tail itself wriggles convulsively for several minutes, distracting the predator and improving the tail-less lizard's chance of escaping unharmed.

Species capable of this feat have a "fragile" tail, with fracture planes in one or more of the vertebrae. A wall of connective tissue or cartilage passes through each such vertebra, making a weak point, where muscles and blood sinuses are also modified to allow an easy break. The lizard slowly grows a new tail, never quite the same as the original. It does not have bony vertebrae with fracture planes, but apart from autotomy it has all the functions of the original, assisting in running, swimming, balancing or climbing, camouflage, courtship, mating and fat-storage. If the tail breaks at any other place than a fracture plane, regeneration is slight.

Losing a tail, though it may save its owner's life, is not without costs. For example, the fat stored in the tail is normally broken down and used for growth and maintenance when food is scarce or no longer available, especially in winter or during drought. One species of gecko, the Australian marbled gecko, is known to live longer when it has a tail. In addition, the fat stored in a female lizard's tail appears to be important in yolk production; individuals lacking tails produce eggs with lower mass and less energy, and the offspring survive less well.

Tail regeneration itself may require substantial energy, an expenditure that could be used instead for reproduction, perhaps making larger eggs. In the Texas banded gecko, at least, reproduction is known to have energetic priority over tail regeneration. This may be true for other short-lived species of lizards, especially when the probability of producing offspring is low.

At least some species of 11 out of the 16 families of lizards are capable of tail autotomy, which appears to be absent in all species of chameleons, beaded lizards, the Bornean earless lizard, monitors and xenosaurs.

across the surfaces of ponds and small streams. The Fringe-toed lizard and the Fringe-toed lacertid have toe modifications for running on loose sand.

Tree-dwelling lizards display some of the most impressive adaptations for locomotion. The flying dragons of Southeast Asia glide from tree to tree on a membrane joining the fore- and hind limbs (see p94). Like birds, chameleons improve their grip in the trees with "zygodactyl" feet, some toes facing forward and some back. Specifically, in chameleons the inner three and outer two digits of the forefeet are bound together and oppose one another, while it is the inner two and outer three toes of the hind feet that are opposed. The toe modifications which allow many geckos to climb sheer surfaces can be exceedingly elaborate (see p98).

Several species of lizards have prehensile tails which they wrap around vegetation to steady themselves as they move through their environment. In effect, they have five "limbs." Chameleons are the lizards best known for this adaptation; however, it is of much wider occurrence. Even the heavy-bodied Giant Solomon Island skink curls its tail around the branches of fig trees. Some species of geckos have the scales on the undersurface of their prehensile tails modified like those on their toes, so that it more firmly grasps the vegetation. The scale at the very tip of the tail even looks like a claw in some species of lizard, and it may function as such.

Defense

A much more characteristic tail modification in lizards results in the remarkable phenomenon of voluntary tail-loss, or autotomization (see box), but camouflage, or crypsis, is by far the most effective way to avoid predation. Many lizards exhibit patterns and coloration that blend with their background. Chisel-teeth lizards and chameleons can change in a few seconds from display to camouflage coloring by movement and expansion of pigment in the skin. Crypsis is further enhanced if the lizard remains motionless, but when directly confronted by predators, such as mammals, birds and other reptiles, several other behavioral and physical defense strategies are employed.

Lizards are well known for their agility and swiftness. Typically, when under attack most species attempt to escape, but the slow and clumsy blue-tongued skinks of Australia almost invariably threaten the predator with a gaping mouth, strong jaws, bright blue tongue and bouts of hisses. The beaded lizards, venomous and usually slow moving, also gape and hiss. Such behavior seems to be very effective and adults of these species have few enemies.

The Australian frilled lizard displays a large collar of loose skin and inflates its body when startled by a predator. Monitors use their speed, powerful jaws, limbs and whip-like tail to deter predators. The basilisks use their powerful, long hind limbs and expanded toes to run on the surface of water to escape land-bound predators. They are also good swimmers, and can stay submerged for very long periods of time. Skin and skeletal modifications allow flying dragons to glide from tree to tree or to a distant spot on the ground; however, they are incapable of the powered flight found in birds, bats and insects. Many species of lizards escape predators by climbing trees, rocks or man-made structures. The special feet and tail modifications of geckos and anoles permit them to climb almost any surface. Several species of geckos move with ease, upside down, across ceilings.

Many lizards live much of their lives underground, and thereby avoid predators. Underground species are found in such diverse families as the skinks, snake lizards and glass lizards. Those that are active on the surface from time to time escape by rapidly diving, burrowing or sinking into soft soil. Many are most active at night, when their potential predators are not about.

Another ploy in avoiding predation is to "play dead" or, alternatively, to become very rigid ("tonic immobility"). Some predators stop their attack when the prey becomes limp or rigid and appears lifeless. They rely on behavioral cues in performing their attack, and a "dead" lizard does not supply these.

The horned lizards of North America and the moloch of Australia are especially spiny, offering attackers an unpalatable mouthful of sharp scales. Many predators actually avoid prey that are especially spiny.

▶ **Threat display.** An Australian frilled lizard erects a rufflike collar of skin around its neck, greatly increasing its apparent size and making it more intimidating to enemies.

▶ **Courting pair** of European sand lizards (*Lacerta agilis*) BELOW RIGHT. The male has green on his flanks.

▼ **Upside-down feeding.** An anole drinks sap from a banana flower.

Feeding Behavior

Many lizards are themselves predators. They feed mostly on insects, mammals, birds and other reptiles. The Komodo dragon is a scavenger-predator that subdues goats and even water buffalos. Its teeth are laterally compressed with serrated edges, resembling those of flesh-eating sharks. The dragon literally cuts chunks of flesh from its large prey. Its highly flexible skull allows it to swallow large items. The Caiman lizard eats snails. Its rigid skull and molar-like teeth provide a base for breaking shells.

Only about 2 percent of all known species of lizards are primarily herbivorous. The iguanas consume a wide variety of plant material, especially as adults. Herbivory reaches its zenith in the Marine iguana of the Galapagos Islands. This species dives 15m (50ft) or more underwater to feed on algae, kelp and other marine plants that grow near the rocky shores where it lives.

Various Australian skinks feed on plants and their fruits. Many species of lizards shift their diets with maturity and seasonal changes in the availability of food.

Social Behavior

Many lizards issue threat displays to their own species and others that indicate territorial ownership or aggressive intent. Color changes, body inflation and push-ups, jaw-gaping, tail-waving and species-specific head movements are important signals. The colorful throat fan, or dewlap, of anoles is distended when males encounter each other or their enemies. Holding a territory is beneficial in several respects, but there are costs, such as the increased risk of being taken by a predator while repeatedly displaying from the same place. Visual predators such as snakes feed more frequently on male anoles than on the inconspicuous females.

Combat often occurs when lizards are

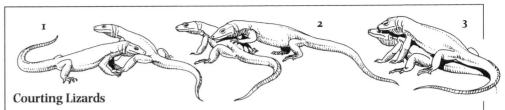

Courting Lizards

Like all vertebrates, lizards have courtship rituals that help them to find suitable partners and win their cooperation in mating. In lizards it is always the male that courts, but he can only progress if his partner provides him with the right stimuli. She must behave like a female, and like one of his own species; with a female of the wrong species his reproductive investment would yield sterile hybrids, if any offspring at all. She must also signal that she is receptive—with mature ova ready for fertilization.

Many lizards use distinctive visual signals in courtship. In the Green anole, the male begins by bobbing his head and expanding the dewlap under his throat. Often, he will approach the female with a stiff-legged walk. If receptive she remains still and then arches her neck when he is near. If unreceptive she simply runs away. In the Arizona alligator lizard, the male makes side-to-side movements of the head. Receptive females approach displaying males and nudge and walk over them performing head-jerks. Unreceptive females retreat, waving their tails.

Visual signals are often important in gecko courtship—in the Western banded gecko, males approach females in a prostrate position, undulating their tails—but in some species, eg the Indian wall gecko, vocalizations are produced by both sexes.

Monitors use very few auditory or visual signals. The male Komodo dragon, for example, approaches a female, presses his snout to her body (1) and flicks her with his long, forked tongue to obtain chemical information about her receptivity. He then scratches her back with his long claws (2), making a ratchet-like noise. If unreceptive she raises and inflates her neck and hisses loudly.

Males often bite, scratch or lick females that have signalled their receptivity. Anguid species such as the slowworm and Arizona alligator lizard grasp the female's neck or head in the mouth while attempting copulation. The Green anole parallels the female's body and, as he firmly grasps her neck with his mouth, typically his hind limbs clasp the base of her tail. The Western banded gecko pushes against his mate with his snout and either licks her or bites her tail and flanks. Eventually he obtains a bite-hold on her neck and aligns his body and his fore- and hind limbs with hers. In the Komodo dragon the male crawls onto the female's back (3) and, flicking his tongue on her head, rubs the base of her tail with his hind limbs to stimulate her to raise it.

attaining or defending a territory or a mate. Male Marine iguanas acquire territories during the onset of the mating season and fiercely fight intruding males. When a territory has been repeatedly defended, neighboring males become less frequently involved in boundary disputes. Larger males usually hold bigger and better territories and they mate more often. Courtship behavior is an important part of the mating ritual (see box). Females of some species are also territorial and fight.

Hatchling and juvenile lizards often emerge together from the nest-hole (eg the Green iguana), an anti-predator strategy in which many eyes are better than two and large numbers make individual capture less likely. Young iguanas often remain in groups and one of them may temporarily behave as leader. They engage in mutual tongue-licking and grooming, dewlap extension and body and chin rubbing. At

night they often sleep together on branches.

Social communication in lizards sometimes involves chemicals. Although the lizard's skin completely lacks mucus glands, other types of glands may be found on the belly, the undersurfaces of the thighs and in the region of the cloaca (the common reproductive and excretory opening). These glands tend to be larger in reproductively mature males. Their secretions are believed to attract females and mark territories. In few species do females have them.

Basking, or voluntary exposure to sun, is very commonly observed in lizards (see pp70–71).

Reproduction

A few lizards are unisexual (see box). In species with both males and females, there is copulation, and fertilization is internal. Males achieve intromission into the female's reproductive tract with one of their two hemipenes, each part of a separate reproductive tract with a single testis, which is located within or near the middle of the body cavity. A hemipenis is not structurally comparable to the mammalian penis, being a membranous pouch (often ornamented with spines, nipple-shaped projections or cups) which is turned outward through the male's cloacal opening during copulation. One hemipenis may be used 3–4 times before the lizard switches to the other, probably because the supply of mature sperm to the first is depleted.

Fertilization of one or more eggs occurs inside the female's oviducts, and the embryo achieves some maturity prior to laying. In a few species, eg Jackson's chameleon and Peron's hemiergis, sperm is stored in the oviducts for long periods of time, thereby making paternity difficult to establish. A female typically lays her eggs beneath a log or rock where the humidity is relatively high. Other species retain their eggs until the embryos are well developed. The young emerge fully developed from thick membranes.

In the Brazilian skink, the young develop inside the oviduct and possess a placental connection with the mother. The lizard placenta, like that of mammals, is important in providing nourishment and removing waste products. The young are born fully developed with little or no extra-embryonic tissues.

Most lizards exhibit little maternal care, except for finding and excavating a suitable site for egg laying. There are, however, several species in which the female broods or guards her eggs. Some clean and rotate their eggs. In a very few species, eg the Great Plains skink, the Desert night lizard and California alligator lizard, the mother may assist hatchlings from the fetal membranes and defend them from predators.

Some lizards have a well-defined period of annual reproduction, whereas others reproduce throughout the seasons. Most species in temperate climates are cyclic, while many tropical forms are continuous breeders. Environmental conditions such as temperature, rainfall and humidity, food availability and light cycles are very important factors in all species.

Lizards and Man

Folklore and fables concerning lizards abound. Many harmless species, especially geckos and skinks, are feared by uninformed people because they firmly believe them to be venomous. Although the beaded lizards are indeed venomous, the beliefs that they possess a venomous tail and that they are capable of spitting poison are false. One ancient superstition is that lizards bite the shadows of unsuspecting people, who are then doomed to die. Lizard tails were part of the recipe for a love potion among the Salish Indians of North America, and some Asian cultures hold that a long and prosperous life is guaranteed if a gecko calls from the bedroom of newlyweds.

Man has relentlessly exploited lizards for food and his social needs. Throughout the tropics of the New World, the Green iguana and Pectinate ctenosaur are killed for their flesh and eggs. West Indian rock iguanas, many of which are severely endangered, suffer a similar fate. In India monitors are eaten, and they are also a source of leather. Live monitors are used in India in fertility rites, or serpent festivals. There is little doubt that this ritualized use harms them.

The pet trade probably has a minor effect on the decline of most lizard populations, but certain species have been depleted by this industry. Rare or unusual forms like the Gila monster and the Banded iguana are eagerly sought by field collectors.

The greatest threat to lizard populations is permanent habitat alteration or destruction, especially in complex and poorly understood regions of the Tropics and Subtropics. In southern Florida, for example,

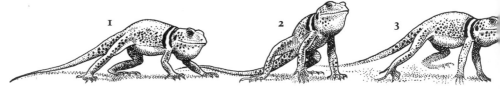

▲ **New generation** of the Crested iguana (*Brachylophus vitiensis*) pushing its way out of parchment-like eggs. Like most lizard hatchlings, these will fend for themselves, without parental care.

▼ **Reproductive and urinary organs.** A male lizard's hemipenes are pouches which are turned outward during copulation. Only one is used at each mating.

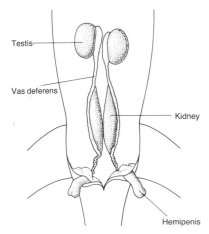

Testis

Vas deferens

Kidney

Hemipenis

◄ **Wrestling match** ABOVE between Bengal monitors fighting for possession of females in the breeding season. Dominance is established by pushing a rival over.

◄ **Lizard aggression.** Preparing for battle with a rival, a male Collared lizard (*Crotaphytus collaris*) (**1**) sees his rival, (**2**) bobs vigorously, his feet leaving the ground, and (**3**) charges.

Unisexual Lizards

Parthenogenesis, or "virgin birth," occurs in many invertebrates, such as flies and earthworms, as well as in some species of vertebrates, including fish, amphibians and lizards. All-female populations, producing viable offspring from eggs unfertilized by males, have been found among rock lizards, geckos and whiptails and racerunners.

The chameleons, chisel-teeth and night lizards have species which are believed to consist mostly, or entirely of females, but the absence of males even from well-sampled populations is inconclusive evidence of unisexual reproduction. It is through observation in laboratory settings that species such as the well-studied New Mexico whiptail have been established to be parthenogenetic. These whiptails never reject skin grafts from others of their species, evidence that all the individuals used in experiments are nearly identical in their genetic make-up. The most compelling results have come with the laboratory production of generations of unisexual lizards.

Pseudosexual behavior has been observed in captive parthenogenetic species, eg whiptails and racerunners. In the Desert grasslands whiptail, for example, some females pursue, mount, and grip other, reproductively active females with their limbs and jaws. This behavior may help to synchronize ovulation and egg-laying in the population.

All unisexual vertebrates that have been studied closely are believed to be of hybrid origin. Typically, both the male and female offspring resulting from hybrid matings are sterile, but, by some unknown mechanism, one or more hybrid females may have retained the ability to reproduce. It is believed that the unisexual New Mexico whiptail arose from hybridization between the Western racerunner, a desert inhabitant, and the Little striped whiptail, a grassland species. A second theory claims that all-female forms arise by way of mutation.

There appear to be certain advantages in being parthenogenetic. Parthenoforms probably are more successful colonizers than bisexuals, because only a single parthenogenetic individual is required to found a new population, as opposed to one of each sex. This form of reproduction may act as a buffer against certain harmful mutations, and when advantageous mutations arise, they are transmitted more quickly to future generations. Parthenoforms are able to increase their numbers more rapidly than bisexuals, as every member of the population can bear young.

However, there are substantial disadvantages in being parthenogenetic, which account for its rarity. Unisexual populations lack the reproductive mechanisms for rapid genetic change and may, therefore, be less likely to survive rapid changes in the environment and the changing character of parasites and diseases.

there is a near ecological collapse and it is due entirely to man's actions. Although the introduction of exotic species of lizards to southern Florida has been blamed for the decline of some native lizards, there is no firm evidence to substantiate these claims. (Exotics occupy man-made environments, new niches that native forms are unable to shift into.) There is no doubt, however, that non-reptilian introductions, in any habitat, are very harmful to many forms of lizards. Among other native species, the rock iguanas of the West Indies have suffered the effects of mongooses, feral dogs, cats, goats and cattle. The remaining populations of the Anegada ground iguana and the related *Cyclura collei* may consist of only old adults incapable of reproduction. With so little knowledge available on the population dynamics of many species, it is difficult to assess the damage, and its correction.

Families of Lizards

Chisel-teeth lizards are a diverse family of more than 300 species from Africa, Asia and Australia. They are mostly insectivores or carnivores, including eggs in their diets, but the Egyptian spiny-tailed lizard is mainly herbivorous. Their vision is well developed, in keeping with their day-active terrestrial or tree-dwelling life-style.

One species, the Australian frilled lizard, runs away on its hind legs when escaping predators. The flying dragons, common in the forests of Southeast Asia, are famous for their ability to glide from perch to perch. This extraordinary form of locomotion is made possible by a large, thin fold of skin extending from each side of the body between the fore- and hind limbs. It is sup-

ported by several elongated, bony ribs. These skin folds act more like parachutes than wings. In each species of flying dragon the wings are adorned with different patterns of bright colors, which seem to serve as signals between the sexes. When gliding, the animal steers with its tail.

Other chisel-teeth lizards have compressed tails and are well adapted for swimming (eg the Eastern water dragon). The

▷ **With turret-like eyes** OVERLEAF the Mountain chameleon (*Chamaeleo montium*) of West Africa can watch out all around for its staple diet of insect prey.

◁▼ **Representative species** of three lizard families. (**1**) Flying dragon (*Draco volans*); Agamidae. (**2**) Green anole (*Anolis carolinensis*); Iguanidae. (**3**) Texas horned lizard (*Phrynosoma cornutum*); Iguanidae.(**4**) Fringe-toed lizard (*Uma notata*); Iguanidae. (**5**) Arabian toad-headed lizard (*Phrynocephalus nejdensis*); Agamidae. (**6**) Spiny-tailed lizard (*Uromastix acanthinurus*); Agamidae. (**7**) Flap-necked chameleon (*Chamaeleo dilepsis*); Chamaeleontidae.

Chameleon dragon has a prehensile tail that it wraps around vegetation to steady itself as it moves through the trees.

Most chisel-teeth lizards perform an elaborate courtship, and males are quite often aggressive towards competitors. The males of many species have brightly colored heads, dewlaps and crests, and interactions between males involve highly ritualized movements and displays. Godeffroy's dragon is quite unusual in that females are more brightly colored than males.

Two groups, the Sri Lanka prehensile-tail lizard and the toad-headed lizards of the Near East, give birth to living young; the remainder lay 1–27 eggs per clutch. At least some populations of the Butterfly lizard of Southeast Asia consist only of females.

The family gets its common name from its rather specialized teeth. The bases are not in sockets, nor do they rest loosely on shelves or against walls of bone, as they do in most other lizards; instead the bases are firmly fixed to the surfaces of the major tooth-bearing bones. The teeth at the front of the head are often compressed and fused, incisor-like, or are exceptionally long and fang-like. Other teeth are truncated blunt cylinders, or are compressed, with irregularly wavy shearing margins.

Chameleons are limited to the Old World, mostly the tropics of India, Africa and Madagascar, and possess numerous adaptations for moving and feeding in trees. They climb slowly and deliberately, gripping the vegetation firmly with zygodactyl feet (toes of the same feet face opposite ways). Their prehensile tail provides an additional appendage steadying the animal and assuring its grip. Even the compressed body is thought to

provide further stability, because much of
the animal's weight can be centered
immediately over the narrow twig or
branch along which it is moving.

Chameleons prey on insects, spiders and
scorpions, although some of the larger
species feed on small birds and mammals.
The chameleon's large turret-like eyes can
independently survey the environment or
they can be turned forward and focused on
one object. This allows a form of binocular
vision, which improves depth perception,
and probably accounts for the chameleon's
incredible accuracy in securing prey with its
tongue. The rapid tongue flick operates by
both hydraulic and muscular forces. The
sticky mucus on the tip of the tongue
ensures that the prey does not escape as it
is withdrawn into the mouth.

A chameleon's movements can be so slow
that much of the time they are imperceptible, and it has an ability to blend with
the colors and patterns of its surroundings.
These are important advantages when it
searches for food. Even the body shape
appears to be leaf-like in outline and may
serve as additional camouflage. The same
traits must also reduce detection by predators. At night, when perched inactively on
a branch, some species instantly drop to a
lower branch or the ground when they are
agitated. This "perch release" may be a
defense against snakes and lemurs. When
stump-tailed chameleons are disturbed they
move gently back and forth, much like a leaf
in a soft breeze. This lineage has become terrestrial; stump-tailed chameleons walk
rather clumsily on the same zygodactyl feet
that their arboreal relatives use for climbing
trees.

Chameleons mate periodically or throughout the year. Courtship occurs in most species and is usually assertive. Females store
sperm for long periods between mating and
egg-laying. Most chameleons lay eggs, 4–40
per laying (70 in Meller's chameleon); however, a few species of pygmy chameleons
give birth to living young. Some bear young
still surrounded by the transparent egg
membrane.

Although they are mostly solitary,
chameleons have well-developed social
systems. Males are territorial and they
engage in long and deliberate fights. Horned
species use their distinctive bony appendages in combat. European chameleons often
bite each other while in copulation.

Iguanas are widely distributed in the New
World, with three genera in Madagascar
and Fiji. This is a very diverse family of terrestrial and tree-dwelling lizards, all of

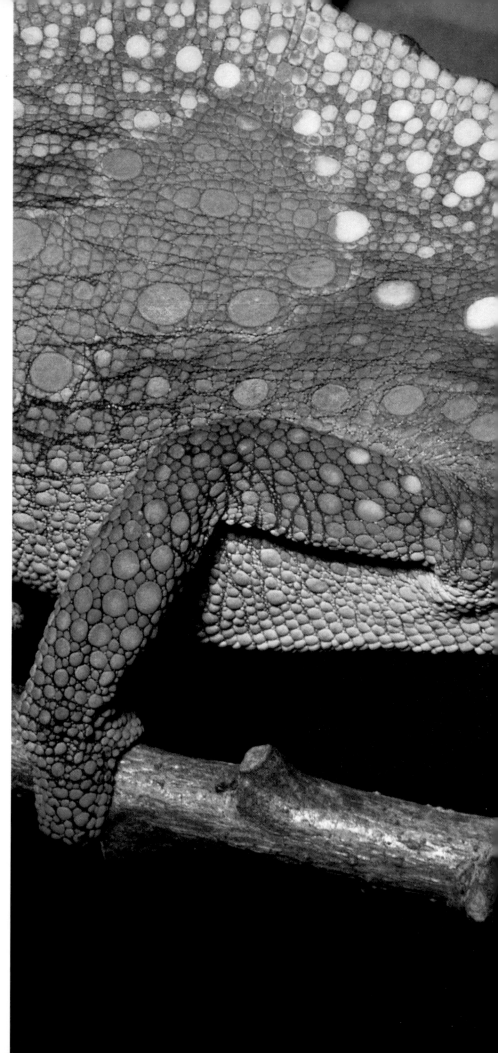

which are active by day. Some of those living in vegetation have prehensile tails and complex gripping surfaces on the undersides of their toes, like geckos. A few species are burrowers; they rapidly dig into sand when approached by potential predators. Some are excellent swimmers and divers, staying submerged for long periods of time. The smaller species are mostly insectivorous, occasionally carnivorous or omnivorous, while the large forms are herbivorous. The Marine iguana of the Galapagos Islands feeds on tidal and subtidal algae, its rounded snout, webbed feet and compressed tail helping to make it an excellent swimmer. It has glands in the nasal cavity which excrete excess salt.

Other iguanas also have modified toes for specialized locomotion. The Leafy plum-tree basilisk has a fold along the side of the toes, which appears to help it to run across the surfaces of ponds and small streams. The toes of the Fringe-toed lizard are thought to be adapted for running on loose sand.

Basking is commonly observed, and at least some iguanas can withstand, at least for short periods, temperatures as high as 47°C (117°F) without dying. Most species have well-developed social systems, which usually involve visual displays. As might be expected in species that are active during the day, iguana behavior is quite varied, and there is considerable sexual dimorphism and dichromatism. Males usually defend territories, and in doing so, they periodically rise up on extended forelimbs, bob their heads, extend their throat fans, erect crests, inflate or compress their bodies, snap their tails and even hiss. The throat and belly are often brightly colored with reds and blues. Most of the territorial behavior is ritualized, and actual combat is uncommon.

Most iguanas lay eggs. The number of eggs per clutch varies from one in anoles to 45 in the Green iguana. Live birth is believed to have arisen independently at least 10 times within the family, with one species of horned lizard, *Phrynosoma douglassi*, bearing up to 31 young at a time.

Geckos are notable for their abilities to vocalize and to climb, even on vertical panes of glass. Widely distributed in both the Old and New Worlds and oceanic islands, they are especially diverse in the Tropics. Their toes vary from narrow and straight, with unmodified scales on the undersides, to bent, or dilated and covered below with rows of hair-like projections. At least one species, the Web-footed gecko, has nearly fully webbed feet. Individual rows of scales on the undersides of a tokay's toes consist

of 150,000 or more projections called setae, which vary from about 30–130 micrometers (0.001–0.005in) in length. A seta, in turn, branches into several hundred bristles, each of which may terminate in a saucer-shaped endplate, or spatula, which measures approximately 0.2 micrometers (0.000008in) in diameter. Considering all four feet, 20 toes, the number of rows and setae and surface area of the endplates, the tokay has an enormous surface area in contact with the climbing surface. Blood-filled sinuses are believed to push the endplate against and around tiny irregularities in the climbing surface and secure a firm grip.

Several species of tree-dwelling geckos have prehensile tails, and it is not uncommon to find the undersurface of the tip of the tail modified into rows of hair-like projections similar to those on the toes. These special modifications are not absolutely essential for life above ground; some arboreal geckos have rather ordinary, unmodified, straight toes and tails.

Most geckos are active at night and, as might be expected, their color and skin patterns tend to be relatively undistinguished.

▲ **Basking in the sun,** Marine iguanas raise their body temperature before diving into the cool sea to feed.

▶ **Breaking camouflage.** Normally cryptic against the tree bark where it hunts for its insect prey, an Eastern spiny-tailed gecko of Australia stands out against a dark surface.

▼ **Sole of a gecko's foot** has ridges for gripping tiny irregularities, making it possible to run up and down vertical surfaces and even to run upside-down across ceilings. The name 'gecko' probably derives from the calls of these lizards, produced by clicking the broad tongue against the roof of the mouth.

these regions of lost skin are regenerated.

Most geckos have well-formed vocal cords, and numerous species including the tokay and the Talkative gecko have an elaborate vocal repertoire. Hearing is particularly well-developed in the nocturnal species, for which visual cues are not readily available. Some geckos produce a series of modulated chirps and clicks, which vary according to the social situation, such as territorial defense and mating.

Geckos typically lay one or two eggs with calcareous shells. A few lay eggs with leathery shells, and still fewer give birth to living young. Baby geckos break out of the egg by piercing it with sharply pointed, paired egg teeth at the tip of the snout, which drop off shortly after birth. Communal egg-laying sites are typical of many species. Nearly 100 Fan-toed gecko eggs were found in one crevice in Israel.

Even though the gecko tongue is not especially long, most species have been observed frequently to lick their spectacle, the transparent covering of their eyes. Most are insectivorous, although a few will eat small mammals and birds; others eat nectar and sweet exudate from tree bark. Many regularly eat their shed skin as well.

Although it may seem unlikely from external appearances, the **snake lizards** of Australia and New Guinea are more closely related to geckos than to any other family. Some of the more prominent features that relate the two groups are small, paired sacs and associated bones that lie at the base of the tail, unique paired egg-teeth, a broad, fleshy, but highly extensible tongue that is frequently observed to lick the region of the eyeball, and a well-developed repertoire of vocal signals.

Snake lizards are partly or fully burrowing. Some are capable of "sand-swimming," others occupy crevices and several frequent terrestrial spider burrows. A few species are found in hummocks of spiny grass and other low lying, dense vegetation. Peak activity for most species is at night.

All are insectivorous, but the two species of sharp-snouted snake lizards prefer other small lizards, especially skinks and geckos. These species are similar to snakes in swallowing prey whole.

All snake lizards lay two, rarely one, elongated, leathery-shelled eggs. Their limb-flaps, once thought to be functionless, are used in a limited way by some species during locomotion, mating and threat displays. Species with black heads such as the Western scalyfoot are said to mimic certain venomous species of front-fanged snake.

The few species active in daytime, such as the day geckos of Madagascar, are much more brightly colored and strikingly patterned. These forms often exhibit marked sexual dichromatism, and, as in many animals, adult males are the more colorful. Those geckos that are active at night have very large eyes, and the shape of the pupil can be adjusted to different light intensities, reduced to a very narrow vertical slit in direct sun or to a large, round opening on moonless nights.

Except for their secretive nature and ability to shed their tails, geckos have few defenses against predators. However, several species in Australia have evolved a novel deterrent. Williams's diplodactyl, for example, is able to eject a viscous fluid from crypts located on the upper surface of its tail. These projectiles travel several centimeters, become sticky and entrap the predator, such as a lycosid spider or a snake lizard. The flying geckos of Southeast Asia, with extensions of skin along the body and tail, can avoid predation by gliding to a distant perch. The Common house gecko sheds large portions of skin, even when lightly grasped, and

Whiptail lizards are mostly active by day, inhabiting swamps, deserts, savanna and tropical rain forests of the New World. They may be terrestrial, partially tree-dwelling or burrowing.

High daylight temperatures lead to short, but fast-moving periods of activity in the desert and savanna species. Some, such as the Caiman lizard and Dragon lizard, are semiaquatic. A few live largely in caves. Some were once thought to have so-called "light organs," but these are no more than rows of light-reflecting scales arranged along the sides of their bodies.

Whiptail lizards feed on small mammals, birds, fish, adult frogs and tadpoles, other lizards, insects, snails and plant material. Some, such as the jungle runners and tegus, readily come to baits, and are frequently captured in traps by South American Indians who eat them or use their fat and flesh in traditional medicines.

Particularly in jungle runners and racerunners, males acquire striking coloration during the breeding season, apparently to advertise their territories.

Whiptails lay 1–7 eggs; the Common tegu is exceptional in laying 32. The eggs are deposited in soft soil or termite nests. If the termites seal off the opening thus made in their nest, the young dig themselves free upon hatching. Several populations of racerunners consist only of females.

The **wall and sand lizards** are conspicuous lizards wherever they occur, in Africa, Europe and Asia. Primarily terrestrial, they are alert and active daytime reptiles, usually living in sandy, open spaces. A few are found in montane grasslands or in dense tropical vegetation, and many are rock-dwellers and agile climbers. Crevice inhabitants tend to have a slightly depressed body form, and some of the desert-dwelling species have toe modifications for running on loose sand. Wall and sand lizards operate at high body temperatures and consequently are active for only a limited part of the day and of the year. However, in the northern part of its range, the Viviparous lizard occurs above the Arctic Circle, the farthest north of any lizard. Members of this family eat a wide variety of prey. Most feed on insects and

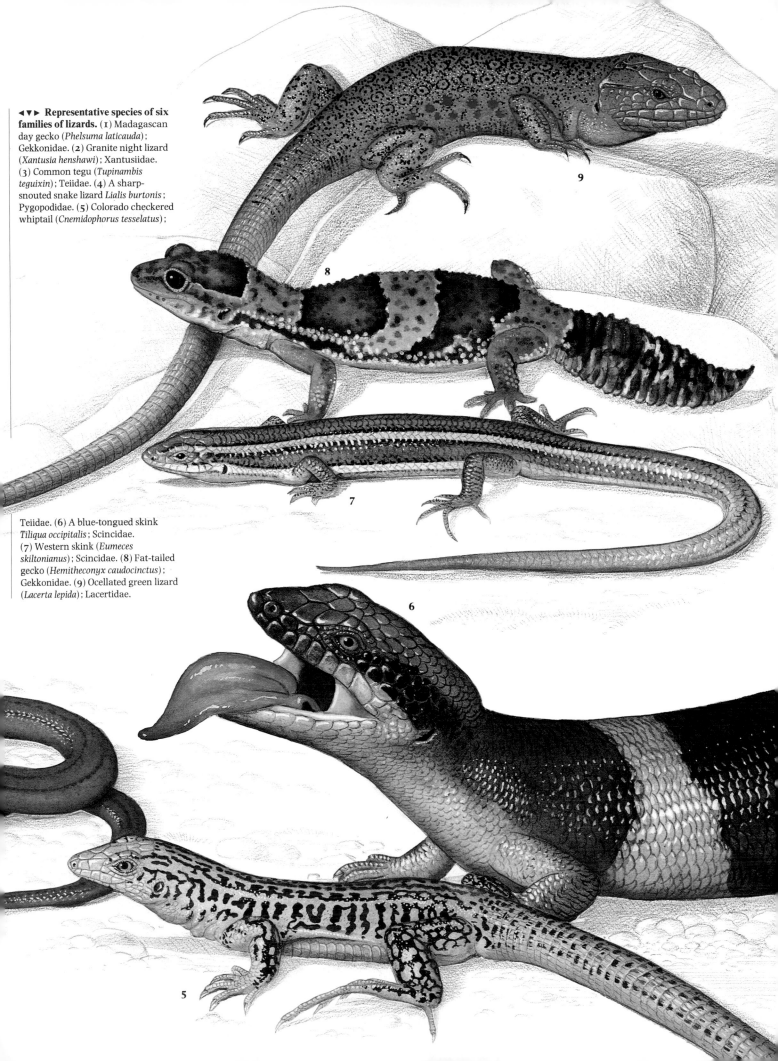

◄▼► Representative species of six families of lizards. (1) Madagascan day gecko (*Phelsuma laticauda*); Gekkonidae. (2) Granite night lizard (*Xantusia henshawi*); Xantusiidae. (3) Common tegu (*Tupinambis teguixin*); Teiidae. (4) A sharp-snouted snake lizard *Lialis burtonis*; Pygopodidae. (5) Colorado checkered whiptail (*Cnemidophorus tesselatus*);

Teiidae. (6) A blue-tongued skink *Tiliqua occipitalis*; Scincidae. (7) Western skink (*Eumeces skiltonianus*); Scincidae. (8) Fat-tailed gecko (*Hemitheconyx caudocinctus*); Gekkonidae. (9) Ocellated green lizard (*Lacerta lepida*); Lacertidae.

other small invertebrates, such as snails and worms. A few take lizards, snakes, small rodents, fruits, seeds and flowers.

Many species are known to be quite social. Males have larger heads than females, are more brightly colored, mainly during the breeding season, and often fight. Most males have characteristic threat postures, in which the head is tilted downward, the throat region inflated and the body compressed and fully presented to the antagonist, showing off the bright colors.

All except the Viviparous lizard and two unrelated species of racerunner lay eggs. Even the former species lays eggs in a limited part of its range. There are 4–11 young per litter or 1–23 eggs per clutch. The eggs are deposited under stones or in shallow holes dug in the earth, which the mother covers. The young of many true lizards are brightly colored, even more so than the adults. At least five species consist only of females.

Wall and sand lizards are rather long-lived; 20 years in captivity has been recorded for the Ocellated green lizard.

Night lizards, discontinuously distributed in the southwestern United States, Mexico, Central America and the West Indies, are mostly terrestrial insectivores active at night. They are very secretive, hiding by day in caves, in crevices, and under slabs of limestone or granite, logs and clumps of low-lying vegetation. The Desert night lizard is commonly found beneath yucca and agave plant debris. The Island lizard prefers plant food, seeds and parts of flowers, on which it uses its shearing, tricuspid teeth; it is mainly active by day.

All species of night lizards appear to give birth to living young, and a definite placental connection has been found in at least four species. The gestation period is about 90 days for the Desert night lizard. Usually 1–3 offspring are born at a time, but the Island night lizard gives birth to 4–9. Costa Rican and Panamanian populations of the Middle American night lizard consist only of females.

Skinks, widely distributed in the New and Old Worlds and on oceanic islands, are as varied in their habits as they are in form and structure. They occur in a variety of habitats from deserts to forests, and can be terrestrial, tree-dwelling or burrowing. The small terrestrial species are usually extremely active. Burrowers tend to be small and secretive, and very readily "swim" through sand. Many of the burrowing species have the lower jaw sunk within the upper, and they exhibit various stages of limb reduction. Some of them have fringed toes.

Skinks are often found on rocky slopes, under piles of debris or logs. Some are found along water courses, and they are excellent swimmers. The Marine skink inhabits rocky shorelines. It readily takes to the sea, where it dives and remains underwater for several minutes to escape predators. It feeds on intertidal crabs and isopods.

At least some tree-dwelling species have specialized glandular structures on the bottoms of their feet which may assist them in their arboreal niche. The Giant Solomon Island skink has well-developed limbs and claws. It is arboreal, nocturnal, completely herbivorous and very aggressive. It bears a single young that is one-third the size of the mother. Skinks are mostly active by day, although some, particularly the burrowing forms and some arboreal species, are active at dusk or at night.

The Green-blood skink is completely arboreal and unique among vertebrates in that it has a green pigment in its blood. The pigment may be related to bile. When this species gapes, it exposes a green tongue and similarly colored mucosal tissues. The eggs, also green, are laid in trees. The upper surface of the adult is green, the belly yellow.

Small skinks eat insects, including termites. The large species, like the blue-tongues of Australia, are herbivorous and may include seeds in their diet. A few are omnivorous.

Viviparity is thought to have arisen independently at least 22 times within the family. Oviparous skinks lay 2–23 eggs per clutch or bear 1–24 live young at a time. The eggs are deposited in rotten wood or loose soil. In some species, eg the Five-lined skink, clutches are watched and guarded by

▲ **With an impressive length of tail,** *Takydromus sexlineatus*, of the wall and sand lizard family, makes its way through long grass.

◄ **Swimming through sand.** The sandfish (genus *Scincus*), is a desert dwelling skink that moves quickly through sand, just below the surface, where it is protected from the direct heat of the sun and where it preys on beetles and millipedes.

► **Biting into its earthworm prey,** a slowworm wins another meal. Slowworms give birth to fully-formed young after a very variable gestation period. In a cool summer, the young may not be born at all but are retained within the mother's body until the following year.

the mother until hatching. Other species such as the Great Plains skink lick the young clean after they have emerged from the eggs.

The **girdle-tailed lizards** are restricted to Africa and Madagascar. They are a family of day-active, terrestrial species adapted to arid environments. They exhibit three radically different body forms correlated with habitat. Typical members of this family, such as the Armadillo girdle-tailed lizard, are very spiny rock-dwellers with a somewhat depressed shape. When they wedge themselves in rock crevices they are difficult to remove. They may also defend themselves by forming a ball with the body and tail. A second type, exemplified by the Cape red-tailed flat lizard, is a less spiny rock-dweller with an extremely depressed shape. It is often found in the narrowest spaces. A third form, represented by species of sweepslangs, is long-bodied, long-tailed and cylindrical, with no limbs or only short appendages; they inhabit grass savanna or sand dunes.

Many girdle-tailed species lay 4–5 eggs; however, several bear 1–6 live young in mid-summer to early fall. Flat lizards lay only two extraordinarily elongated eggs in cracks in rocks.

Most species are insectivores. Some of the largest are carnivorous, and at least two groups are plant-eating. One, *Angolosaurus skoogi*, consumes seeds that are blown onto the sand dunes where it lives.

The more spiny girdle-tailed lizards, such as the sungazer, defend themselves against predators by slapping them with their spiny tails, but some play dead when attacked.

The **blind lizards** comprise three Asian and one Mexican species with eyes concealed beneath the skin. The biology of these secretive burrowing reptiles is virtually unknown. They occupy humid tropical and pine-oak forests, where they burrow into rotten logs and hide beneath stones; some burrow in sand and loose soil. All appear to be insectivorous. They lay rounded eggs with calcareous shells. The paddle-like hind limbs are thought to be used to clasp the female during copulation.

The **xenosaurs** of China, Mexico and Guatemala are mainly terrestrial and rather sedentary. They occasionally climb 1–2m (3.3–6.6ft) above ground, but readily enter water. They are found in a variety of microenvironments, from narrow crevices and holes in rocks to hollow logs and holes in trees. It is not unusual to find them submerged in shallow streams or puddles beneath rocks. They occur from dry scrub to wet or cloud forest, in limestone or volcanic mountainous regions.

Very secretive, they are mostly active in the shade or at dusk and during the early evening. However, the Chinese xenosaur has been observed basking in open vegetation overhanging water. Other species have been observed to leave their retreats when it rains.

Food preferences of the xenosaurs vary from insects, especially winged ants, to tadpoles and small fishes. They bite ferociously and gape widely in a threatening manner when approached. Their tiny red eyes accentuate their intimidating behavior. Some native people erroneously believe that xenosaurs are venomous. All species bear 4–7 living young. Birth takes place in late spring to midsummer.

The **anguids** have a covering of bony-plated scales, even on the undersides, that makes them look and feel rigid. They are widely distributed in the New and Old Worlds and vary in shape from short and stout to long and slender. Some species have short limbs, some (eg the slowworm) have none at all, while others display various intermediate stages in limb reduction. All have functional eyes, although these are small to modest in size.

Most are terrestrial like the slowworm, but some live in trees and these may possess a prehensile tail (eg the tree anguids of Mexico and Central America). The tree-dwellers are often found in epiphytic bromeliads as high as 40m (130ft) above ground. The Southern alligator lizard has an ordinary fat, cylindrical tail, which does not appear to be prehensile, but it has been observed hanging by its tail while feeding on birds' eggs in a nest.

A few anguids burrow in sand or loose, loamy soil. They are also found in litter, under rocks and logs and in rotting vegeta-

◀▼▶ **Representative species** of seven families of lizards (1) Southern alligator lizard (*Elgaria multicarinata*); Anguidae. (2) Bornean earless lizard (*Lanthanotus borneensis*); Lanthanotidae. (3) Gila monster (*Heloderma suspectum*); Helodermatidae. (4) Sungazer (*Cordylus giganteus*); Cordylidae. (5) Chinese xenosaur (*Shinisaurus crocodilurus*); Xenosauridae. (6) An Asian blind lizard *Dibamus novaeguinae*; Dibamidae. (7) Common Asiatic monitor (*Varanus salvator*); Varanidae.

tion. Some live in rather hot and dry environments, while others are adapted to cool and very humid coniferous or pine and oak forests. All of them seem to be secretive, both the day-active and night-active species.

Anguid diets are extraordinarily variable. They are known to eat small lizards and mice, the eggs and young of birds, tadpoles, earthworms, spiders, scorpions, sow bugs, grasshoppers, moths and wasps and a variety of insect larvae. The sheltopusik of Europe prefers slugs and snails, and farmers recognize it as the natural predator primarily responsible for controlling these and other pests. The California legless lizard is a burrower which feeds by suddenly thrusting its snout through the soil surface to take insects and spiders.

Most anguids lay eggs, 2–12 at a time. At least one species of glass lizard deposits them in vacated mammal burrows, while others are known to brood their clutches. Other anguids bear up to 26 living young per litter. Males are quite aggressive during the breeding season, when they often engage in extended bouts of biting rival males.

The more northern species enter winter torpor; one winter retreat was found to contain 30 slowworms. At least some anguids are long-lived; well over 50 years in captivity is the record.

The two **beaded lizards,** the Gila monster and the Mexican beaded lizard, are found in arid to tropical habitats in the Colorado River drainage in the United States and along the Pacific slopes of Mexico. They are mildly venomous, but their painful bite is very rarely fatal to humans in good health. The venom is produced by modified, paired salivary glands, and it affects the nervous system. It begins with local pain and numbness, which can lead to cardiac and respiratory paralysis. Unlike those of snakes, the venom glands are confined to the lower jaws. Each is located on the outer side of the jaw, toward the tip of the snout, just below the skin. The venom empties into a fleshy groove between the inner edge of the lip and the outer margin of the jaw. From there it passes to the grooved teeth, which draw the venom into the wound by capillary action as the lizard chews its victim.

Both species eat a wide variety of small mammals, birds, lizards, frogs, reptile and birds' eggs, insects, earthworms, myriapods and carrion. Their prey is swallowed whole, except for eggs, which they break first. The tail of both species is used as an energy store, presumably an adaptation to highly unpredictable food resources. Chemosensation, by

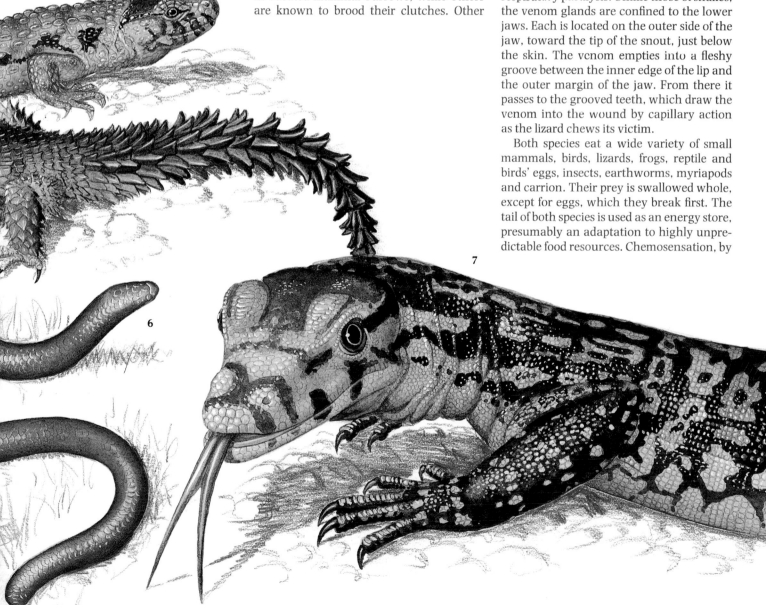

way of the tongue and vomeronasal organ, seems to play a large role in prey location (see p87). The venom is very effective in subduing mammals and birds, but has much less effect on frogs.

Beaded lizards are primarily terrestrial. They prefer cooler temperatures, and are most active at dusk and at night. They are generally inactive during the winter months, especially in the United States. While generally sluggish, they are capable of quick movements when provoked. They frequently inhabit semiarid rocky regions near foothills, and they are often found on rock ledges. They are also found in abandoned mammal burrows, and frequent sources of permanent water. Mating occurs mostly in spring, and lasts 30–60 minutes. Females lay 3–13 long eggs in mid to late summer and bury them at a depth of about 12.5cm (5in) in areas exposed to the sun. Incubation lasts 117–130 days.

Superficially, the **Bornean earless lizard,** sole member of its family, resembles the beaded lizards. The body, tongue and teeth are very similar in shape, but it can be distinguished by its nostrils, placed on top of the snout rather than on the sides. It also differs in not having an external ear opening, venom apparatus or a fold of skin across the throat. Unlike beaded lizards, it has pits in the larger scales which may function as tactile organs. Unfortunately, little is known

about the life of this enigmatic creature. Almost all observations have been made on captives kept under artificial conditions.

This lizard appears to be partly aquatic and partly a burrower. It readily enters water, where it stays for very long periods. It drinks considerably and appears to become dry rapidly. A good swimmer, its movement on land is labored. It uses sideways undulations of the body, somewhat snake-like, on both land and in the water. The forelimbs are used in swimming as well. The tail is slightly prehensile and may serve as a hold-fast in swift moving water. Most of the known specimens were collected after severe flooding, and they are thought to be common in ditches adjacent to rice fields.

On land, the Bornean earless lizard is capable of moving rapidly, but only for short distances. Its forelimbs seem to be used more in steering, while the hindlimbs appear to assist in pushing the animal along. The body is not lifted off the ground. The lizard burrows by thrusting its snout into the earth.

In captivity, the earless lizard eats some marine fish, earthworms and yolks of seaturtle and birds' eggs. It frequently senses the environment, especially potential foods, with its elongated tongue. Its slow rate of growth, at least in captivity, and its generally lethargic and unaggressive nature, imply that it has a low rate of metabolism. It is nocturnal and an egg-layer.

▲ **Terrestrial monitor,** Gould's monitor inhabits coastal and desert areas of Australia. It lives in a burrow and rears up on its hind legs when threatened by an enemy or a rival.

◄ **Sunbathing monitor,** ABOVE an Australian Mitchell's water monitor (*Varanus mitchelli*) basks in the sun. Monitors hunt for their prey by day, and this species, very agile in the water, feeds on a variety of aquatic animals, including fish.

► **Giants among lizards,** Komodo dragons can grow to a length of 3m (10ft) and prey on animals as large as deer and wild pigs. Despite their size, they are fast-moving and agile. They are good swimmers and climb trees.

Monitor lizards vary from 12cm (4.7in) in the Short-tailed monitor to 1.5m (57in), and over 165kg (364lb), in the Komodo dragon, the largest living lizard. This dragon regularly kills prey as large as pigs and small deer, and has been known to bring down a 590kg (1300lb) adult Water buffalo. It can engulf large amounts in one gulp, and has a prodigious appetite. A 46kg (101lb) Komodo dragon ate a whole 41kg (90lb) wild pig in one meal. This species is reported to attack and kill humans.

Monitors tend to swallow their prey whole, like snakes. Some authorities have claimed that they partly fill the large mammalian carnivore niche, especially in places like Australia where they are common. Twenty-four of the 31 species occur there and also in other localities without terrestrial carnivorous mammals.

Monitors are daytime lizards and most species actively search for food. The tongue is freqently employed, as in the beaded lizards, in food searching. The Komodo dragon often hides and waits for its prey. Some species eat carrion, giant land snails, grasshoppers, beetles, whip scorpions, crocodile and birds' eggs, crabs, fish, other lizards, snakes, nestling birds, shrews and squirrels.

Many species hold their heads erect on their long necks, which gives them the appearance of being alert. They intimidate predators by lashing out with their tails, inflating their throats, hissing loudly, turning sideways and compressing their bodies.

They are mostly terrestrial, but many are agile climbers and good swimmers. Several species are strong runners, and Gould's monitor can outrun a human over a short distance. The tail is somewhat compressed in tree-dwellers, very compressed in semiaquatic monitors. At least one species, the Common Asiatic monitor, has been seen swimming far out to sea. It can remain submerged for an hour, and often dives into water to escape potential predators.

Combat between males is frequently observed during the breeding season in some species. Monitors lay 7–35, and perhaps more, soft-shelled eggs, usually deposited in holes in riverbanks or in trees along water courses. The Nile monitor often lays its eggs in termite nests. There is little or no sexual dimorphism.

Monitors live in rocky and sandy deserts, in savannas and in forest, riverbank or mangrove environments. Some species, such as the Bengal and Cape monitors, become dormant during periods of drought or cool weather. AGK/GS

THE 16 FAMILIES OF LIZARDS

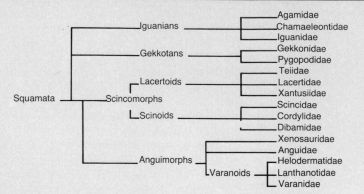

Lizard classification is unstable and is currently undergoing major revision. While most families are well described their interrelationships are poorly documented. Only a tentative phylogenetic hypothesis is available (see ABOVE). The better founded relationships include: iguanians, gekkotans, lacertoids, scincoids, and varanoids. The Xenosauridae and Anguidae are probably closely related to the varanoids, and together form the anguimorph assemblage. Anguimorphs and snakes are probably relatives. The Dibamidae may be scincoid. Lacertoids and scincoids are usually placed together as scincomorphs, which are thought to share a common ancestry with anguimorphs. The iguanians and gekkotans are almost certainly the most primitive groups of lizards.

Chisel-Teeth Lizards
Family: Agamidae
Three hundred species in 53 genera.

Distribution: throughout Africa and Australia and all areas between, N to 52°, except Madagascar; up to more than 3,600m. Length: 4–35cm. Color: generally brown, gray or black; many species sexually dichromatic; some capable of rapidly changing color. Scales: most keeled or drawn out into spines; in many species males and females with different head ornaments, throat fans, neck frills and folds, crests or enlarged spines on back and tail. Body form: head large and set off from neck; body cylindrical, compressed or depressed; 5th toe absent or reduced; tail long

and not fragile. Eyes and lids: well developed. Ears: external opening rarely covered with scales. Tongue: thick and fleshy, blunt and slightly notched at tip. Teeth: acrodont (fixed to tooth-bearing bones); at front often incisor-like, or long and fang-like; others truncated blunt cylinders or compressed, with irregularly wavy shearing margins. Wide variety of skin glands on belly and undersides of thighs in many species. Species and genera include: **Australian frilled lizard** (*Chlamydosaurus kingii*), **Butterfly lizard** (*Liolepis belliana*), **Chameleon dragon** (*Chelosania brunnea*), **Common bloodsucker** (*Calotes versicolor*), **Eastern water dragon** (*Physignatus lesueurii*), **Egyptian spiny-tailed lizard** [*] (*Uromastyx aegyptius*), **flying dragons** (genus *Draco*), **Godeffroy's dragon** (*Gonocephalus godeffroyi*), **moloch** or **Horny devil** (*Moloch horridus*), **Sri Lanka prehensile-tail lizard** (*Cophotis ceylanica*), **Sail-fin lizard** [V] (*Hydrosaurus pustulatus*), **toad-headed lizards** (genus *Phrynocephalus*). Total threatened species: 1.

Chameleons
Family: Chamaeleontidae
Eighty-five species in 4 genera.

Distribution: Madagascar and neighboring Indian Ocean islands, Sri Lanka, India, Pakistan, S Arabian Peninsula, Crete, S Spain, Africa except the Sahara; up to 4,260m. Length: 2–28cm. Color: predominantly brown, green or yellow; can quickly change color, even to extremes of white and black.

Scales: small, juxtaposed, without bony plates. Body form: head and body compressed; neck not defined; head often with horns or crests; limbs tending to be long and slender; feet zygodactyl (with some toes bound together and opposed); tail slender, prehensile in most species, never fragile. Eyes: protruding, covered with scaly lids, with only a tiny slit for vision. Ears: middle ear cavity and external opening absent. Tongue: long and slender, can be extended more than head-body length. Teeth: acrodont. Skin glands absent from belly and undersides of thighs. Species and genera include: **African chameleon** [*] (*Chamaeleo chamaeleon*), **European chameleon** (*C. vulgaris*), **Jackson's chameleon** [*] (*C. jacksonii*), **Meller's chameleon** [*] (*C. melleri*), **pygmy chameleons** (genus *Microsaura*), **stump-tailed chameleons** (genus *Brookesia*).

Iguanas
Family: Iguanidae
Six hundred and fifty species in 55 genera.

Distribution: S Canada to Argentina; a few species on Madagascar, Fiji and Tonga; up to 5,000m. Length: 5–45cm. Color: in general, brown, gray or black; several species mostly bright green or blue. Scales: variable; bony plates absent; throat fans, crests on back and fringes on toes common. Body form: variable; limbs typically well developed and five-toed; tail usually fragile. Eyes: moderately large, with well-developed lids. Ears: external opening usually present. Tongue: thick and fleshy, slightly grooved at tip. Teeth: variable between species. Species and genera include: **Anegada ground iguana** [*] [E] (*Cyclura pinguis*), **anoles** (genus *Anolis*), **basilisks** (genus *Basiliscus*), **banded iguanas** (genus *Brachylophus*), **Blunt-nosed lizard** [E] (*Gambelia silus*), **Fiji banded iguana** [*] [E] (*Brachylophus fasciatus*), **Fringe-toed lizard** (*Uma notata*), **Galapagos land iguana** [*] [V] (*Conolophus subcristatus*), **Giant anole** [E] (*Anolis roosevelti*), **Green anole** (*A. carolinensis*), **Green iguana** [*] (*Iguana iguana*), **horned lizards** (genus

Phrynosoma), **Leafy plumb-tree basilisk** (*Basiliscus plumifrons*), **Marine iguana** [*] [R] (*Amblyrhynchus cristatus*), **Pectinate ctenosaur** (*Ctenosaura pectinata*), **spiny lizards** (genus *Sceloporus*), **West Indian rock iguanas** [*](genus *Cyclura*). Total threatened species: 13. Total threatened subspecies: 1.

Geckos
Family: Gekkonidae
Eight hundred species in 85 genera.

Distribution: worldwide between 50°N and 47°S; up to 2,130m. Length: 1.5–24cm. Color: usually brown, gray or black; a few species yellow, orange or green. Scales: almost always small, comprising a soft skin; strongly keeled tubercles and spines sometimes scattered among them; without bone, rarely overlapping; enlarged, symmetrical head shields exceptional. Body form: typically with depressed head, body and tail; tail varying considerably in shape and ornamentation, fragile in all but some knob-tailed geckos; limbs short, with 5 toes which are especially variable in shape and scalation. Eyes: usually large with lids fused to form transparent covering. Ears: external opening may be small. Tongue: short, broad, slightly notched at tip. Teeth: cylindrical and pointed, in a few species with blunt crowns. Skin glands in males on belly next to cloacal opening or on underside of thighs; peculiar tiny paired sacs and associated bones present at base of tail in most species. Species and genera include: **Australian marbled gecko** (*Phyllodactylus marmoratus*), **Brook's half-toed gecko** (*Hemidactylus brookii*), **Common house gecko** (*Gehyra mutilata*), **day geckos** [*] (genus *Phelsuma*), **Fan-toed gecko** (*Ptyodactylus hasselquistii*), **flying**

▶ **Visual impact** of display postures and movements in Boyd's rain forest dragon (*Gonocephalus boydii*), from the tropical rain forests of Australia, is enhanced by bright colors, crest and dewlap.

geckos (genus *Ptychozoon*), **Green tree gecko** (*Naultinus elegans*), **Indian wall gecko** (*Hemidactylus flaviviridis*), **knob-tailed geckos** (genus *Nephrurus*), **Rodriguez day gecko** ▣ E (*Phelsuma edwardnewtonii*), **Talkative gecko** (*Ptenopus garrulus*), **Texas banded gecko** (*Coleonyx brevis*), **tokay** (*Gekko gecko*), **Web-footed gecko** (*Palmatogekko rangei*), **Western banded gecko** (*Coleonyx variegatus*), **Williams's diplodactyl** (*Diplodactylus williamsi*). Total threatened species: 4.

Snake Lizards
Family: Pygopodidae
Thirty-one species in 8 genera.

Distribution: Aru, New Britain, New Guinea, Australia except Tasmania; up to 750m. Length: 6.5–31cm. Color: usually brown, gray or black. Scales: on head large and symmetrical in almost all species; overlapping above on trunk and tail, usually smooth; on underside large rectangular shields; bony plates absent. Body form: snake-like in appearance; forelimbs absent, hind legs persisting as small to large flaps held tightly against body near cloacal opening; tail fragile. Eyes: modest in size, with fused lids forming transparent covering; pupil usually a vertical slit. Ears: with external opening; inconspicuous in a few species. Tongue: short, broad and thick; slightly notched at tip. Teeth: conical; stout to slender. With peculiar small paired sacs and associated bones at base of tail, like geckos. Species and genera include: **sharp-snouted snake lizards** (genus *Lialis*), **Western scalyfoot** (*Pygopus nigriceps*).

Whiptails and Racerunners
Family: Teiidae
Two hundred and twenty-seven species in 39 genera.

Distribution: S USA through S America and W Indies except

Patagonia and southern forests; up to 3,962m. Length: 3.7–45cm. Color: predominantly green, brown, gray or black. Scales: in most species large and symmetrical on head, small and granular on body and in rectangular, hexagonal plates on belly; bony plates absent. Body form: variable, stout with large head and well-developed limbs to elongated with small head and reduced limbs; usually with pointed snout and long, fragile tail. Eyes: moderately large, with oval pupils; lids well developed, movable and usually covered with scales; lower lids transparent in some. Ears: open or completely covered with scales. Tongue: long, narrow, covered above with fleshy protuberances, deeply forked at tip. Teeth: conical at front, variable at sides. Femoral skin glands usually present. Species and genera include: **Caiman lizard** (*Dracaena guianensis*), **Common tegu** (*Tupinambis teguixin*), **Dragon lizard** (*Crocodilurus lacertinus*), **jungle runners** (genus *Ameiva*), **Desert grasslands whiptail** (*Cnemidophorus uniparens*), **Little striped whiptail** (*C. inornatus*), **New Mexico whiptail** (*C. neomexicanus*), **St. Croix ground lizard** E (*Ameiva polops*), **Western racerunner** (*C. tigris*). Total threatened species: 2.

Wall and Sand Lizards
Family: Lacertidae
Two hundred species in 25 genera.

Distribution: Europe, Africa, Asia, Indo-Australian Archipelago; up to 3,810m. Length: 4–22cm. Color: green, yellow, blue, brown, gray or black. Scales: may be enlarged and symmetrically arranged on head, containing thin bony plates usually fused to skull; on back small and sometimes irregular; belly with large, smooth, rectangular plates in well-defined rows; in whorls on tail, where enlarged into spines in some species. Body form: head conical and distinct from body; snout pointed; usually with fold of skin across throat; body long, with well-developed limbs typically five-toed; tail long and fragile. Eyes: moderately large, with movable lids; some species with transparent window in lower lid. Tongue: long and narrow, deeply forked at tip, covered above with small projections or folds. Teeth:

tending to be cylindrical; some on palate. Femoral and preanal glands usually present. Species and genera include: **fringe-toed lacertids** (genus *Acanthodactylus*), **Hierro giant lizard** E (*Gallotia simonyi*), **Ocellated green lizard** (*Lacerta lepida*), **racerunners** (genus *Eremias*), **Rock lizard** (*Lacerta saxicola*), **Viviparous lizard** (*L. vivipara*). Total threatened species: 1. Total threatened subspecies: 1.

Night Lizards
Family: Xantusiidae
Sixteen species in 4 genera.

Distribution: E Cuba, Panama to C Mexico and SW USA; up to 2,600m. Length: 3.5–12cm. Color: predominantly somber shades of brown, gray or black. Scales: on head very large, with bony plates in some species; on upper surfaces of body and tail much smaller, juxtaposed; underside of body covered with large, rectangular plates. Body form: head quite depressed in several species; body long and slightly depressed; limbs short and typically five-toed; tail long and fragile. Eyes: small, with vertical pupil and transparent, fused lids. Ears: with external opening. Tongue: long and slightly notched at tip. Teeth: cylindrical and either blunt or with 3 cusps; absent from palate. Femoral glands present, preanal glands absent. Species include: **Cuban night lizard** (*Cricosaura typica*), **Desert night lizard** (*Xantusia vigilis*), **Island night lizard** R (*X. riversiana*), **Middle American night lizard** (*Lepiodophyma flavimaculatum*). Total threatened species: 1.

Skinks
Family: Scincidae
One thousand two hundred and seventy-five species in 85 genera.

Distribution: all tropical and temperate regions, especially in Africa, S Asia, Indo-Australian Archipelago, New Guinea, Australia, New Zealand and from S Canada to N

Argentina; up to 4,800m. Length: 2.8–35cm. Color: brown, gray and black predominating; some species green or blue. Scales: on top of head usually enlarged to form series of symmetrical shields; on body usually smooth, flat and overlapping each other in regular order. Body form: very variable, in general elongated and somewhat depressed, with a small, flattened head and short legs. Eyes: modest to small and nonfunctional; pupil usually round; lids well developed, movable or fused; lower lids with transparent disk or covered with scales. Ears: external opening present or covered by scales. Tongue: short, broad, flat and fleshy; scaly or ridged; slightly notched at tip. Teeth: very variable. Preanal and femoral skin glands absent. Species and genera include: **blind worms** (genus *Typhlosaurus*), **blue-tongued skinks** (genus *Tiliqua*), **Brazilian skink** (*Mabuya heathi*), **casqueheads** (genus *Tribolonotus*), **Five-lined skink** (*Eumeces fasciatus*), **Giant Solomon Island skink** (*Cornucia zebrata*), **Great Plains skink** (*Eumeces obsoletus*), **Green-blood skink** (*Prasinohaema virens*), **Marine skink** (*Emoia atrocostata*), **Peron's hemiergis** (*Hemiergis peronii*). Total threatened species: 3.

Girdle-Tailed Lizards
Family: Cordylidae
Fifty species in 10 genera.

Distribution: Africa S of the Sahara, Madagascar; up to 3,500m. Length: 5–27.5cm. Color: bluish- or yellowish-green, brown, gray or black. Scales: on head large symmetrical shields with bony plates; on body usually in regular series, rectangular and overlapping, usually keeled on upper surfaces. Body form: stout to snake-like; cylindrical or depressed; limbs absent in some species; tail fragile, short to very long. Eyes: well developed, with conspicuous lids; lower lid with transparent window in some species. Ears: external opening distinct. Tongue: short to moderately elongated; pointed; may be feebly notched at tip. Teeth: nearly cylindrical, with tapering tips or 2 cusps; frequently compressed at sides and curved inwards; present on palate. Femoral glands with conspicuous external pores in most species. Species and genera include: **Armadillo girdle-tailed lizard** ▣ (*Cordylus cataphractus*), **Cape red-tailed flat lizard** (*Platysaurus capensis*), **flat lizards** (genus *Platysaurus*), **Leathery crag lizard** ▣ (*Pseudocordylus microlepidotus*), **sungazer** ▣ (*Cordylus giganteus*), **sweepslangs** (genus *Chamaesaura*).

Blind Lizards
Family: Dibamidae
Four species in 2 genera.

Distribution: New Guinea to Indochina; E Mexico; up to 1,525m. Length: 12–16.5cm. Color: flesh-color tones or violet purplish-brown predominating. Scales: on head large and plate-like, especially on snout and lower jaws; on body and tail smooth, overlapping, with concentric lines of growth; without bone. Body form: snake-like; forelimbs absent; hind limbs small and paddle-shaped, present only in males; tail fragile, extremely short. Eyes: lidless and concealed beneath skin. Ears: external opening covered with scales. Tongue: short, wide, not divided at tip. Teeth: small and pointed, curving inwards; absent from palate. Preanal glands in some species. Species and genera include: **Asian blind lizards** (genus *Dibamus*), **Mexican blind lizard** (*Anelytropsis papillosus*).

Xenosaurs
Family: Xenosauridae
Four species in 2 genera.

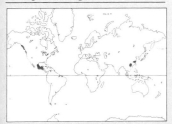

Distribution: E Mexico S to Guatemala; S China; 300–2,100m. Length: 10–15cm. Color: predominantly brown, gray or black. Scales: minute to large, with small to large disks of bone; some species with a series of enlarged scutes on midline of nape and trunk, which may continue to tail. Body form: head compressed in Chinese xenosaur, depressed in New World species; body

stout, with well-developed limbs; tail moderately long, not fragile. Eyes: of modest size, with round pupil. Ears: with very large opening, conspicuous or inconspicuous depending on scale covering. Tongue: with a long slender portion forked at tip and at least partially retractable into more fleshy basal portion. Teeth: fang-like, with slight inward curve, or blunt and cylindrical; tips of some with sharp cutting edges; absent from palate. Femoral and preanal glands absent. Species and genera include: **Chinese xenosaur** (*Shinisaurus crocodilurus*), **New World xenosaurs** (genus *Xenosaurus*).

Anguids
Family: Anguidae
Seventy-five species in 8 genera.

Distribution: SW Canada and much of N USA to N Argentina, including W Indies; Britain to China, Sumatra and Borneo, between Arctic Circle and NW Africa in the west and S Asia in the east; absent from Sri Lanka and Arabian Peninsula; up to more than 4,260m. Length: 6–30cm. Color: bright green, brown, gray, silver or black. Scales: smooth or moderately keeled; most with well-developed bony plates, including those on underside; on head large and juxtaposed; on body smaller, overlapping and disk-shaped. Body form: most species with streamlined shape; some with prominent skin folds; limbs short when present; tail usually very long and fragile. Eyes: functional but small to modest; lids movable, lower ones sometimes with transparent window. Ears: external opening covered with scales in a few species. Tongue: long, slender portion with forked tip may be extended; less retractable fleshy portion found well back in the mouth. Teeth: crushing and close-set to fang-like, inwardly curved and widely separated; absent from palate. Skin glands absent from region of anal opening and underside of thighs. Species and genera include: **Arizona alligator lizard** (*Elgaria kingii*), **Black legless lizard** ⒠ (*Anniella pulchra nigra*), **California alligator lizard** (*Elgaria multicarinata multicarinata*), **California legless lizard** (*Anniella pulchra*), **glass lizards** (genus *Ophisaurus*), **Panamint alligator lizard** ⓚ (*Elgaria panamintinus*), **sheltopusik**

(*Ophisaurus apodus*), **slowworm** or **blindworm** (*Anguis fragilis*), **Southern alligator lizard** (*Elgaria multicarinata*), **tree anguids** (Genus *Abronia*). Total threatened species: 1. Total threatened subspecies: 1.

Beaded Lizards
Family: Helodermatidae
Two species in 1 genus.

Distribution: SW USA through W Mexico to Guatemala; up to 2,000m. Length: 33–45.5cm. Color: typically brown or black, light colors such as yellow predominating in some individuals. Scales: on upper surfaces large and convex, juxtaposed, each surrounded by a ring of granules, arranged in horizontal and diagonal rows; small and rectangular in rows across underside; thick disks of pitted bone in most large scales, often fused to skull. Body form: almost cylindrical; head massive, depressed, with blunt snout; distinctive fold of skin across throat; body stout, with limbs short and five-toed; tail short to moderately long, not fragile, tending to have blunt tip. Eyes: small, with round pupils and thick, well-developed, movable lids. Ears: external opening exposed. Tongue: with a longer, deeply forked portion and a basal portion covered with fleshy projections. Teeth: elongated, inwardly curved and sharply pointed, somewhat compressed, deeply grooved on snout-facing edge, with groove slight or absent on opposite edge. Skin glands absent from belly and underside of thighs. The only venomous lizards, with a bite that is painful but rarely fatal to humans. Species: **Gila monster** ▣ Ⓥ (*Heloderma suspectum*), **Mexican beaded lizard** ▣ Ⓘ (*H. horridum*).

Bornean Earless Lizard
Family: Lanthanotidae
One species, *Lanthanotus borneensis*.

Distribution: near sea level on Borneo. Length: up to 20cm. Color: rather drab, uniform dark brown or black. Scales: small and undifferentiated on head except in region of temples where there are 3 rows of much enlarged tubercles, with 3–5 rows continuing along midline of back and tail; otherwise small and flattened on body with irregularly scattered tubercles. Body

form: head slightly depressed, with small nostrils high on snout, moderately distinct from body; body and tail cylindrical and of nearly equal length; limbs short, five-toed, forelimbs appearing weaker than hind limbs; tail not fragile. Eyes: small, with round pupils and well-developed lids; transparent window in lower lid. Ears: external opening absent. Tongue: like beaded lizards. Teeth: recurved and fang-like; attached to jaw; palate with a few small teeth.

Monitor Lizards
Family: Varanidae
Thirty-one species in 1 genus.

Distribution: Africa to S Asia, Indo-Australian Archipelago, Philippines, New Guinea, Australia; up to 1,830m. Length: 12cm–1.5m. Color: largely drab brown, gray or black. Scales: mostly small, pebble-like granules which may form rings around larger, juxtaposed scales with conspicuous pits; thin disks of bone in some. Body form: distinctive, with long neck and relatively short body; head usually very long and narrow, frequently with pointed snout and slit-like nostrils placed near eyes; skin fold across throat; limbs strongly built, five-toed; toes and curved claws long and strong; tail long and muscular, not fragile, usually compressed. Eyes: large, pupils almost circular, lids movable. Ears: external opening exposed. Tongue: very long and slender, deeply forked, no basal portion. Teeth: usually compressed, with sharp cutting edges, fang-like; absent from palate. Femoral and preanal glands absent. Species include: **Bengal monitor** ▣ (*Varanus bengalensis*), **Cape monitor** ▣ (*V. exanthematicus*), **Common Asiatic monitor** ▣ (*V. salvator*), **Gould's monitor** (*V. gouldii*), **Komodo dragon or ora** ▣ Ⓡ (*V. komodoensis*), **Nile monitor** ▣ (*V. niloticus*), **Short-tailed monitor** ▣ (*V. brevicauda*). Total threatened species: 2.

SNAKES

Suborder: Serpentes (Ophidia)
Two thousand three hundred and eighty-nine
species in 417 genera and 11 families.
Distribution: worldwide except Arctic regions,
Antarctica, Iceland, Ireland, New Zealand, and
some small oceanic islands.

Length (snout to tip of tail): from 15cm–11·4m
(6in–37.5ft), but most are 25cm–1.5m
(10–60in).

Most terrestrial, but many burrowing, aquatic,
marine or tree-dwelling; legless with long,
flexible, scaly body, lacking eyelids and external
ear openings, but with highly sensitive tactile
and chemical receptors; some with organs for
sensing infrared (heat) emissions. Color: mostly
brown, gray, or black, but some with bright
red, yellow or green bodies or markings that
vary from spots and blotches to rings,
crossbands, and stripes.

Reproduction: fertilization internal by means of
paired male hemipenes (only one inserted at a
time); most lay eggs but many bear live young;
some have true placental connection with
mother; a few snakes guard eggs, but no young
and few eggs receive parental care.

Longevity: even small snakes may live as long
as 12 years; large species may live 40 years,
perhaps longer.

▶ **An extreme example** of the modifications in
the reptilian body form shown by all snakes,
this Grass-green vine snake (*Dryophis prasinus*)
of Southeast Asia, Indonesia and India is
several feet long but little thicker than a pencil.
Vine snakes are a tree-dwelling form in the
harmless snake family and feed largely on
young birds. Their shape and color enable them
to hide undetected among creepers and vines.

DESPITE having no legs, eyelids or
external ears, snakes are a remarkably
successful group. About 2,400 species of
these long, scaly reptiles occur in a wide
variety of habitats on all continents except
Antarctica.

Because of their strangeness, and because
many can kill humans, they are feared or
revered wherever they occur. The fact that
an old and wrinkled snake can shed its skin
and appear bright and youthful again lends
powerful symbolism to these creatures in
many cultures. Pythons are sacred to
Australian aborigines and to many peoples
of Africa. The Egyptian cobra, or asp, was
a sign of imperial power in ancient times,
and Cleopatra is supposed to have taken her
life by allowing an asp to bite her; in Mexico
a rattlesnake represented an Aztec god, and
the intertwined snakes of the Greek cadu-
ceus are still used as a symbol of healing by
the medical profession.

The Serpentine Body Plan

Underneath their scaly skin, snakes have
bones and muscles, heart and intestines,
liver and lungs much like those of other
vertebrates. Most of these organs have been
modified, however, for the snake's special
mode of life, in particular for its habit of
swallowing prey whole (see p120) and its
need for rapid locomotion, both to catch its
prey and to avoid predators.

The body has been lengthened by the
addition of extra vertebrae to the spinal column. Most species have more than 200
vertebrae and some have more than 400.
Each is connected to the adjacent one by no
fewer than ten articulating surfaces, forming a strongly reinforced, but supple system
that is moved by complicated sets of interlocking muscles. Each vertebra bears a pair
of ribs that curve over the internal organs
of the body and are held in place by ligaments and muscles.

Many of the paired internal organs have
either been reduced or offset from one
another to fit more easily within this slender
construction. The primitive boas and
pythons are the only snakes that retain a
pair of lungs. In most snakes the left lung
is greatly reduced or absent. The kidneys
have been repositioned, with the left kidney
lying behind the right. Females of very
slender species, such as the thread snakes
and crowned snakes, have even lost one of
their oviducts.

Locomotion

Although some snakes are highly specialized for movement on land, or for swimming
or climbing in trees, almost any is adept at
all three of these. A minority of species are
specialized for burrowing. It used to be
thought that, when moving on land, snakes
"walked on their ribs," moving them back
and forth like so many pairs of legs. It is now
known that the ribs remain still and the real
"walking" in most snakes is done by movement of the enlarged ventral scutes that
cover the belly. Each scute is attached to two
or more pairs of ribs by muscles that allow
it to be tilted in or out and to be pulled back
and forth. Since each overlaps the front edge
of the next one (like the shingles on a roof),
the free edge of the scute is positioned to
push against the ground when pulled back,
and to slide over the ground freely when it
is pulled forward.

By moving its ventral scutes in groups,
with some pushing back against the ground
while others slide forward, a snake can
move slowly over the ground in a straight
line. Only by looking carefully can one see
the back-and-forth movement of the scutes.
This "rectilinear mode" of travel is most
often used by heavy-bodied snakes such as
pythons or vipers (eg the Puff adder), when
they are not in a hurry. It is also often used
in combination with some of the other
modes of locomotion.

The rectilinear mode of locomotion is too
slow for most snakes, which move in a
quicker "lateral undulatory mode." The
body, laid out in a series of S-shaped curves,
appears merely to slide forward while the
head lays out additional curves. The same
movement is used in swimming. On land the
hind part of each curve is pushed against
small irregularities in the ground to give this
forward motion. Because several pushing
points are used, the snake progresses very
smoothly. Close observation may also show
that at each of the hind parts of the curves,
the ventral scutes are being pushed back by
their individual muscles. Thus, a swift snake
such as an American racer or a Eurasian
whipsnake gains most of its speed from the
lateral undulatory mode but uses rectilinear
movements to help to retain its grip on the
ground.

While many tree-dwelling snakes use one
or both of the methods described, some, such
as the tropical American tree boas, have
developed a special "concertina mode" of
tree-climbing. Most of these snakes have a
prehensile tail. To climb the smooth trunk
of a tree, the boa coils around it, and while
holding on with its tail and the rear part of
its body, it reaches up some distance with
its head and hooks its neck around the trunk
at that point. When it has a firm purchase

with its neck, it loosens its hold with the tail and pulls the rear part of the body up to near the level of the neck. By repeating this process, the boa can climb trees (or the trunks of bamboo) that lack sufficient irregularities to allow for other forms of locomotion.

Perhaps the most bewildering form of travel used by snakes, however, is the "sidewinding" of desert dwelling species such as the African Horned viper and the American sidewinder. The snake makes an arc with the front part of its body and "throws" its head some distance before it touches the sand. It then transfers the rest of its body across that arc, meanwhile laying out another arc with its head. The snake looks something like a rolling spring and faces at an angle to its actual direction of travel: it appears to be headed in one direction while it is actually going in another. Sidewinding has the advantage of allowing the snake to progress across soft sand without attempting to push against it, while keeping much of the body off the surface, which may be dangerously hot.

Most snakes do not travel as fast as they appear to. A rattlesnake's gait has been measured at about 3km per hour (2mph) and even the racers move at speeds of less than 6.5km per hour (4mph). The record appears to be held by an African Black mamba that was clocked at 11.2km per hour (7mph) while chasing a man who had been teasing it. The snake was shot before it caught the man.

Feeding Behavior and Sensory Perception

All snakes eat animals; there are no vegetarians among them. Boas and pythons mainly feed on mammals, which they kill by constriction—from mice to deer, depending upon the size of the snake. Mammals and birds are the favored prey of many other snakes as well, including most of those that immobilize their prey with venom (see pp130–131), but there are species that have exotic tastes.

Besides those that will eat only frogs or only fishes, there are species, such as the tropical American cat-eyed snakes and the Asian snail-eaters, that eat nothing but snails. Their lower jaws are modified,as tiny grapple-hooks to pull the snail out of its shell. There is an African egg-eating snake that can swallow an egg twice the size of its head. Besides its powers of engulfing, it has the pointed ends of its neck vertebrae protruding into its esophagus to slice the egg open, so that it can save stomach room by regurgitating the shell. The little Redbelly snake of North America has no obvious

Sense Organs in Snakes

Snakes have the usual senses of touch, taste, smell, sight and hearing, but in addition they have some very uncommon ways of collecting information about their environment. Although sight and hearing are limited in some species, all have a special extension of their sense of taste and smell, and some can detect infrared radiation.

A snake seems to have a "glassy stare" because it lacks eyelids; instead, the eyes are covered with a transparent window, the brille. The eyes vary a great deal in their sensitivity. In some of the "blind snakes" they merely distinguish between light and dark, but some of the day-active terrestrial and tree-dwelling species have very acute vision—although they appear to recognize movement more readily than shape and form. Many nighttime snakes have eyes with vertically elliptical pupils that open up very wide in dim light.

There are no external ears in snakes; the single earbone is attached to the jaw rather than to a tympanic membrane. Although snakes can hear low-frequency sounds very well, they cannot hear those in the higher ranges. Thus, a rattlesnake cannot hear its own rattle.

Surprisingly, snakes can compensate for such sensory deprivations with their tongues. The flicking out of the forked tongue is a typical action of snakes, seen BELOW in the Toad-eater snake (*Xenodon rabdocephalus*) of

Costa Rica, but its use was not at first well understood. Often the snake will touch the ground with the tongue tips but at other times the tongue is merely waved in the air. Why does this happen?

It has been found that the tongue, although also an organ of touch, is more important for picking up chemical signals. Whether touched to the ground or waved in the face, it collects chemical molecules which are brought back into the mouth and then inserted into the paired pockets of the vomeronasal or Jacobson's organ in the roof of the mouth. This organ analyzes the chemical signals and allows the snake to trail a prey animal, recognize a predator or find a mate.

Some snakes, including pit vipers and most boas and pythons, have a sensory system for the reception of infrared heat rays. These are the "pits" on the side of the face in pit vipers, eg in the Totonacan rattlesnake (*Crotalus durissus totonacus*) RIGHT ABOVE. In boas and pythons, eg the Green tree python RIGHT MIDDLE, pits occur on the lips. With these, the most sensitive heat receptors known in the animal world, the snake can distinguish not only the direction of an object that differs in temperature from the background, but also its distance, sensing changes of less than 0.001 Celsius degrees (0.002 Fahrenheit degrees). Thus, a rattlesnake can find a mouse and strike it accurately in total darkness.

feeding modifications, but eats nothing but slugs. The Annulated sea snake feeds only on the eggs of certain fishes, and American green snakes eat grasshoppers and caterpillars. Thread snakes eat ants and their larvae and termites.

On the other hand, American garter snakes will eat almost any animal that they can catch and subdue: grasshoppers, earthworms, frogs, mammals, birds. With neither venom nor powers to constrict, they can feed on only the smaller vertebrates.

With such a diversity of food items, different snakes must use different senses to find their prey. Observation of an American racer or Eurasian whipsnake tracking a frog through a meadow reveals that the snake is using its eyes to follow the frog's movements—dashing after the frog when it hops, stopping when it stops. Such snakes have large eyes with round pupils. Many of those which go out in bright sunlight have amber-colored lenses in their eyes, apparently to protect the retina from too much light. Most snakes, however, whether night-active or day-active, have eyes that are only moderate in size, or even small, and except for burrowing snakes that may hear their prey scraping through the earth, snakes in general do not appear to use their ears for finding prey. They depend mainly on other senses (see box).

Life History
For snakes in the temperate regions, the beginning of the year is marked by the spring thaw. In the tropics it may be the onset of the rainy season. Commonly a snake will have spent the winter in company with others of its kind, so that clusters of snakes may be seen at the entrances to dens at this time.

Usually the first activity after basking in the sunlight is to shed last year's outer skin. Triggered by hormonal action, the semi-transparent epidermal layer loosens around the mouth and then is rubbed against a rock or log and pushed back over the head. While the old skin is held back by these objects, the snake can slowly crawl out of it, leaving it behind as a complete inside-out replica showing every scale and often a trace of the color pattern.

In those female snakes that have mature eggs in their oviducts, the molting of the skin releases a chemical signal that they are ready to mate (see p117). After mating, the snakes disperse to various parts of their range to resume their normal activities—moving between sun and shade to regulate body temperature, avoiding predators, and capturing and feeding on prey. Snakes are not social creatures during most of their active life.

If the snake is of an egg-laying (oviparous) kind, such as rat snakes or racers, several weeks after mating the female will seek an appropriate place to lay her developing eggs. It may be in the soft heart of a rotten log or in sandy soil under a rock. Whatever the place, the requirements for the nest site are the same—it must be damp but not wet, and warm but not hot. Most such snakes merely clear out a cavity in a secluded place, lay their eggs, cover them and leave. In a few species the female remains with the eggs until they hatch (see p116).

Another approach is shown by species such as the garter snakes, water snakes and pit vipers. These, instead of laying their eggs, retain them in their bodies until they hatch; they give birth to living young. In a few of these live-bearers (eg American water snakes) there is even a placenta between mother and young, which serves to nourish them. After hatching or birth, however, the young are on their own—no maternal care is known in snakes.

Typically, the young are born or hatch 3–4 months after mating has taken place. In some species, however, mating may occur in the fall and the sperm are retained in special areas of the female's oviduct (spermathecae) until spring, when the eggs are mature and fertilization takes place. In such snakes birth or hatching can take place almost a year after mating. In some tropical snakes (which do not overwinter in groups), the females may retain sperm for 3–4 years and produce young long after separation from males of their species.

As in most ectothermic ("cold-blooded") vertebrates, the growth of the young is heavily dependent upon the amount of food available. Many snakes of temperate regions, which typically hatch or are born in the fall, may not eat until the following spring and show little or no growth for six months or more. Others begin to eat immediately and may double their size in 3–4 months. After a rapid growth period of 2–5 years, the snake becomes sexually mature and growth slows. It never ceases entirely, however, and almost imperceptible growth may still occur in long-lived species after 20 years.

Snakes, like other ectothermic animals, have slow metabolic rates (about one-tenth that of birds and mammals). They thus have slower, but longer lives than birds or mammals of equivalent size. Whereas few mice live more than three years, a small snake such as a Milk snake has been known to live 18 years. The larger Boa constrictor has lived 30 years in captivity, and pythons in the wild are believed to live even longer.

The smallest of adult snakes is undoubtedly one of the burrowing thread snakes— only 15cm long and no bigger around than a matchstick. The record for the largest snake is more difficult to determine since all of the "records" are based on observations in the field, rather than specimens brought back for examination. Reticulated pythons of Southeast Asia over 6m (20ft) long often appear in zoos, and a 10m (33ft) specimen has been reported from the Indonesian island of Celebes. On the other hand, whereas captive anacondas from South America are seldom longer than 4.6m (15ft), a Green anaconda killed in Colombia was reportedly measured at 11.4m (37.5ft). If weight is considered, the record size undoubtedly would belong to such a snake. Even a 6m anaconda would weigh more than a 10m python. Its great weight and aquatic habitat may be the reasons why only smaller specimens reach civilization.

All of the records of snakes 10m or more in length were made in the early part of this century. With the current commercial value of skins and the widespread use of modern rifles, it is unlikely that any snake now living will survive long enough to attain the previously reported dimensions.

Families of Snakes

The anatomy of snakes tells us that we must search for their ancestors among the lizards—or from some stock closely related to lizards. Snake fossils first appear during the Cretaceous (136–65 million years ago), the last period of the Age of Reptiles. Some workers think that the ancestral snake was a small burrowing animal. They emphasize that the loss of limbs, eyelids and external ears is common in burrowing lizards. Others believe that snakes were derived from large marine reptiles such as mosasaurs or aigialosaurs. Most fossil remains of snakes are no more than isolated vertebrae, however, and this dispute is still not resolved.

Primitive snakes. Four living families of snakes retain a number of features that relate them to lizards, or some lizard-like ancestral reptile. In none of these families do the ventral scutes extend as far toward the sides as they do in "typical" advanced snakes (see p129). Also none of the primitive snakes has the typical pattern of head scutes. Most do, however, have the separate brille covering the eye. Most of them also

Brooding Behavior in Snakes

No snake provides care for its young and only a few show any interest in their eggs after they are laid. Oddly, it is among the primitive snakes—specifically the pythons—that the most elaborate care of eggs is found. The females of many kinds of pythons, from Africa, Asia and Australia, have been reported to coil around their eggs after laying, and to remain with them until they hatch. Although this habit has not been reported for all species of pythons, it is obviously a widespread habit and may be characteristic of all.

The actual incubation of eggs (ie providing them with heat) is not necessary in most of these species because most live in the tropics. An African Rock python in captivity was observed to remain with her eggs most of the time until they hatched, but she left them for brief periods to drink water and at least once to defecate and shed her skin.

Some of the Australian pythons range well into temperate climates, however, and have adapted to cooler conditions. A female Carpet python was observed to leave the eggs regularly, bask to raise her body temperature and then return and recoil about the clutch. It is not known if this is typical of this species only or of all Australian pythons.

The only other python that ranges well into temperate regions is the Indian. The female of this species has modified her habits even further, and actually produces body heat to aid in the incubation of the eggs. She accomplishes this by rhythmic contractions of her body muscles. In pythons of this species studied in captivity, it was found that if the temperature was kept at about 30°C (86°F), the snake merely remained coiled about the eggs, but if the surroundings became cooler the female began to contract her body muscles. The number of contractions increased as the temperature was lowered. Experiments showed that a female could

maintain a temperature differential of 5–7 Celsius degrees (9–12.5 Fahrenheit degrees) by violently contracting the body muscles (described as hiccups by observers) at a rate of more than 30 per minute—the eggs remaining at the desired 30°C. She was never seen to leave the eggs during almost 90 days of incubation. No other snake (in fact, no other reptile) incubates in this way.

Among the advanced snakes there are only a few scattered species that provide some care to the eggs.

Females of the two North American mud snakes merely coil around their eggs and remain with them until they hatch. Both sexes of Asian cobras are reported to cooperate in digging out a nest cavity in the ground, and to defend the eggs from possible predators.

The King cobra is unique among snakes in the complexity of the nest that it provides. The female scrapes together a large pile of leaves, grasses and associated soil and forms a nest cavity in the top of the pile, where the eggs are laid. She then covers the egg mass with leaves and makes another cavity on top—remaining there on guard until the eggs hatch.

No examples of brooding are known among true vipers, and but a single species of pit viper is known to provide care, the Mountain viper of Southeast Asia. The female remains coiled on or near the eggs for the month or so that it takes them to incubate.

have vestiges of hind limbs that appear as "spurs" on either side of the cloacal opening. These are larger and easier to see in males. (No snake has any trace of front limbs.)

The main features that distinguish primitive snakes, however, are internal. All have an extra bone, the coronoid, in the lower jaw. Most of them have two lungs, unlike the advanced snakes and blind snakes, which have only one usable lung.

Pythons are widely distributed in the Old World tropics in humid rain forest and thorn scrubland. They feed mainly on birds and mammals. Some of the larger pythons commonly feed on pigs or deer. An Indian python is recorded as having eaten a fully grown leopard. There are a few Asian and African records of humans (usually children

▲ **Guarding her clutch.** A Black-and-white-lipped cobra (*Naja melanoleuca*) of Africa brooding her eggs.

▶ **Suspended mating** ABOVE in a pair of Black rat snakes (*Elaphe obsoleta obsoleta*) of North America.

▶ **Guarding her brood,** a female Asp viper (*Vipera aspis*) of Europe. Active by day and night, Asp vipers are relatively slow-moving and feed on mice, lizards and nestling birds. After a gestation period of four months, a female gives birth to between five and fifteen young. The Asp viper's bite is painful but rarely fatal to humans.

Courtship and Aggression in Snakes

Ordinarily, snakes appear to be oblivious to others of their kind. However, when the mating season arrives, all of this changes. Male snakes become aggressive to one another and the scent of an attractive female may send them into a frenzy.

Not every female of a species can mate every year, but if food has been abundant perhaps half the adult females will have mature eggs in their oviducts, and (usually upon shedding their skins) they will exude a chemical secretion (a pheromone) signalling that they are ready.

In gregarious species such a female may attract numerous courting males. In species that live as lone individuals, however, her scent trail may be picked up by only a single tongue-flicking suitor.

In either case the male, upon finding the female, moves forward to bring his chin onto the nape of her neck, with his body overlapping or alongside hers, pressing against her along his entire length. The tongue flicks become more rapid and are nearly continuous as his body approaches hers. He rubs his chin over her nape and vibrates the entire rear of his body against hers, at the same time striving to bring his tail beneath hers. If she finds him suitable she

raises her tail and opens her cloaca for the insertion of one of the male's two hemipenes. After it is inserted, the pair may remain mated from ten minutes to more than 24 hours, depending on the species.

In boas and pythons, another element is introduced, with the male using his "spurs" (rudiments of pelvic limbs) to scratch the female in the cloacal region as an additional stimulus. The males of some of the advanced snakes, which are spurless, may also grasp the female's neck in their jaws.

In American water snakes, garter snakes and the related European Grass snakes, many males may compete to mate with a single female. Sometimes there are so many that they form a "snake ball" with their intertwined bodies. Male aggression in these species amounts to no more than trying to push one another from the mating position.

Males of less gregarious species show ritualized aggression in pushing contests, often without females present. They face one another with their heads raised, then each advances and attempts to press the head of the opposing snake to the ground. As each rises higher and higher to get above the other, they form a conspicuous figure, and the contest may last for more than an hour.

◄▲▼► **Representative species** of the eight families of primitive and blind snakes. (**1**) Coral pipesnake (*Anilius scytale*); Aniliidae. (**2**) Mexican burrowing python (*Loxocemus bicolor*); Pythonidae. (**3**) Calabar python (*Calabaria reinhardtii*); Pythonidae. (**4**) Texas blind snake (*Leptotyphlops dulcis*); Leptotyphlopidae. (**5**) A shieldtail snake, *Uropeltis ocellatus*; Uropeltidae. (**6**) Cuban Island ground boa (*Tropidophis melanurus*); Tropidophiidae. (**7**) An Asian pipesnake, *Cylindrophius rufus*; Aniliidae. (**8**) Schlegel's blind snake (*Typhlops schlegelii*); Typhlopidae.

or small adults) killed and eaten by some of the larger species.

Some pythons, eg the dwarf Children's python of Australia, are less than 1m (3.3ft) long. Most are 3–6m (10–20ft), and the Reticulated python of Southeast Asia is one of the longest snakes, up to 10m (33ft).

Three small pythons have, probably independently of each other, taken up a burrowing life. Each is about 1m (3.3ft) in length, but has different features and occupies a different region. The Mexican burrowing python is the only American representative of the pythons. It occurs along the Pacific coast of Central America from Mexico to Costa Rica. The Sunbeam python of Southeast Asia is unusual among primitive snakes in lacking any vestige of hind limbs. Its ventral scutes are reduced even more than in other primitive snakes. The Calabar python of West Africa is one of the "two-headed" snakes. It has a small head and broad blunt tail. When disturbed it hides its head in a ball of coils and uses its head-like tail to "strike" at the aggressor.

The **pipesnakes** are specialized snake-eating burrowers. The Coral pipesnake of the Amazon Basin is ringed with red and black, like the coral snakes of that region. It differs from most other snakes in lacking a transparent brille over each eye. Instead, the small eyes are shielded by an irregular scute. The Asian pipesnakes, burrowers in damp soils and often found in rice fields and swamps, are a glossy black. They feed on eels as well as other snakes. Many hide their heads and wave their tails (which are brilliant red underneath) to distract predators.

Some of these species are reported to be live-bearing.

The **boas** are live-bearers, with some large species producing up to 80 young. Widely dispersed, they include terrestrial species on Fiji and arboreal tree boas and aquatic anacondas in tropical America. There are some species on Madagascar. Asian and African sand boas burrow in loose sand in desert and arid regions. The Rubber and Rosy sand boas lead similar lives in drylands and pine forests of western North America. Sand boas are seldom more than 1m (3.3ft) long and often only half that length. Most other boas are 2–4m (6.5–13ft), but anacondas may reach a length of more than 11m (36ft). Unlike most pythons, many boas have a slender body and a long tail, but anacondas become very heavy with increasing length and a large individual might weigh more

How a Snake Swallows its Prey

Although some snakes have taken up a burrowing life and specialize in eating small insects and worms, most eat animals that are large in proportion to their own size. In fact it would seem that the major features that distinguish snakes from other animals are those that allow the capture and swallowing of large animals. Large prey and their slow metabolism give snakes the advantage of not having to eat so often. Few eat more than once a week, many eat only 8–10 times per year, and a large python can go for 12 months or more without eating.

Snakes' teeth in general are no more than sharply pointed, inwardly curving cones used to hold a prey animal and drag it back into the esophagus. All of the jaw bones (with the exception in some species of the premaxillary bones at the front of the upper jaw) bear numerous teeth of this kind. Besides this, these bones are attached to the skull only by muscles and ligaments, so that each bone can be moved individually—up and down, back and forth, or from side to side. The two halves of the lower jaw are not fused at the front but are connected only by ligaments and muscles.

Thus, each half of the lower jaw as well as each of the six toothed bones of the upper jaw and palate is independently movable.

If the prey animal is dangerous (eg a rat) it is usually killed by venom, constriction or a hard bite, but if it is relatively harmless (a worm or a frog) it may be swallowed live.

The snake grasps the prey animal and generally turns it to go down the gullet head-first. Then the toothed bones of the jaw work alternately, "walking" the prey into the esophagus. The snake then forms a sharp curve in its neck behind the prey animal and pushes it downward into the stomach.

The snake's body skin is flexible enough to let a large animal stretch it on the way down without tearing it. Snakes have dispensed with the pectoral girdle associated with front limbs in other vertebrates, so it does not obstruct the passage of food through the esophagus. Also, they have lost the sternum, which connects the front ends of the ribs in most animals. Without any obstruction, the prey can slip easily from the mouth to the pit of the stomach, with flexible skin and ribs spreading to make room.

▲ **Crushed to death** in the coils of a Pygmy python (*Liasis perthensis*) of Australia, a mouse is killed before being swallowed. Geckos are more common prey of this snake, which lives in rock crevices and termite mounds.

▲ **Mortal combat.** ABOVE An African python subduing a crocodile.

◄ **Head-first.** A Hog-nosed viper (*Bothrops nasutus*) begins to swallow a frog, the start of a lengthy process.

▷ OVERLEAF A 4m (13ft) Oenpelli python (*Python oenpelliensis*) in northern Australia.

than 500kg (1,100lb). Perhaps the most familiar of all the giant snakes is the smaller, tree-dwelling Boa constrictor, which occurs from Argentina to southern Mexico. It has been reported to reach 5.5m (18ft) in length, but few exceed 3m (10ft).

Anacondas live in tropical South America along large rivers and in swamps and lakes, often basking in the sun on branches overhanging the water. They are known to eat turtles and caimans as well as the birds and mammals preyed upon by other boas. Some species of West Indian boas feed largely on bats in caves. Sand boas stay in their burrows during the heat of the day and come out in the evening to feed on small mammals or lizards. Some refugees of the Russian Revolution fleeing across Asian deserts are reported to have survived only through the sudden nightly appearance of this source of protein.

The poorly-known **protocolubroid snakes** have large head scutes which resemble those of the advanced snakes. They also approach the advanced snakes in the elongation of the hyoid bone in the throat and in having only one lung. The American woodsnakes, one in Mexico and two in South America but most in the West Indies, are secretive, mainly night-active creatures, all under 1m (3.3ft). Feeding on lizards and small mammals, they are mainly terrestrial but sometimes climb trees. They are usually found under rocks or logs or crossing a road at night.

The two Mauritius snakes, the Round Island and the Round Island keel-scaled snakes, are now found only on tiny Round Island near Mauritius in the Indian Ocean, but previously they occurred on Mauritius itself. They differ from all other snakes in having the maxillary bone of the upper jaw divided into two. Little is known of their habits and the few museum specimens were mostly collected more than 100 years ago. A recent survey of the island discovered only a single Round Island snake but several dozen Round Island keel-scaled snakes.

Blind snakes. The four families of blind snakes differ even more from the typical description of a snake than the primitive snakes do. Their strange characteristics have been ascribed to a primitive state by some researchers, by others to a high degree of specialization for their burrowing lifestyle. It has even been suggested that they are not snakes at all, but burrowing lizards.

Most of them retain some primitive features, such as pelvic vestiges and coronoid bones, but they have lost most of their teeth as well as the left lung. The bones of the skull have been fused to form a hard burrowing instrument, and in all families the rostral scute is enlarged, while the other scutes are so reduced and changed in shape as to be virtually unrecognizable. The tiny eyes, of no use below ground, are vestiges hidden beneath head scutes rather than lying under transparent brilles. The ventral scutes, no longer needed for locomotion, are reduced to the same size and shape as the dorsal scales. With the head the same diameter as the cylindrical body and with an indistinguishable, stubby tail, these snakes look more like the earthworms many of them eat than like reptiles. Blind snake families are distinguished from one another most easily by the disposition of teeth in their tiny mouths.

Two families, comprising the bigjaw blind snakes, have the maxillary bone fused to the skull. **Shieldtail snakes,** burrowers in damp soils of hilly areas in Sri Lanka and southern India, have teeth in both upper and lower jaws and an enlarged scute or series of scutes of distinctive character on the upper surface of the tail. Most **thread snakes,** found in tropical rain forest as well as thorn scrub and desert areas of both the Old and New Worlds, feed on ants and termites. They have teeth only in the lower jaw. All are oviparous, laying 1–4 elongated eggs. There is one report of a member of this family brooding its eggs.

In weakjaw blind snakes, the toothed

maxilla is movable and lies transversely in the palate. The little-known **dawn blind snakes,** which have one or two teeth in the lower jaws, are burrowers in tropical rain forests of Central and South America. **Typical blind snakes,** with toothless lower jaws, are found in the tropics of both Old and New Worlds. They inhabit grassland and thorn scrub as well as rain forest, feeding mainly on ants and termites, occasionally taking other insects or their larvae. Both egg-laying and live-bearing species are known, with 5–10 eggs comprising the usual clutch. However, Schlegel's blind snake, a large African species, is reported to lay as many as 60 eggs. The tiny Flowerpot snake, which has been accidentally introduced in many parts of the world, is thought to be an all-female species.

Advanced snakes. In none of the three families of advanced snakes is there any rudiment of pelvic vestiges or a coronoid bone. Only the right lung is functional. A great many species have given up constriction in favor of speed or venom for the capture and immobilization of prey (see pp130–131). About 83 percent of all snakes belong to the advanced families, permitting their characteristic arrangement of head scutes (see p129), their lightly built skeletons, long body muscles and highly flexible bodies to be regarded as typical of snakes in general.

The saliva of many snakes is toxic, but most of the snakes of the huge family known as **harmless snakes** have neither the apparatus to inject significant amounts of saliva-venom nor saliva of sufficient toxicity to be dangerous to humans. Only a few unusual species, all found in tropical Asia or Africa, are deemed a hazard. Species of harmless snakes range in length from 12cm (4.5in) to 3.6m (11.7ft).

Many attempts have been made to break this large assemblage, with its numerous species and varied life-styles, into meaningful smaller groups. No fewer than twenty tribes, subfamilies and families have been proposed by various workers. They are divided here into six subfamilies that differ in their internal structures, in habits and in geographic distribution.

Ethiopian snakes (subfamily Lamprophiinae, 185 species in 51 genera) inhabit tropical rain forest and thorn scrub, mainly in Africa south of the Sahara and on Madagascar. A few species are found in Southeast Asia. Most are terrestrial or partly tree-dwelling, but some live underground. Both egg-layers and live-bearers are included. Most feed on other vertebrates, but

with difficulty on land, they live mainly in fresh water, but have been able to travel through the sea from Asia to Australia. They feed mainly on fish (one feeds on crabs). This aquatic group is live-bearing, with the larger members giving birth to 25–35 young. A few associated species are slender egg-laying burrowers in moist soil and feed on worms.

The water snakes and garter snakes (subfamily Natricinae, 138 species in 39 genera) are mostly aquatic or semiaquatic, with some generalized forms inhabiting many different habitats. Garter snakes live by ponds and streams from Canada to Costa Rica, emerging from torpor very early in the spring and remaining active late into the fall. They are commonly kept as pets. Water snakes occur throughout the Northern Hemisphere and southward through Asia into northern Australia. They include the Grass snake, the most common snake of Europe. Most are excellent swimmers and can remain submerged for long periods. Some species are highly selective in their diet, specializing in earthworms or slugs, crayfish or frogs. Others will take almost any animal of appropriate size, from insects to mammals. All New World species bear live young—some having been found to have a true placental attachment between embryo and mother. Most Old World species lay eggs.

Rat snakes and racers (subfamily Colubrinae, 548 species in 88 genera) occur mainly in the Northern Hemisphere, but there are some in South America and Africa and from Southeast Asia to northern Australia. Most are terrestrial or semiarboreal, but some burrow in sand or loose soil. Most of the rat snakes feed principally on rodents, occasionally eating birds or their eggs. When disturbed they may coil and strike, with tail vibrating rapidly, but they are not venomous. The closely related racers can sound like rattlesnakes when they vibrate their tails in dry leaves. These excitable snakes can bite painfully, but their needle-sharp teeth inject no venom. More

some, such as the Asian snail-eaters, specialize in eating snails or slugs. Burrowing asps (the atractaspids) are among the venomous exceptions to the rule that this is a harmless family.

Neotropical snakes (subfamily Xenodontinae, 620 species in 96 genera, including cat-eyed and mud snakes) inhabit tropical rain forest to desert scrub, mainly in the New World tropics, but with a few species

in temperate North America. Most are terrestrial but some live in trees, underground, or in water. Most feed on snails or worms, fish, frogs, or other reptiles. A few eat birds and mammals. Only a few are live-bearing.

The stout-bodied species making up most of the Asian wartsnakes (subfamily Acrochordinae, 37 species in 11 genera) are covered with tiny three-spined scales. The ventral scutes are greatly reduced. Moving

than their speed of up to 6.5km per hour (4mph), their ability to quickly dodge and turn makes them difficult to catch. Most feed on small vertebrates such as frogs, lizards and mice, but some eat insects and worms. With few exceptions, all lay eggs.

The sand snakes and their allies (subfamily Psammophiinae, 34 species in 7 genera) are terrestrial inhabitants of grassland, scrubland and semidesert, mainly in Africa south of the Sahara, with some species ranging into southern Europe and Asia. They are fast-moving, day-active snakes that feed usually on frogs, lizards and small mammals, which they immobilize with their toxic saliva. All lay eggs.

Two groups of **front-fanged snakes,** the cobras and their allies and the sea snakes, are sometimes recognized. Recently it has been suggested that the Australian front-fanged snakes form another separate group. All have short tubular fangs on a long maxillary bone, which may also bear other teeth behind the fangs. Their quick-acting venom is much more toxic than that of the vipers, and usually affects the nervous system.

Cobras and their allies, the mambas, kraits, and coral snakes, usually live in forests but some are found in grassland, thorn scrub or desert. Most are terrestrial but a few live in trees, enter water or burrow. Coral snakes are found both in eastern Asia and the Americas. They have potent venoms but are not aggressive and their short fangs do not inject the venom easily. Thus they must inflict several bites or hang on to their victim to be effective. The colorful Eastern coral snake of the southern United States has alternating rings of red, yellow, and black. It can be distinguished from its non-venomous mimics by the order of the colorful rings ("red on yellow, kill a fellow").

The King cobra of India, at 5.5m (18ft) is the longest venomous snake. Cobras and

the smaller and more numerous kraits deliver many thousands of fatal bites each year in India and other parts of Asia. In Africa, mambas are a serious cause of fatalities, as are the cobras—including spitting cobras that can squirt venom up to 3m (10ft) into the eyes of a threatening human or animal.

When disturbed, cobras rise up and spread long, thin neck ribs to tighten loose skin into a "hood." A cobra suddenly thrust into the open by an Indian snake charmer assumes this position, and while keeping its gaze on the end of a constantly moving, seemingly threatening flute, appears to "dance" to the music—most of which is outside its range of hearing. Most cobras eat frogs and other snakes, but a few eat rodents and other vertebrates. All but a few lay eggs, which are guarded by the female in some species (see p116).

Australian venomous snakes make up more than 80 percent of all snakes on the Australian continent. (Most of the others are pythons and blindsnakes.) They also occur in New Guinea, Fiji and the Solomon Islands. The rare and aggressive taipans are the largest, up to 3.5m (12ft), but the venom of tiger snakes is the most deadly. The Death adder differs from most in resembling a

► ▲ ▼ **Representative species** of two families of advanced snakes. (1) Pelagic sea snake (*Pelamis platurus*); Elapidae. (2) Asian wart snake or Arafura file snake (*Acrochordus arafurae*); Colubridae. (3) Asian cobra (*Naja naja*); Elapidae. (4) A sand snake, *Psammophis condenarus*; Colubridae. (5) Death adder (*Acanthophis antarcticus*); Elapidae. (6) Southern hognose snake (*Heterodon simus*); Colubridae. (7) Plainbelly water snake (*Nerodia erythrogaster*); Colubridae. (8) Racer (*Coluber constrictor*); Colubridae. (9) African house snake (*Lamprophis fuscus*); Colubridae.

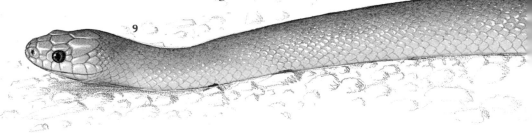

viper. Although the Eastern brown snake and others flatten the neck when disturbed, none has a hood like a cobra. Only a few of the Australian venomous snakes are live-bearers. The most common prey are lizards and small mammals. Mainly terrestrial, some of these snakes live partly under-ground; a few species live in trees.

The sea snakes, which may have arisen from the Australian venomous snakes, mainly inhabit shallow seas. Most spend their entire lives in salt water, where they give birth to live young, but sea kraits lay eggs, often in caves above the tide level, and sometimes prowl uninhabited islands. All sea snakes are fish eaters, some specialists eating only eels or only the eggs of certain fish species. The family is centered in the Malaysian region of the southwest Pacific

and eastward to Australia. A few species range west to Saudi Arabia, north to Japan and east to the Solomons. A single species, the Pelagic sea snake extends this range from the east coast of Africa to the Pacific coast of tropical America. Most of these snakes seldom bite humans, even when handled, but a few are aggressive. Their venom is stronger than a cobra's—the snake must subdue its prey quickly to avoid losing it in the depths of the sea.

Snakes of the **viper** family bear a single pair of long hollow fangs on the very short maxillary bones of the upper jaw. The max-illa can be rotated to bring the fangs forward for biting. Large jaw muscles squeeze the venom (which mainly acts on the tissues and blood of the victim) from glands on either side of the snake's head. The bulkiness

▲ **On the Wyoming prairie,** a Western rattlesnake (*Crotalus viridis*) hides in low brush.

▶ **Poisonous spray** ABOVE from a Black-necked spitting cobra (*Naja nigricollis nigricollis*) of South Africa is usually aimed at the eyes of the victim. This behavior is primarily defensive and can leave an adversary permanently blinded.

▶ **Geometrical skin patterns** CENTER of the Gaboon viper give it camouflage in leaf litter on the forest floor in tropical Africa, where it lies in wait for rodents, frogs and birds.

▶ **Threat display** of a Parrot snake (*Leptophis depressirostris*) of Costa Rica.

Circle in Norway. Distribution is spotty in southern Asia, with one species, Russell's viper, reaching Java and Komodo Island. Due to its abundance in populated areas it is believed to cause more human deaths than any other kind of snake.

The Gaboon viper of tropical Africa, up to 2m (6.2ft) long with a body 15cm (6in) in diameter, is the largest. The Puff adder, belonging to the same genus, is only one of many Old World vipers that puff up their bodies with air and hiss loudly when disturbed. A few species are tree-dwellers and one has taken up a burrowing life. Some desert species bury themselves in the sand to escape the excessive desert heat. A few, including some of the desert dwellers, lay eggs.

Pit vipers have a deep pit in the loreal region (on each side of the face) between the nostril and the eye. It is associated with an excavation in the maxillary bone in this region and contains heat-sensitive nerve-endings (see p114). This group is most abundant in the New World (where the true vipers do not occur) and also in eastern Asia. One species ranges west to eastern Europe. They live mainly in forested regions and many are tree-dwellers.

The cottonmouth, or Water moccasin, is semiaquatic, living in swamps and along lakes and streams in the southeastern United States. A less dangerous relative is the copperhead, which is the most common venomous snake of the eastern United States. The copperhead bites more humans than any other venomous snake in North America, but fatalities are rare because of its only mildly toxic venom.

The bushmaster of Central and South America, at 3.5m (12ft), is the longest of the vipers and the only one in the Americas that lays eggs.

Most familiar of the pit vipers are the rattlesnakes, which add a horny segment to the end of the tail each time they shed their skin. These segments buzz against one another when a disturbed rattler vibrates its tail. The warning thus given to potential enemies is one worth taking: within an hour of delivery, venom for a diamondback rattlesnake can kill a man weighing 100kg (220lb). Ranging from southern Canada to Argentina, rattlesnake species are concentrated in dry habitats in the southwestern United States and northern Mexico.

The pit vipers are often recognized as a separate family from the Old World vipers, and recent biochemical evidence suggests that they may have a separate origin despite several similarities. HGD

of these muscles and glands gives the head a typically wide, triangular shape. Vipers usually obtain their prey by a quick strike. They rapidly inject venom and then await the death of the animal before seizing it again. Tree-dwelling species that feed on birds cannot do this, however, and retain their hold after biting. In most vipers the head scutes are reduced in size or broken up so that the greater part of the head is covered with small scales. These mainly terrestrial snakes tend to have heavy bodies. They feed on vertebrates such as frogs, lizards and mammals up to the size of a hare. They range in length from 25cm (10in) to 3.5m (12ft). Most give birth to living young.

The Old World vipers are found in Africa and in Eurasia from England to Japan. The European adder ranges north of the Arctic

THE 11 FAMILIES OF SNAKES

Abbreviations: Length = length from snout to tip of tail. ▣ CITES-listed Ⓔ Endangered Ⓡ Rare Ⓥ Vulnerable.

Total threatened species = number of species endangered, vulnerable, rare, threatened or of indeterminate or unknown status. Approximate nonmetric equivalents: 10cm = 4in. 1m = 3.3ft.

Primitive Snakes
(Infraorder Henophidia)

Pythons ▣
Family: Pythonidae
Twenty-seven species in 9 genera.*

Distribution: Old World tropics and subtropics from Africa through Southeast Asia and the East Indies to Australia. A single species in Mexico and Central America. Length: from under 1m to more than 10m; most 3–6m. Color: uniform brown or bright green to boldly patterned with blotches or diamonds. Scales: small ventral scutes, paired on underside of tail. Body form: cylindrical, with short tail and vestiges of hind limbs; two lungs; eyes with vertically elliptical pupils. Most have paired subcaudal scutes, teeth on the premaxilla, a postfrontal bone above the orbit of the eye, and spineless hemipenes with flounces (ruffles) and apical awns (small pointed tips). All lay eggs. Species include: **Calabar python** (*Calabaria reinhardtii*), **Carpet** or **Diamond python** (*Morelia spilotes*), **Children's python** (*Liasis childreni*), **Green tree python** (*Chondropython viridis*), **Indian** or **Burmese python** Ⓥ (*Python molurus*), **Mexican burrowing python** (*Loxocemus bicolor*), **Reticulated python** (*Python reticulatus*), **Rock python** (*P. sebae*), **Sunbeam python** (*Xenopeltis unicolor*). Total threatened species: 1.

*The pythons are sometimes included in a single family with the boas. The Calabar, Mexican burrowing and Sunbeam pythons are sometimes classed as separate single-species families.

Pipesnakes
Family: Aniliidae
Eleven species in 3 genera.*

Distribution: the Amazon Basin; Burma and Indochina S to E Indies. Length: 1m or less. Color: red and black in some combination, sometimes in rings, in others black

above and red below. Scales: ventral scutes not larger or hardly larger than dorsal scales. Brille absent in American species. Body form: head grading indistinguishably into body; tail short and broad. Species include **Coral pipesnake** (*Anilius scytale*).

*Some authorities include the Mexican burrowing python. Some count the 10 species of Asian pipesnakes as a subfamily of the shieldtails.

Protocolubroids
Family: Tropidophiidae
Twenty-two species in 6 genera.

Distribution: most West Indian, one found in Mexico, two in mainland S America, two on Round Island in the Indian Ocean. Length: most 30–60cm, none attaining 1m. Color: most brown with indistinct darker markings; *Exiliboa* polished black; a few with distinct light crossbands. Scales: some large head scutes resembling those of advanced snakes. Body form: boa-like, with small distinct head, vertically elliptical pupils, and tiny, hook-like remnants of hind limbs, but with only one lung. Round Island snakes differ from all other snakes in having a divided maxillary bone in the upper jaw.

Species include: **Round Island snake** ▣ Ⓔ (*Bolyeria multocarinata*), **Round Island keel-scaled snake** ▣ Ⓔ (*Casarea dussumieri*). Total threatened species: 2.

Boas ▣
Family: Boidae
Thirty-nine species in 12 genera.*

Distribution: W N America, New World tropics, Africa, Madagascar, W Asia, Fiji, Solomons, New Guinea. Length: most 2–4m; Green anaconda reported to reach more than 11m. Scales: many rows of dorsal scales, ventral scutes small, single row under tail. Body form: relatively slender with fairly long tail (but large species

becoming heavy with increasing length); vestiges of hind limbs; no teeth on premaxillary. Most with heat-sensitive pits on lips. All live-bearing. Species and genera include: **African and Asian sand boas** (genera *Eryx, Gongylophis*), **American tree boas** (genus *Corallus*), **anacondas** (genus *Eunectes*), **Boa constrictor** (*Boa constrictor*), **Fijian boas** (genus *Candoia*), **Green anaconda** (*Eunectes murinus*), **Madagascan boas** (genera *Acrantophis, Sanzinia*), **Puerto Rican boa** Ⓔ (*Epicrates inornatus*), **Rosy boa** (*Lichanura trivirgata*), **Rubber boa** (*Charina bottae*), **West Indian boas** (genus *Epicrates*). Total threatened species: 7.

*The 14 species of sand boas form a group which has been separate from other boas for more than 50 million years. They are sometimes counted as a separate family, the Erycidae.

Blind Snakes
(Infraorder Scolecophidia)

Bigjaw Blind snakes
(Superfamily Uropeltoidea)

Shieldtail Snakes
Family: Uropeltidae
Forty-four species in 8 genera.

Distribution: S India, Sri Lanka. Length: less than 90cm; most 20–50cm. Color: irridescent black or brown, often marked above or below with brilliant yellow, red or white. Body form: like typical blind snakes except all species slender, maxillary bone of upper jaw fused to braincase, some teeth in both upper and lower jaws, upper surface of tail with scute or series of scutes of distinctive shape.

Thread Snakes
Thread snakes or slender blind snakes
Family: Leptotyphlopidae
Seventy-eight species in 2 genera.

Distribution: S America N to Bahamas and SW USA; Africa E through Saudi Arabia to Pakistan. Length: 15–41cm; most 20–30cm. Color: grayish, black or pink, some with light markings. Body form: like typical blind snakes except very slender, with maxilla fused to skull and with teeth in lower jaw only.

Weakjaw Blind Snakes
(Superfamily Typhlopoidea)

Dawn Blind Snakes
Family: Anomalepidae
Twenty species in 4 genera.

Distribution: S C America and tropical S America. Length: 11–30cm; most 13–16 cm. Color: brown or black, some with yellow or white head and/or tail. Body form: like typical blind snakes with toothed movable maxilla, short tail and indistinct head; skull bones less fused and with 1–2 teeth in lower jaw.

Typical Blind Snakes
Family: Typhlopidae
One hundred and sixty-three species in 3 genera.

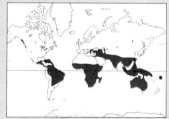

Distribution: tropical S America N to Mexico and the Bahamas, Africa S of Sahara, SE Europe across S Asia to Taiwan and Australia. Length: 15–90cm; most 20–50cm. Color: pink, yellow, brown or black; solid or with darker or lighter blotches, bands or lines. Body form: cylindrical, with indistinct head, reduced eyes under head scutes, movable toothed maxilla, lower jaw toothless, tail short. Small species tend to be slender, individuals of some large species become rather thick-bodied. Species include: **Flowerpot snake** (*Rhamphotyphlops braminus*), **Mona blind snake** Ⓡ (*Typhlops monensis*), **Schlegel's blind snake** (*Rhinotyphlops schlegeli*). Total threatened species: 1.

Advanced Snakes
(Infraorder Caenophidia)

Harmless Snakes
Family: Colubridae
One thousand, five hundred and
sixty-two species in 292 genera.*

Distribution: all continents except
Antarctica, from near Arctic Circle in
Scandinavia and Siberia S to Terra del
Fuego (S America), Cape of Good
Hope (Africa) and NE Australia. On
most islands except Ireland, Iceland,
New Zealand and small oceanic
islands. Length: 13cm–3.5m; most
50cm–2m. Color: most brown, gray
or black; some bright green or red;
most with spots, blotches or stripes.
Body form: most with distinct head
and tapering body; burrowers
cylindrical with indistinct head; eyes
small to large, with brille; pupil
horizontally or vertically elliptical in
some, round in most. None has
functional left lung, coronoid bone or
pelvic vestiges. All generalized species
have "typical" head scutes (see
RIGHT). Vertebral hypapophyses
absent in most; present in water
snakes and some others. Hemipenes
usually ornamented with spines, often
also with calyces, rarely
unornamented; sulcus forked or
simple (see RIGHT). Species and genera
include: **Aesculapian snake** (*Elaphe
longissima*), **American green snakes**
(genus *Opheodrys*), **American water
snakes and garter snakes** (genera
Nerodia, *Thamnophis*), **Asian snail-
eaters** (genus *Pareas*), **atractaspid
snakes or burrowing asps** (genus
Atractaspis), **cat-eyed snakes** (genus
Dipsas), **crowned snakes** (genus
Tantilla), **egg-eating snakes** (genus
Dasypeltis), **Eurasian whipsnake**
(*Coluber gemonensis*), **Grass snake**
(*Natrix natrix*), **Milk snake**
(*Lampropeltis triangulum*), **mud snakes**
(genus *Farancia*), **racer** (*Coluber
constrictor*), **rat snakes** (genus *Elaphe*),
Redbelly snake (*Storeria
occipitomaculata*), **San Francisco garter
snake** Ⓔ (*Thamnophis sirtalis
tetrataenia*). Total threatened
subspecies: 8.

*Some authorities recognize up to 6 different
families of harmless snakes.

Front-fanged Snakes
Family: Elapidae
Two hundred and thirty-six species in
61 genera.*

Distribution: N and S America, Asia,
Africa, Australia; seasnakes ranging
from coasts of Asia to E Africa,
Australia and tropical America.
Length: 38cm–5.6m; most 75cm–
1.5m. Color: most gray, brown or
black, often with collars or
crossbands; some bright green; coral
snakes ringed with red, yellow and
black. Body form: from thick-bodied
with broad head to slender, racer-like;
sea snakes with tail compressed to oar
shape, often thick-bodied with small
head; all with fixed, hollow fangs,
often with several teeth behind them.
Species include: **Annulated sea snake**
(*Emydocephalus annulatus*), **Asian
cobra** (*Naja naja*), **Black mamba**
(*Dendroaspis polylepis*), **Central Asian
cobra** Ⓔ (*Naja oxiana*), **Death adder**
(*Acanthophis antarcticus*), **Desert
taipan** (*Oxyuranus microlepidotus*),
Dubois's reef snake (*Aipysurus duboisii*),
Eastern brown snake (*Pseudonaja
textilis*), **Eastern coral snake** (*Micrurus
fulvius*), **Egyptian cobra** or **asp** (*Naja
haje*), **Fiji snake** Ⓥ (*Ogmodon vitianus*),
King cobra (*Ophiophagus hannah*),
kraits (genus *Bungarus*), **mambas**
(genus *Dendroaspis*), **New World coral
snakes** (genera *Micruroides*,
Micrurus), **oriental coral snakes**
(genus *Calliophis*), **Pelagic sea snake**
(*Pelamis platurus*), **sea kraits** (genus
Laticauda), **spitting cobras** (*Naja
nigricollis*, *N. mossambica*, *Hemachatus
haemachatus*), **tiger snakes** (*Notechis
scutatus*, *N. ater*). Total threatened
species: 2.

*Seasnakes are sometimes counted as a
separate family, the Hydrophiidae and the
Australian venomous snakes as the family
Acanthophiidae.

Vipers
Family: Viperidae
One hundred and eighty-seven species
in 17 genera.*

Distribution: Canada to Argentina,
S Siberia and Japan S to E Indies and
Africa, W to Scandinavia, England,
and Spain. Length: 25cm–3.65m;
most 60cm–1.2m. Color: from bright
green with red markings to solid
brown or black; most with pattern of
dark blotches on lighter background.
Body form: generally heavy-bodied
with distinct head and eyes with
vertically elliptical pupils; single pair
of hollow fangs on very short maxilla
can be rotated to bring fangs forward
to bite. Species and genera include:
Asian tree vipers (genus
Trimeresurus), **bushmaster** (*Lachesis
muta*), **Central American fer-de-lance**
(*Bothrops asper*), **copperhead**
(*Agkistrodon contortrix*), **cottonmouth**
(*A. piscivorus*), **diamondback
rattlesnakes** (*Crotalus adamanteus*,
C. atrox), **European adder** (*Vipera
berus*), **Gaboon viper** (*Bitis gabonica*),
Horned viper (*Cerastes cerastes*),
jararaca (*Bothrops jararaca*), **Latifi's
viper** Ⓔ (*Vipera latifii*), **Mountain
viper** (*Trimeresurus monticola*), **New
Mexico ridge nose rattlesnake** Ⓔ
(*Crotalus willardi obscurus*), **Puff adder**
(*Bitis arietans*), **pygmy rattlesnakes**
(genus *Sistrurus*), **Russell's viper**
(*Vipera russelli*), **saw-scaled vipers**
(genus *Echis*), **sidewinder** (*Crotalus
cerastes*), **Southern fer-de-lance**
(*Bothops atrox*). Total threatened
species: 6. Total threatened
subspecies: 5.

*The 142 species of pit vipers are sometimes
split off as a separate family, the Crotalidae.

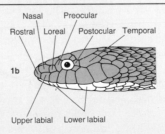
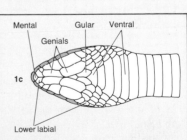

▲ ◀ ▼ **Scales and hemipenes.** (1) The typical arrangement of scales on an
advanced snake's head and upper body (a) from above, (b) from side, (c)
from below. (2) Anal and tail scutes of an advanced snake. (3) Single
hemipenis (a) with apical awns, (b) with spines and calyces, (c) with spines
only, (d) with flounces, (e) with apical disks, (f) with capitations.

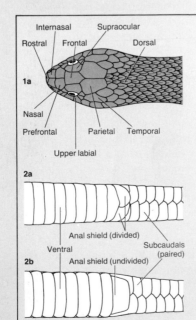

Vipers, Rattlesnakes and Cobras
Venomous snakes

A rattlesnake strikes, its fangs entering and leaving its prey in a fraction of a second, but long enough to inject a lethal dose of poison. The snake retreats to a hiding place and only later searches for its now dead prey. The poison has worked in two ways—killing the prey, and aiding the process of digestion. This would be a typical scenario of a hunt. Man can hardly be regarded as prey, so why do so many people die from snake bites—the answer is that when confronted with an aggressor, the snake's weapons of attack become those of defense.

Venoms are a recently evolved item of snake weaponry. Representatives of more than 100 genera are believed to have them to at least some extent, but none of the pythons, boas or members of other "primitive" families do. Most venomous snakes belong to "advanced" families. They include all vipers, all front-fanged snakes (cobras, sea snakes and Australian venomous snakes) and some species in the harmless snake family.

Being legless, snakes have no way of tearing apart large prey. They have had to develop a number of special mechanisms to be able to incapacitate large animals and feed on them. Constriction, among the more primitive families, is one of these mechanisms. Venoms are another.

There is reason to think that snake venoms evolved from digestive juices. Their digestive action seems still to be important, but the principal function of venoms is the subjugation of prey, enabling the snake to feed upon animals that would otherwise be unavailable. Active or potentially dangerous creatures are weakened or disoriented, while hard-to-get-at prey in burrows or crevices can be paralyzed and extracted.

Venom also deters enemies, and a few snakes, for example the spitting cobras, seem to use it primarily for this purpose. Other snakes have evolved sounds, colors, and behavior patterns that warn possible predators of their dangerous nature, and this in turn has led to mimicry of venomous snakes by nonvenomous species.

Snake venoms are produced by glands located in the upper jaw or temporal region except in a few species that have tubular glands extending well into the body. Space for venom storage is greatest in vipers and some cobras and least in the so-called harmless snakes. Venom glands are usually associated with teeth modified for injection.

In many of the harmless snakes, the dental modification is simply an enlargement of one or two pairs of back teeth. In others,

these teeth have grooves on the front or sides. In the front-fanged snakes the venom-conducting teeth are in the front part of the upper jaw, and the grooves are closed for at least part of their length. In vipers and burrowing asps (actractaspids) the fang can be folded against the roof of the mouth. The fangs of these snakes are proportionally longer than those of front-fanged snakes, except for a few Australian venomous snakes. The longest fangs are those of the Gaboon viper, which measure 2.9cm (1.2in) in a 1.3m (51in) snake.

Snake venoms are colorless to amber liquids containing 18–67 percent solids, nearly all of which is protein. The amounts that can be obtained by venom extraction, or "milking," vary from a few microliters (millionths of a liter) to 6–7ml (0.2–0.24fl oz), with dry weights varying from a fraction of a milligram to about 1.5g (0.05oz). The smallest yields are obtained from harmless snakes and sea snakes, the largest from pit vipers such as the diamondback rattlesnakes and neotropical fer-de-lance. Experimental evidence suggests that snakes never inject more than half their venom in a bite.

Snake venoms contain many proteins and polypeptides with biological activity. Best known are the polypeptide neurotoxins of which about 70 have been identified, most of them in venoms of front-fanged snakes. The neurotoxins act by blocking the

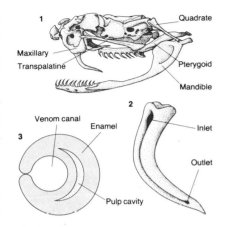

▲ Fang equipment. (1) Rattlesnake skull, showing specialized teeth in the upper jaw. (2) Fang of a rattlesnake showing the inlet for the poison and its outlet near the tip. (3) Cross section of a cobra's fang, showing cavity through which the poison is conducted.

◄ Threatening fangs of a Toad-eater snake (*Xenodon rabdocephalus*) of Costa Rica. The forward position of the opening to the larynx allows the snake to breathe even when very large prey is lodged in its throat.

▼ Lethal strike by a Western diamondback rattlesnake (*Crotalus atrox*).

transmission of nerve impulses to muscles. Another group of polypeptide toxins affect cell membranes.

Enzymes occur in all snake venoms. They can affect the prey by destroying blood clotting factors, by producing thrombosis and internal bleeding and by breaking down skeletal muscle and intercellular cementing substances. Other interesting proteins in snake venoms include a factor that promotes growth of nerve fibers and a substance that inactivates complement, an important component of the immune system. Some of these snake venom components are used by biochemists, pharmacologists, immunologists and molecular biologists in their research. They have a very limited role in clinical medicine, although an important antihypertensive drug was first found in the venom of the jararaca, a South American pit viper.

The components of snake venoms act in concert to produce their effects. Damage to small blood vessels and destruction of clotting factors cause hemorrhage. A fall in blood pressure may result directly from venom or be secondary to a loss in blood volume. Paralysis results from blocking the transmission of nerve impulses to muscles. Tissue such as skeletal muscle may be broken down directly by venom or may be damaged indirectly through impaired circulation. Products of tissue breakdown often affect heart and kidney function.

The most lethal snake venoms are those of two Australian land snakes, the Desert taipan and Eastern brown snake, and Dubois's reef snake. For all these species, the lethal dose for a 20g (0.7oz) mouse is less than 1 microgram (1 millionth of a gram).

More than 50 species, belonging to 33 genera are reported to have poisoned humans, from very mildly to fatally. Statistics compiled by the World Health Organization indicate 30,000–40,000 deaths annually from snakebite. The incidence of snakebite is highest in rural agricultural and pastoral populations of Southeast Asia, West Africa, and parts of tropical America. Leading killers are the saw-scaled vipers, Asian cobra, Russell's viper, and the large neotropical lancehead vipers, the Southern and Central American fer-de-lance. SAM

WORM-LIZARDS

Suborder: Amphisbaenia
Worm-lizards or ringed lizards.
One hundred and forty species in 21 genera
and 4 families.
Distribution: subtropical regions of N America,
W Indies, S America, into Patagonia; Africa,
Iberian Peninsula, Arabia, W Asia.

Habitat: burrowing reptiles highly specialized
for digging.

Size: length (snout to tip of tail) from 10–
75cm (4–30in), but most are 15–35cm (6–14in).

Color: reddish-brown to brownish black, black
and white.

Reproduction: fertilization internal; some lay
eggs, in others the eggs develop inside female.

Longevity: generally 1–2 years in captivity,
some longer.

Species include: **Florida worm-lizard** (*Rhineura
floridana*).

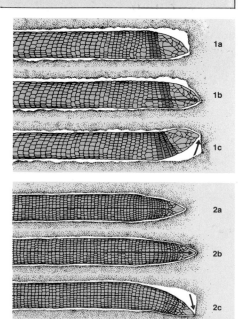

WORM-LIZARDS are the only true burrowers among the reptiles. Some other reptiles live underground for part of their lives, and some of those use tunnels dug by other animals, but only worm-lizards are exclusively subterranean. They generate their own tunnels, many of them driving passages through very hard soils, and their digging adaptations, among other features, are distinctive. They first appear in the fossil record of the North American Paleocene (65 million years ago). Other early specimens have been found in Belgium and the largest known fossil forms are from Tanzania.

Three of the four worm-lizard families lack all traces of limbs and may even have lost remnants of the internal pelvic and pectoral girdles which other legless reptiles retain. A fourth family, the Mexican worm-lizards (Bipedidae), have retained and even increased the size of their forelimbs; their body has become elongated behind the shoulder girdle and gives the impression that the hands are not only large but on the head, so that the folk name is *lagartijas con orejas* ("little lizards with big ears"). The hands help the animals move above-ground and also generate the initial divot from which they burrow into the soil.

All worm-lizards form tunnels by forceful movements of the head. Heads are formed into various kinds of digging tools, and the skulls are more solid than those of other reptiles of equivalent size. In some species, the skull is shielded by hard keratin, in others by scales with a low-friction surface that facilitates penetration of the soil. The eyelids are fused. The eyes lie deep below the translucent skin. There are no external ear openings and the nostrils point backward so that pressure tends to close them, which prevents sand entering during burrowing. The upper lip extends over the lower lip and the lower jaw normally closes with the head in such a way that it is likely to be pushed closed rather than open as the head drives into the soil at the end of the tunnel.

Under the ground, worm-lizards propel the body by concertina and rectilinear movements. The skin, in rings around the body, is relatively free from the trunk and can slide over it, folding like a bellows. In rectilinear motion, portions of the skin are fixed against the tunnel wall and the attaching muscles pull up the trunk, generating the force required for a penetrating stroke into the tunnel's end.

Once the head is driven into the end of the tunnel it may be wriggled and then withdrawn slightly before the next stroke. However, about half of the species have

▲ **Exclusively a burrower,** a worm-lizard such as this *Amphisbaena* has small eyes deep beneath translucent skin, no external ear openings and nostrils that point backward so that pressure closes them during burrowing.

▶ **Forelimbs of the Mexican worm-lizard** (*Bipes biporus*) are used below and above ground.

◀ **Two worm-lizard digging methods.** (1) In shovel-snouted species, at the start of the stroke (a) the rings of scales behind the head are close together. During penetration (b), these rings separate, pushing the head forward. In tunnel-widening (c), the head is lifted against the tunnel roof. (2) In keel-snouted species, the tunnel-extending stroke (a,b) is similar, but the tunnel is widened either (c) near the snout by bending the head or (d) around the back of the skull by bending the body sideways.

disadvantage that less than half of the neck muscles can be used for compression; the spade-headed species are larger and more numerous.

The Florida worm-lizard, sole living member of the family Rhineuridae that has an extensive fossil record across the North American continent, also shows a spade-snouted pattern. It digs in a pattern similar to that of the true worm-lizards and its head segmentation also shows similarities. However, it differs profoundly from the pattern of the African and South American species in the nature and arrangement of the bones involved in forming the spade.

The Trogonophidae are a family of edge-snouted worm-lizards that burrow in a rotating, oscillatory pattern. Their face tends to be a flattened plate before the eyes. The edges of this plate form scrapers that shave a layer of soil off the end of the tunnel so that the side of the trunk can force it into the tunnel's wall in the next movement. As the penetrating strokes produce torsional forces between body and tunnel wall, these are the only worm-lizards that have opted for a triangular or beam-shaped cross-section of the body (and the tunnel). The method is highly effective in the friable sandy soils of the Arabian peninsula and the Horn of Africa where the most specialized species are found.

Worm-lizards are formidable predators. With large, interlocking upper and lower teeth they bite their prey, crushing it, and withdraw down the tunnel pulling the victim, so that pieces are ripped out as the body is dragged along.

Prey (small arthropods, worms and even vertebrates) are recognized by scent and sound. The ears are modified so that sound is detected through a substitute eardrum that lies on the side of the jaws, allowing worm-lizards to hear airborne sounds transmitted down the tunnel before them. Experiments suggest that they respond to sounds made by the movements of prey. They get some of their moisture from the food, but certain species can apparently collect soil water, pulling it in by capillary action between their lips and tongue.

Worm-lizards reproduce like snakes and lizards, with hemipenes (see pp92, 129) allowing internal fertilization. Some species lay eggs, a few in ant and termite colonies, and in some the eggs develop within the female before live birth. As in snakes, the embryos are complexly coiled within the egg. Unlike snakes, the posterior end of the embryo remains coiled into a relatively small spiral until shortly before birth. CG

separated the effort of tunnel extension from that of widening it. They first drive the head into the tunnel's end and then use different muscles arranged in a complicated pulley system to press the soil into the tunnel's roof and floor. They thus avoid having to dump soil on the surface and can spend most of their lives underground.

Members of the commonest family, the true worm-lizards (Amphisbaenidae), found in the Mediterranean region, Africa and the Americas, have specialized their widening system. They either form the head into a vertical keel, swinging this to left and right after penetration, or into a horizontal spade that is lifted to compress soil into the roof of the tunnel. Keel-headed species have the

TUATARA

Sphenodon punctatus R
Family: Sphenodontidae
Sole living member of order Rhynchocephalia.
Distribution: about 30 small islands and rock
stacks off the coasts of New Zealand.

Size: Males up to 61cm (24in) from snout to tip
of tail, weight 1kg (2.2lb); females up to 45cm
(18in); weight 0.15kg (1.1lb).

Night-active burrower in areas of low forest
and scrub, usually associated with colonies of
burrowing seabirds. Color: adult background
color olive-green, gray, or dark pink, with an
overall speckling of gray or white; newly
hatched animal brown or gray, with a pale
head shield, striped throat and sometimes
distinctive markings on the tail.

Reproduction: lays eggs, 6–15 per clutch with
incubation of approximately 15 months.

Longevity: unknown, but probably 120 years
or more.

R Rare

Tuataras are relics of a bygone age now found only in isolated parts of New Zealand. Among their many curious features are a third "eye" in the top of the head, eggs that take 15 months to hatch and a life-span in excess of a century.

The tuatara is the sole surviving member of an entire reptilian order, the Rhynchocephalia, which came into being in the Mesozoic (220 million years ago)—well before the first dinosaurs appeared. Rhynchocephalians lived in Europe, Asia, North and South America, and southern and East Africa, but all except the tuatara were extinct by the end of the Mesozoic (65 million years ago). It is almost identical in structure to a form that existed about 140 million years ago, which makes it of exceptional interest to scientists, who study it for clues to the physiology and anatomy of reptiles that lived over 200 million years ago.

Although it superficially resembles a lizard, the tuatara has a number of features which clearly distinguish it: the structure of the skull, which has two pairs of arches like a crocodilian's; the vertebrae, which are hollow at each end; a small projection on the back of each rib (the uncinate process); a bony skeleton in the abdominal wall; the jaw teeth, which are not separate structures but serrations of the jaw bone; the absence of an ear drum (tympanum) and of a middle ear, and the absence of a male copulatory organ. Some features of the tuatara's brain and of its locomotion resemble conditions in amphibians, and its heart is more primitive

than that found in any other reptile group.

Some of the tuatara's specialized features appear to be associated with a change in habitat since the days of its early ancestors. This reptile is now a nocturnal burrower with specializations of the visual cells, including a "duplex retina" containing two types of visual cell, which presumably enable the animal, like crocodiles and turtles, to see by night as well as by day. The retina is backed by a *tapetum lucidum*, a layer which reflects light back through the sense cells a second time. Tuataras have a low metabolic rate, a capacity for low temperature activity and long, slow growth.

Like a lizard's (see p86), the pineal body in the tuatara's brain is connected to a "third eye" on the top of the head: the parietal, a structure found below the skin in

▲ Living, but endangered, "fossil." The tuatara once occurred widely on the two main islands of New Zealand but is now restricted to about 20 small islands and 10–12 islets and rock stacks, off the northern and eastern coasts of the North Island, and in Cook Strait, between the North and South Islands. Many of the colonies consist only of adult animals, with a minority of the islands supporting successful breeding populations.

◄ Threat display. "Tuatara" is a Maori word meaning "peaks on the back," a reference to the triangular folds of skin that form a conspicuous crest along the back and tail of the male, and a rudimentary crest on the female. The crest is normally soft and pliant, but can be raised and stiffened in a threat display by the male when alarmed. Females are very timid, retreating hastily when disturbed.

Large populations of burrowing seabirds (for example, petrels, prions, and shearwaters) come ashore each year to nest. By their burrowing they provide shelter for the tuataras (although they can dig their own burrows) and by defecation and shuffling movements on the forest floor they encourage a high concentration of ground insects, especially beetles, which provide a large part of the tuatara's diet. The tuatara's diet also includes spiders, earthworms, slaters, slugs, snails, geckos and skinks and the chicks and eggs of seabirds. Adults occasionally eat young tuataras.

Apart from coming out of their burrows on sunny days to bask in or near their burrow entrances, tuataras are active at night. They mate in January (Southern Hemisphere summer), and in October or November (spring) the females excavate burrows 10cm (4in) deep or more, in which they lay 6–15 eggs. The eggs are bluntly oval, about 25–30mm (1–1.2in) long, and enclosed in a parchment-like covering. The incubation period is approximately 15 months—the longest known for any reptile. During incubation the eggs are vulnerable to predators, and to damage from extreme changes in climatic conditions.

The embryo develops a horny, bluntly thorn-shaped egg-breaker on the top of its nose. With this it slits the soft shell before emerging. The hatchlings are about 54mm (2.2in) long from snout to vent, and are very active—a necessary feature for survival, as they are almost immediately dependent on their own efforts to find food. They may dig small burrows for themselves, or hide under stones or logs. The egg-breaker disappears about two weeks after hatching.

Growth is long and slow; tuataras reach sexual maturity at about 20 years of age, and growth continues until 50–60 years of age. It is likely that tuataras may live for over 120 years; but this has yet to be proven, and views that tuataras live to be 200-300 years of age are sheer speculation.

The tuatara's survival in New Zealand, while its relatives became extinct in all other parts of the world, is probably due to the fact that New Zealand became separated from other land masses about 80 million years ago, before any of the later evolving land predators reached it. Apart from man, the tuatara's main enemy may now be the kiore, or Polynesian rat (*Rattus exulans*); the best self-maintaining populations occur on rat-free islands. The tuatara is absolutely protected by the New Zealand Wildlife Act—protection essential for its survival.

a space between the parietal bones in the roof of the skull. The parietal has many of the structural features of an eye, including a lens, retina and nervous connections to the brain, but experimental work has shown that, although sensitive to light, it cannot contribute to the formation of visual images. The pineal body in the tuatara is not known to be sensitive to light, but it also has a structure which would permit light sensitivity.

The islands where the tuatara survives today are all wholly or partially cliff-bound, with boulder beaches, and the seas surrounding them can change rapidly. Landing on the islands is difficult, helping to protect them from interference by man. On islands that are more readily accessible, the tuatara has been eliminated through disturbance of habitat and introduction of predators.

JR

CROCODILIANS

ALLIGATORS, crocodiles and the gharial are a vestige of the great Age of Reptiles, relics of an ancient, much larger group that existed in the Mesozoic era (225–65 million years ago). They have changed little in the last 65 million years, but far from being out of place in the modern world and thus doomed to extinction, they remain masters of their environment. Only human exploitation has hampered their success.

Any member of this order is instantly recognizable by its characteristically crocodilian appearance. However, the most important features distinguishing crocodilians are internal. Despite their antiquity, they have brains and hearts which are more advanced than those of any other living reptiles. The ventricles of the heart are completely divided and there is no mixture of arterial and venous blood within the heart. A more oxygenated blood supply is thus available to the brain, and it has a true cerebral cortex, allowing more learned, as opposed to merely instinctive, behavior.

Similar life-styles in the different species make for many shared characteristics. All of these aquatic and semiaquatic predators have eyes and nostrils set high on the head so that they can see and breathe when lying or floating almost totally submerged. A "third eyelid" (nictitating membrane) sweeps sideways across the eye to give more protection during diving. It is transparent and does not interfere with the animal's sharp vision. Nostrils and ears close under water. When the ears are out of water, hearing is acute. A "false palate" (basihyal throat valve), consisting of a wide flap of skin at the back of the mouth, closes the glottis and allows the animal to feed while submerged, without the risk of swallowing water and drowning.

The most obvious adaptation for locomotion is the large, compressed tail, used to propel the animal through water. The limbs, folded back along the body during swimming, are primarily for movement on land. Front legs are usually weak. The back legs vary in strength between species: some (eg the gharial and the Saltwater crocodile) seldom move more than their own length from the water's edge, while others, such as the mugger, can wander long distances over land if a home pond dries up. By contrast with the "unimproved" gait of lizards (see p68), crocodilians have a "high walk," in which limbs are brought in towards the body and lift it well clear of the ground. Actual galloping across land has been observed in the Australian freshwater crocodile. There is no webbing on the fore-limbs, but webbing on the hind feet allows a swimming crocodilian—by a sudden upward movement of the feet with toes fully spread—to sink quickly downwards and backwards when danger threatens.

Crocodilians are found throughout the tropical and subtropical areas of the world, almost wherever there is water, but the tropical regions are especially favored. The American alligator in the southeastern United States and the Chinese alligator, in the Yangtse River and its tributaries, can stand colder winters than most crocodiles and all other members of the alligator family. However, both the mugger, a crocodile, and the gharial occur across northern India and into Nepal, including areas with cold winters. They do not hibernate, but on cold nights avoid extremes of cold by sleeping at the bottom of rivers or ponds. Metabolism slows greatly during this sleep and oxygen is not supplied to most tissues, but if the supply of oxygen to the heart and brain threatens to become inadequate, the animal will surface to breathe. Like all reptiles inhabiting areas with variable environmental temperatures, such crocodilians need to bask in the sun to regulate their body temperature (see pp70–71).

Distribution is also affected by tolerance to salt water, the sea being an effective barrier to the spread of freshwater species. The Cuban crocodile is restricted to two swamps in Cuba, but the American crocodile, an estuarine species which is saltwater-tolerant and occasionally swept by storms across open seas, occurs on a range of Caribbean islands and from the extreme south of Florida through Central America, on both the Atlantic and Pacific coasts, to northern South America. Intervening sea, despite its narrowness and its islands, has allowed completely different freshwater species to inhabit New Guinea and northern Australia, but the Saltwater crocodile, the estuarine species of the Old World, has an enormous distribution from Cochin in southwest India east to southern China and then south through Malaysia, Indonesia and the Philippines to New Guinea and northern Australia.

Most of a crocodilian's day may be spent hauled out on the bank basking, but in the early evening it becomes active, especially for feeding. It is a carnivore and will eat almost any animal that it can overcome. However, many species have very definite food preferences or are limited to a fairly limited choice of food items. The larger species show the greatest feeding diversity, their preferred prey changing as they grow;

▲ **By keeping its mouth open** this basking Orinoco crocodile allows the heat of the sun to reach areas where blood is closest to the skin surface.

▶ **Swamp navigation.** OVERLEAF An American alligator progressing through its domain.

▼ **Baby toss.** A female Nile crocodile flips one of her babies into the air to reposition it in her mouth. Mouth transport guarantees safety from predators.

insects, amphibians, fish, mollusks and crustaceans are taken by small individuals, but larger ones may include in their diet a significant proportion of mammals.

Many of the differences between crocodilian species reflect variations in diet. In the gharial an extremely elongated snout is associated with a fish-eating habit. The Australian freshwater and African slender-snouted crocodiles and the False gharial also feed mainly on fish and have long, slender snouts. This shape offers little resistance to the water and allows a quick sideways swipe to catch prey that has come within reach. Alligators and the mugger, by contrast, have short, broad snouts and powerful jaws for tackling a much wider range of prey, including turtles, egrets and small to large mammals. Alligators drag egrets under-water and even take huge turtles in their jaws and crack them. Large, broad-snouted muggers can successfully tackle deer and cattle. The snout is less blunt in generalized feeders such as the Nile crocodile which includes fish, birds and hoofed mammals in its diet. Fish-eaters such as the gharial have

specialized piercing teeth to keep hold of slippery prey. The teeth of more generalized feeders are adapted for tearing and holding. To dismember very large prey which cannot be swallowed whole, crocodiles perform twisting movements which aid their tearing teeth in detatching large chunks of flesh. Crocodilians often lose teeth in encounters with prey, but they are quickly replaced. Each tooth contains a small replacement tooth within its pulp cavity and examination sometimes reveals a further tiny tooth ready to erupt within that.

Surprise is used especially by larger species attacking alert animals such as deer and monkeys, or egrets, herons and other wading birds, which are capable of quick responses to danger. In most species adults are well camouflaged in drab greenish, brownish or blackish tones. Strategies include waiting unseen or moving slowly towards prey without being detected. Large animals are often taken when drinking; facing down the slope of the bank towards the water, they are easily toppled, dragged down and drowned. Even very large crocodiles can often approach unseen under water, especially in muddy conditions.

In all crocodilians, fertilization is internal, and all lay eggs. Males have a single, grooved penis that can be protruded from the cloaca through a longitudinal slit. There are no external characters which allow ready identification of sex in any species except the gharial. The mature gharial male develops a somewhat bulbous pot-like structure at the end of its greatly elongated snout. It is absent in females and has no known function other than sexual identification at a distance. In all species, the male courts the female, often coming alongside her in the water, swimming parallel to her and placing his adjacent fore- and hind limbs over her body. During copulation the pair usually sinks to the bottom. After about two months, the female is ready to lay her eggs, and on ground above the level of any likely flooding during the incubation period (2.5–3 months) she makes a nest under cover of darkness.

Some species, such as the Nile and Australian crocodiles and the gharial, dig a flask-shaped hole in the ground. The eggs have hard, heavily calcified shells like those of birds, and great care seems to be taken not to break any by dropping them onto one another when placing them in the nest. It is thought that each egg is laid onto the mother's rear foot, which, like a hand, lowers it carefully into the hole. When laying is complete the mother carefully covers the eggs with soil. She leaves no traces of the nest, and her own tracks in the fine silt will disappear in even a slight breeze.

Many other crocodilians, including such diverse species as the American alligator and the Saltwater crocodile, build mound nests. Over a period of several nights, the female heaps large quantities of vegetation over the eggs. She may fell suitable items using her jaws or scrape up already fallen material with her front and hind limbs. The completed nest may be 2.5–3m (8–10ft) in diameter and 70–100cm (26–40in) high. It becomes a rotting mass, with a constant temperature of 30–32°C (86–89.5° F). In many crocodilian species the female shows a high degree of parental care during incubation and hatching (see p140).

Growth can be rapid in environments that contain abundant food and are warm all year round. Many individuals grow more than 30cm (12in) in a year, but the young of some of the larger species, such as the mugger in India, can grow from about 25cm (10in) at hatching to more than 1m (3.3ft) by the end of their first year. Reports of monster-sized crocodilians are common, but seldom verifiable. The maximum size in the American alligator, reached only by exceptionally large males, is about 5.5m (18ft). The record for a gharial is 6.6m (21.5ft) and for an American crocodile 6.9m (22.6ft). Calculations made on the basis of the length of a skull owned by the Raja of Kanika in Orissa, India, indicate an overall length of 7.46m (24.25ft) in one Saltwater crocodile.

There has been considerable confusion about maximum adult size in the larger species and its relationship to age. It is probably quite wrong to say that very large individuals are all very old. Although crocodilians grow as they get older, some grow much faster than others, especially when they are young. This may in part be due to advantages of climate and nutrition which vary locally and from year to year, but even under apparently identical conditions in captivity members of a single nest can show marked variation in growth rates.

Little is known about longevity in the wild, but ages of 73 and about 100 have been recorded for the American alligator in captivity.

Humans have sometimes been deceived by crocodilian camouflage and have had difficult escapes after stepping on what they thought were logs. However, these reptiles rarely attack man. In a ten-year study of the Saltwater crocodile in the Bhitarkanika crocodile sanctuary in eastern India, only four attacks, by large males, were recorded in spite of the fact that the sanctuary includes a large human population and some of the largest crocodiles surviving in the world today. American alligators sometimes prey on pets where housing development encroaches on their habitat, and in recent years they have caused a few human fatalities.

A demand for luxury leather led to a decimation of crocodilian populations during the two decades after World War II. The rate of loss surprised even the hunters. Around 1950, and even later in some parts of the world, the resource was enormous. However, what was happening was analogous to mining, not to cropping a resource with a sustained yield. Even in large crocodilians with high reproductive rates the annual sustainable crop is very small. Flooding and predators take a heavy toll of eggs and hatchlings. Many species need long periods of growth before reproduction, and hunters have taken untold numbers before they had a chance to breed. Hunters also often shoot mothers guarding nests, since

they are easy targets, with the loss both of breeding females and orphaned hatchlings. Some species, such as the Cuban crocodile, are vulnerable on account of their small home ranges: disappearing in one locality can mean disappearing altogether.

Endangered late-breeding species include the Saltwater crocodile—which begins breeding at 2.3–2.6m (7.5–8.5ft), probably at about 10 years of age, the American crocodile, the little-known Orinoco crocodile of Venezuela and Colombia and the Black caiman of the Amazon Basin. The American alligator starts breeding at about

eight years in the wild, and in the past has been seriously threatened both by hunters and by habitat destruction through drainage of swamplands for agriculture and housing. However, recovery of the American alligator has been achieved through effective protection, and some states have now reinstated open hunting seasons.

A species pushed to the brink of extinction by hunting is the gharial. In 1974 the government of India and the United Nations Food and Agriculture Organization conducted a survey of its population in India. It was estimated that no more than 50–60 adults

▲ **Ambushed.** Crocodiles commonly lie in wait at water holes and attack prey as it drinks. This Nile crocodile has caught an impala.

▶ **Active conservation.** Young sanctuary-hatched gharials are wrapped in protective padding during transportation before release. Active management of this species involves the collection of eggs for hatchery incubation. Hatchlings are reared to a length of about 1.2m (4ft), when they are safe from predators, before release into the wild.

◀ **Mound nest** guarded by a female Saltwater crocodile.

Watchful Mothers—Parental Care in Crocodilians

A mother crocodilian's brood is vulnerable at three stages. First, an enormous list of mammals and reptiles are persistent egg hunters, including wild and feral pigs, monitor lizards and tribal humans. Next, monitor lizards, foxes and crows take hatchlings before they reach the water, and finally, in the water, the young are prey to large fish and wading birds such as storks and large herons. In response, maternal care in many crocodilians begins as soon as the eggs are laid, and in some it lasts long after hatching.

A mother Saltwater crocodile digs out one or more wallows just beside her mound nest. They fill up with water and she is able to lie unseen on guard. Muggers leave their nests far from the water, but the mother's nocturnal visits are so regular that she creates a conspicuous footpath. The gharial does not emerge from the water to inspect her nest but often appears at the riverbank nearby.

When they are ready, hatchlings of all species studied break their shells, and, with just their snouts poking out, wait for their mother. They will respond to any stimulation,

such as vibrations caused by the mother crawling over the nest area, by calling with loud, high-pitched grunts that can be heard at a considerable distance and are probably the trigger for the mother to excavate the nest. In many species she will pick up eggs which have not hatched and gently crush them in her jaws to liberate the late hatchlings. In captivity, Saltwater males have been observed to help. Females of many species, such as the Nile and Saltwater crocodiles, provide a safe passage to water by gently picking up the young in their mouths in batches and carrying them in the gular (throat) pouch. In Mexico, male caimans have been observed doing this. American alligators carry their hatchlings to specially excavated pools.

Nile crocodile mothers have nursery areas in quiet backwaters where they protect their young for another three months. Hunters have reported approaching a Saltwater crocodile with young that were "eaten up" before the adult dived—evidently this was a mother taking offspring into her mouth for a ride to safety. In the American alligator, care may last as long as one and even two years.

of this species survived, not counting small numbers in Nepal and fewer than 10 in Pakistan and Bangladesh, but effective conservation measures have now made the gharial's future more promising. Massive sanctuaries have been created and active management involves the collection of eggs for hatchery incubation. Hatchlings are reared to a length of about 1.2m (4ft), when they are safe from egg and hatchling predators, before they are released into the wild. Gharial numbers in the sanctuaries have increased to several thousand. Several Indian states operate similar schemes for the mugger. However, the mugger is still listed as vulnerable, due to continued hunting and egg collecting, and the gharial continues to be listed as endangered: most of the released gharials are not yet of breeding age (about 10 years) and a secure breeding population has not yet been re-established.

Many species have not been the subject of such concerted efforts or of such an enlightened attitude as that of the Indian authorities. Even though the Convention on International Trade in Endangered Species of Wild Flora and Fauna (CITES) now bans trade in the skins of most crocodilians, the numbers of some species have been reduced to a mere handful in areas where habitat is not secure, nor law enforcement adequate. There is a danger that such little-known species as the Broad-nosed caiman, the Philippines crocodile and the Siamese crocodile will become extinct, unnoticed except by a few specialists.

Crocodilian Families

The **alligators** can be distinguished from crocodiles by the fourth mandibular tooth: it fits into the upper jaw and cannot be seen when the jaw is closed. Protoalligators arose in the late Cretaceous (ending about 65 million years ago) either in Asia or North America. The caimans first appeared in South America in the Pliocene (65–54 million years ago) and survive today as three genera (*Caiman*, *Melanosuchus* and *Paleosuchus*) in Central and South America. The genus *Alligator* arose in the Oligocene (38–26 million years ago) in North America. Today the critically endangered Chinese alligator survives as a population of only a few hundred at most. The American alligator, the only other member of the

genus, has made an excellent recovery from serious depletion. It occurs in wet habitat throughout Louisiana and Florida, in eastern Texas, in southern parts of Arkansas, Mississippi, Alabama and Georgia and in coastal regions of North and South Carolina. Alligators eat mostly vertebrate prey, usually slow-moving fish but also birds, mammals, amphibians and reptiles that venture into the water.

In **crocodiles** the fourth mandibular tooth is visible when the jaw is closed. This family arose in the late Cretaceous, either in Eurasia or North America, and spread rapidly. Before the end of the Cretaceous, crocodiles were present in Europe, Africa, northern and southern Asia and both North and South America. Today the 12 members of the genus *Crocodylus* include the most widespread crocodilian species: the Nile crocodile, found in wet habitats throughout Africa, and the American and the Saltwater crocodiles (see p136). Two crocodiles belong to genera of their own: the endangered False gharial of Indonesia, Malaysia and possibly Thailand and the African dwarf crocodile of West and Central Africa, reported to be nearing extinction. Throughout much of its extensive range, the American crocodile is likely to become extinct, but in Florida, at least, there are sound conservation programs for the remnant populations.

The **gharial**, often called the "gavial" as the result of a clerical error in copying an early account, gets its name from the pot-like protuberance on the snout of the mature male: *ghara* in Hindi means "pot." It is the sole living member of a family which arose in the Cretaceous and had representatives in South America from the Oligocene into the Pliocene (38–2 million years ago).

HRB

▼ ▶ **Representative species** of the three families of crocodilians. (1) Smooth-fronted caiman (*Paleosuchus palpebrosus*); Alligatoridae. (2) African dwarf crocodile (*Osteolaemus tetraspis*); Crocodylidae. (3) Female False gharial (*Tomistoma schlegelii*) with young; Crocodylidae. (4) Female Gharial (*Gavialis gangeticus*) fishing; Gavialidae. (5) Chinese alligator (*Alligator sinensis*); Alligatoridae. (6) American crocodile (*Crocodylus acutus*); Crocodylidae. (7) Female American alligator (*Alligator mississippiensis*) on nest mound; Alligatoridae. (8) Black caiman (*Melanosuchus niger*); Alligatoridae. (9) Mugger (*Crocodylus palustris*); Crocodylidae. (10) African slender-snouted crocodile (*Crocodylus cataphractus*); Crocodylidae.

Bibliography

The following list of titles indicates key reference works used in the preparation of this volume and those recommended for further reading. The list is divided into a number of categories.

General Works
Bellairs, A. d'A. (1969) *The Life of Reptiles, vols. 1-2*, Weidenfeld and Nicolson, London.
Bellairs, A. d'A. and Cox, C. B. (eds) (1976) *Morphology and Biology of Reptiles*, Academic Press, London.
Carr, A. (1963) *The Reptiles*, Life Nature Library, New York.
Carr, A. (1967) *So Excellent a Fishe. A Natural History of Sea Turtles*, Natural History Press, Garden City, New York.
Cochran, D. M. (1961) *Living Amphibians of the World*, Doubleday and Co, Garden City, New York.
Duellman, W. E. and Trueb, L. (1985) *Biology of Amphibians*, McGraw-Hill Book Co, New York.
Dunson, W. A. (ed) (1975) *The Biology of Sea Snakes*, University Park Press, Baltimore, Maryland.
Engelmann, W.-E. and Obst, F. J. (1981) *Snakes. Biology, Behavior and Relationship to Man*, Edition Leipzig, Leipzig.
Ferguson, M. W. J. (ed) (1984) *The Structure, Development and Evolution of Reptiles*, Academic Press, London.
Frost, D. (ed) (1985) *Amphibian Species of the World*, Association of Systematics Collections and Allen Press, Lawrence, Kansas. (Continuing series.)
Gans, C. et al. (eds) (1969-1982) *Biology of the Reptilia, vols 1-13*, Academic Press, London – a continuing series, now published by John Wiley/ Interscience, New York.
Goin, C. J., Goin, O. B. and Zug, G. R. (1978) *Introduction to Herpetology* (third edition), W. H. Freeman and Co, San Francisco.
Grassé, P.-P. et al. (1970) *Traité de zoologie: reptiles, vols. 1-2*, Masson et Cie, Paris. (*Amphibians* in press, authored by R. Laurent.)
Harless, M. and Morlock, H. (eds) (1979) *Turtles: Perspectives and Research*, John Wiley & Sons, New York.
Klauber, L. M. (1982) *Rattlesnakes* (abridged edition), University of California Press, Berkeley, California.
Neill, W. T. (1971) *The Last of the Ruling Reptiles. Alligators, Crocodiles, and their Kin*, Columbia University Press, New York.
Noble, G. K. (1931) *The Biology of the Amphibia*, McGraw-Hill Book Co, New York. (Reprint Dover Publications, 1954.)
Obst, F. J., Richter, K. and Jacob, U. (1984) *Lexicon der Terraristik und Herpetologie*, Edition Leipzig, Leipzig.
Parker, H. W. and Grandison, A. G. C. (1977) *Snakes, a Natural History*. British Museum (Nat Hist), London, and Cornell University Press, Ithaca, New York.
Peters, J. A. (1964) *Dictionary of Herpetology*, Hafner Publishing Co, New York.
Porter, K. R. (1972) *Herpetology*, W. B. Saunders Co, Philadelphia.
Pritchard, P. C. H. (1979) *Encyclopedia of Turtles*, T. F. H. Publications, Jersey City, New Jersey.
Rhodin, A. G. J. and Miyata, K. (eds) (1983) *Advances in Herpetology and Evolutionary Biology*, Museum of Comparative Zoology, Harvard University, Cambridge, Massachusetts.
Russell, F. E. (1980) *Snake Venom Poisoning*, J. B. Lippincott Co, Philadelphia.
Schmidt, K. P. and Inger, R. F. (1957) *Living Reptiles of the World*, Doubleday and Co, Garden City, New York.
Taylor, E. H. (1968) *The Caecilians of the World*, University of Kansas Press, Lawrence.
Vial, J. L. (ed) (1973) *Evolutionary Biology of the Anurans*, University of Missouri Press, Columbia, Missouri.

Behavior, Ecology and Physiology
Cloudsley-Thompson, J. L. (1971) *The Temperature and Water Relations of Reptiles*, Merrow Publishing Co, London.
Florkin, M. and Scheer, B. T. (eds) (1974) *Chemical Zoology, vol. 9: Amphibia and Reptilia*, Academic Press, London.
Fox, H. (1984) *Amphibian Morphogenesis*, Humana Press, Clifton, New Jersey.
Gans, C. (1974) *Biomechanics*, J. B. Lippincott Co, Philadelphia.
Huey, R. B., Pianka, E. R. and Schoener, T. W. (eds) (1983) *Lizard Ecology*, Harvard University Press, Cambridge, Massachusetts.
Lofts, B. (ed) (1974, 1976) *Physiology of the Amphibia, vols, 2-3*, Academic Press, New York.
Moore, J. A. (ed) (1964) *Physiology of the Amphibia, vol. 1*, Academic Press, New York.
Taylor, D. H. and Guttman, S. I. (eds) (1977) *The Reproductive Biology of Amphibians*, Plenum Press, New York.

Regional Studies, Distribution and Field Identification

North America
Behler, J. L and King, F. W. (1979) *The Audubon Society Field Guide to North American Reptiles and Amphibians*, Alfred A. Knopf, New York.
Bishop, S. C. (1947) *Handbook of Salamanders*, Cornell University Press, Ithaca, New York.
Carr, A. (1952) *Handbook of Turtles*, Cornell University Press, Ithaca, New York.
Catalogue of American Amphibians and Reptiles (1963-1985), Society for the Study of Amphibians and Reptiles, Athens, Ohio (continuing series).
Conant, R. (1975) *A Field Guide to Reptiles and Amphibians of Eastern and Central North America* (second edition), Houghton Mifflin Co, Boston.
Cook, F. R. (1984) *Introduction to Canadian Amphibians and Reptiles*, National Museums of Canada, Ottawa.
Ernst, C. H. and Barbour, R. W. (1973) *Turtles of the United States*, University Press of Kentucky, Lexington.
Smith, H. M. (1946) *Handbook of Lizards*, Cornell University Press, Ithaca, New York.
Smith, H. M. (1978) *A Guide to Field Identification. Amphibians of North America*, Golden Press, New York.
Smith, H. M. and Brodie, E. D., Jr (1982) *A Guide to Field Identification. Reptiles of North America*, Golden Press, New York.
Stebbins, R. C. (1985) *A Field Guide to Western Reptiles and Amphibians* (second edition), Houghton Mifflin Co, Boston.
Wright, A. H. and Wright, A. A. (1949) *Handbook of Frogs and Toads of the United States and Canada* (third edition), Cornell University Press, Ithaca, New York.
Wright, A. H. and Wright, A. A. (1957) *Handbook of Snakes of the United States and Canada, 2 vols*, Cornell University Press, Ithaca, New York. (Vol. 3, Bibliography, was published privately by the authors in 1962 and reprinted by Society for the Study of Amphibians and Reptiles in 1979.)

Middle America and West Indies
Alvarez del Toro, M. (1982) *Los reptiles de Chiapas* (third edition), Instituto Historia Natural, Tuxtla Gutierrez, Chiapas, México.
Duellman, W. E. (1970) *The Hylid Frogs of Middle America, vols. 1-2*, University of Kansas, Museum of Natural History, monograph 1, Lawrence.
Rivero, J. A. (1978) *Los anfibios y reptiles de Puerto Rico*, Editorial Universitaria, Universidad de Puerto Rico, San Juan.
Savage, J. M. and Villa, R., J. (in press) *An Introduction to the Herpetofauna of Costa Rica. Checklist and Keys*, Society for the Study of Amphibians and Reptiles, Athens, Ohio.
Schwartz, A. and Thomas, R. (1975) *A Check-list of West Indian Amphibians and Reptiles*, Carnegie Museum of Natural History Special Publication number 1, Pittsburgh, Pennsylvania.
Smith, H. M. and Smith, R. B. (1971-1980) *Synopsis of the Herpetofauna of Mexico, vols. 1-6*, Eric Lundberg, Augusta, West Virginia. (A continuing series, now published by John Johnson, North Bennington, Vermont.)
Villa, J. (1972) *Anfibios de Nicaragua*, Instituto Geográfico Nacional and Banco Central de Nicaragua, Managua.
Wilson, L. D. and Meyer, J. R. (1982) *The Snakes of Honduras*, Milwaukee Public Museum, Publications in Biology and Geology number 6, Milwaukee, Wisconsin.

South America
Amaral, A. do (1977) *Serpentes do Brasil, Iconografia colorida*, Ediçoes Melhoramentos, Editoria da Universidade de São Paulo, São Paulo.
Duellman, W. E. (1978) *The Biology of an Equatorial Herpetofauna in Amazonian Ecuador*, University of Kansas Museum of Natural History, miscellaneous publication number 65, Lawrence.
Duellman, W. E. (ed) (1979) *The South American Herpetofauna: Its Origin, Evolution and Dispersal*, University of Kansas Museum of Natural History, monograph number 7, Lawrence.
Hoogmoed, M. S. (1973) *The Lizards and Amphisbaenians of Surinam*, W. Junk, The Hague.
Lancini V., A. R. (1979) *Serpientes de Venezuela*, Ernesto Armitano Editor, Caracas.
Medem M., F. (1981, 1983) *Los Crocodylia de Sur America, vols. 1-2*, Colciencias, Ministerio de Educación Nacional, Bogotá.
Peters, J. A., Orejas-Miranda, B. and Donoso-Barros, R. (1970) *Catalogue of the Neotropical Squamata, parts 1-2*, US National Museum bulletin number 297, Washington.
Pritchard, P. C. H. and Trebbau, P. (1984) *The Turtles of Venezuela*, Society for the Study of Amphibians and Reptiles, Athens, Ohio.
Vanzolini, P. E., Ramos-Costa, A. M. M. and Vitt, L. J. (1980) *Répteis das caatingas*, Academia Brasileira de Ciências, Rio de Janeiro.

Europe and Middle East
Alon, A. and Arbel, A. (1984) *Plants and Animals of Israel, vol. 3: Reptiles*, Society for the Protection of Nature, Ministry of Defence Publishing House, Jerusalem.
Arnold, E. N. and Burton, J. A. (1978) *A Field Guide to the Reptiles and Amphibians of Britain and Europe*, William Collins Sons, London.
Basoglu, M. and Baran, I. (1977, 1980) *The Reptiles of Turkey, parts 1-2*, Ege Üniversitesi, Fen Fakültesi, reports 76 and 81, Bornova-Izmir, Turkey.
Böhme, W. (ed) (1981, 1984) *Handbuch der Reptilien und Amphibien Europas, vols. 1-2*, Akademische Verlagsgesellschaft, Wiesbaden. (Continuing series, now published by AULA Verlag, Wiesbaden.)
Frazer, D. (1983) *Reptiles and Amphibians in Britain*, William Collins Sons, London.
Joger, U. (1984) *The Venomous Snakes of the Near and Middle East*, Ludwig Reichert Verlag, Wiesbaden.
Khalaf, K. T. (1959) *Reptiles of Iraq with Some Notes on the Amphibians*, Ar-Rabitta Press, Baghdad.
Matz, G. and Weber, D. (1983) *Guide des amphibiens et reptiles d'Europe*, Delachaux & Niestlé, Neuchâtel, Switzerland.
Welch, K. R. G. (1983) *Herpetology of Europe and Southwest Asia: a Checklist and Bibliography*, Krieger Publishing Co, Malabar, Florida.

Africa and Madagascar
African Amphibians (1981) Fourth International Symposium, Monitore Zoologico Italiano, vol. 15 (supplement), Florence.
Broadley, D. G. (1983) *Fitzsimons' Snakes of Southern Africa*, Delta Books, Johannesburg.
Fitzsimons, V. F. (1943) *The Lizards of South Africa*, Transvaal Museum, Pretoria (reprint Swets & Zeitlinger N. V., 1970).
Guibé, J. (1978) *Les batraciens de Madagascar*, Bonner Zoologische Monographien number 11, Bonn.
Passmore, N. I and Carruthers, V. C. (1979) *South African Frogs*, Witwatersrand University Press, Johannesburg.
Pitman, C. R. S. (1974) *A Guide to the Snakes of Uganda* (revised edition), Wheldon and Wesley, Codicote, England.
Stewart, M. M. (1967) *Amphibians of Malawi*, State University of New York Press, Albany, New York.
Villiers, A. (1975) *Les serpents de l'ouest africain* (third edition), Les Nouvelles Éditions Africaines, Université de Dakar, Initiations et Études Africaines, number 2, Dakar, Senegal.
Welch, K. R. G. (1982) *Herpetology of Africa: a Checklist and Bibliography*, Krieger Publishing Co, Malabar, Florida.

Central and Eastern Asia
Bannikov, A. G., Darevsky, I. S., Ischenko, V. G., Rostamov, A. K. and Shcherbak, N. N. (1977) (*Guide to the Reptiles and Amphibians of the USSR*). Proswescenije, Moscow.
Brown, W. C. and Alcala, A. C. (1978, 1980) *Philippine Lizards, vols. 1-2*, Silliman University, Natural Science, monographs numbers 1 and 2, Dumaguete City, Philippines.

Chinese Snakes, Atlas of (1980), Shanghai Science and Technology Publishing Co, Shanghai.
Kuntz, R. E. (1963) *Snakes of Taiwan*, Quarterly Journal of the Taiwan Museum, volume 16, numbers 1-2, Taipei.
Liu, C.-C. and Hu, S.-Q. (1960) *The Anura of China*, Science Press, Beijing.
Lue, K.-Y. and Chen, S.-H. (1982), *(The Amphibians of Taiwan)*, S.-H. Chen, Taipei.
Mao, S.-H. (1971) *Turtles of Taiwan*, Commercial Press, Taipei.
Nakamura, K. and Uéno, S.-I. (1971) *Japanese Reptiles and Amphibians in Colour*, Hoikusha Publishing Co, Osaka.
Okada, Y. (1966) *Fauna Japonica: Anura*, Biogeographical Society of Japan, Tokyo.
Pope, C. H. (1935) *The Reptiles of China*, American Museum of Natural History, New York.
Sengoku, S. (ed) (1979) *(Amphibians and Reptiles of Japan)*, Japan Wildlife Research Institute, "Light of the Home" Association, Tokyo.
Thorn, R. (1968) *Les salamandres d'Europe, d'Asie et d'Afrique du Nord*, Éditions Paul Lechevalier, Paris.
Zhao, E. and Qixiong, H. (1984) *Studies on Chinese Tailed Amphibians*, Sichuan Scientific and Technical Publishing House, Chengdu.

Indian Subcontinent, Southeast Asia, Philippines and East Indies
Berry, P. Y. (1975) *The Amphibian Fauna of Peninsular Malaysia*, Tropical Press, Kuala Lumpur.
Daniel, J. C. (1983) *The Book of Indian Reptiles*, Bombay Natural History Society, Bombay.
DeSilva, P. H. D. H. (1980) *Snake Fauna of Sri Lanka*, National Museums of Sri Lanka, Colombo.
Inger, R. F. (1954) *Systematics and Zoogeography of Philippine Amphibia*, Chicago Natural History Museum, Fieldiana: Zoology, volume 33, number 4, Chicago.
Inger, R. F. (1966) *The Systematics and Zoogeography of the Amphibia of Borneo*, Field Museum of Natural History, Fieldiana: Zoology, volume 52, Chicago.
Kampen, P. N. van (1923) *The Amphibia of the Indo-Australian Archipelago*, E. J. Brill, Leiden.

Kirtisinghe, P. (1957) *The Amphibia of Ceylon*, published by the author, Colombo, Sri Lanka.
Lim, B. L. (1982) *Poisonous Snakes of Peninsular Malaysia* (second edition), Malayan Nature Society, Kuala Lumpur.
Minton, S. A., Jr (1966) *A Contribution to the Herpetology of West Pakistan*, American Museum of Natural History bulletin 134, number 2, New York.
Rooij, Nelly de. (1915, 1917) *The Reptiles of the Indo-Australian Archipelago, vols. 1-2*, E. J. Brill, Leiden (reprint A. Asher, 1970).
Taylor, E. H. (1922) *The Snakes of the Philippine Islands*, Bureau of Printing, Manila (reprint A. Asher, 1966).
Taylor, E. H. (1962) *The Amphibian Fauna of Thailand*, University of Kansas Science Bulletin 63, Lawrence.
Taylor, E. H. (1963) *The Lizards of Thailand*, University of Kansas Science Bulletin 64, Lawrence.
Taylor, E. H. (1965) *The Serpents of Thailand and Adjacent Waters*, University of Kansas Science Bulletin 65, Lawrence.
Tweedie, M. W. F. (1983) *The Snakes of Malaya* (third edition), Singapore National Printers, Singapore.
Wirot, N. (1979) *The Turtles of Thailand*, Siamfarm Zoological Garden, Bangkok.

Australia, New Guinea, New Zealand and Oceania
Barker, J. and Grigg, G. (1977) *A Field Guide to Australian Frogs*, Rigby Publishers, Adelaide.
Cogger, H. G. (1983) *Reptiles and Amphibians of Australia* (third edition), A. H. & A. W. Reed, Sydney.
Cogger, H. G., Cameron E. E. and Cogger, H. M. (1983) *Zoological Catalogue of Australia, vol. 1: Amphibia and Reptilia*, Australian Government Publishing Service, Canberra.
Goode, J. (1967) *Freshwater Tortoises of Australia and New Guinea (in the Family Chelidae)*, Lansdowne Press, Melbourne.
Jenkins, R. and Bartell, R. (1980) *A Field Guide to Reptiles of the Australian High Country*, Inkata Press, Melbourne.
McCoy, M. (1980) *Reptiles of the Solomon Islands*, Wau Ecology Institute handbook number 7, Wau, Papua New Guinea.

Menzies, J. I. (1976) *Handbook of Common New Guinea Frogs*, Wau Ecology Institute handbook number 1, Wau, Papua New Guinea.
Mirtschin, P. and Davis, R. (1983) *Dangerous Snakes of Australia* (revised edition), Rigby Publishers, Adelaide.
Robb, J. (1980) *New Zealand Amphibians and Reptiles in Colour*, William Collins Publishers, Auckland.
Storr, G. M., Smith, L. A. and Johnstone, R. E. (1981, 1983) *Lizards of Western Australia, parts 1-2*, University of Western Australia Press, Perth.

Conservation, Husbandry and Care in Captivity
Cooper, J. E. and Jackson, O. F. (1981) *Diseases of the Reptilia, vols. 1-2*, Academic Press, London.
Frye, F. L. (1981) *Biomedical and Surgical Aspects of Captive Reptile Husbandry*, Veterinary Medicine Publishing Co, Edwardsville, Kansas.
Groombridge, B. (1982) *The IUCN Amphibia-Reptilia Red Data Book, part 1: Testudines, Crocodylia, Rhynchocephalia*, International Union of Conservation of Nature, Gland, Switzerland.
Marcus, L. C. (1981) *Veterinary Biology and Medicine of Captive Amphibians and Reptiles*, Lea & Febiger, Philadelphia.
Matz, G. and Vanderhaege, M. (1978) *Guide du terrarium. Technique amphibiens reptiles*, Delachaux et Niestlé, Neuchâtel, Switzerland.
Murphy, J. B. and Collins, J. T. (eds) (1980) *Reproductive Biology and Diseases of Captive Reptiles*, Society for the Study of Amphibians and Reptiles, Athens, Ohio.
Reichenbach-Klinke, H. and Elkan, E. (1965) *The Principal Diseases of Lower Vertebrates, books 2-3: Diseases of Amphibians, Reptiles*, T.F.H. Publications, Neptune City, New Jersey.
Reptile Symposium on Captive Propagation & Husbandry (1979-1984), vols. 1-7, Zoological Consortium, Thurmont, Maryland. (Continuing series.)
Townsend, S. (ed) (1980) *The Care and Breeding of Captive Reptiles*, The British Herpetological Society, London.
Townsend, S. and Lawrence, K. (eds) (1985) *Reptiles. Breeding, Behaviour, and Veterinary Aspects*, The British Herpetological Society, London.

Journals and Herpetological Societies
Acta Herpetologica Sinica, Chinese Society of Herpetologists, Chengdu, China.
Alytes, Société Batrachologique de France, Paris, France.
Amphibia-Reptilia, Societas Europaea Herpetologica, Leiden, The Netherlands.
British Journal of Herpetology, The British Herpetological Society, London, United Kingdom.
Bulletin de la Société Herpétologique de France, Société Herpétologique de France, Paris, France.
Copeia, American Society of Ichthyologists and Herpetologists, Gainesville, Florida, USA.
Hamadryad, Madras Snake Park, Madras, India.
Herpetofauna, Australasian Affiliation of Herpetological Societies, Sydney, Australia.
Herpetofauna, Herpetofauna Verlags, Weinstadt, Federal Republic of Germany.
Herpetologica, Herpetological Monographs, Herpetologists' League, Lawrence, Kansas, USA.
Japanese Journal of Herpetology, The Herpetological Society of Japan, Kyoto, Japan.
Journal of Herpetology, Herpetological Review, Catalogue of American Amphibians and Reptiles, Facsimile Reprints in Herpetology, Contributions to Herpetology (monographs), Society for the Study of Amphibians and Reptiles, Athens, Ohio, USA.
Journal of the Herpetological Association of Africa, Herpetological Association of Africa, Humewood, South Africa.
Lacerta, Nederlandse Vereniging voor Herpetologie en Terrariumkunde, Amsterdam, The Netherlands.
Salamandra, Deutschen Gesellschaft für Herpetologie und Terrarienkunde, Frankfurt am Main, Federal Republic of Germany.
The Snake, The Japan Snake Institute, Nittagun, Japan.

A complete listing of world herpetological societies and journals is printed in Herpetological Circular number 13, 1983, published by the Society for the Study of Amphibians and Reptiles.

Picture Acknowledgements

Key: *t* top. *b* bottom. *c* center. *l* left. *r* right.
Abbreviations: A Ardea. AN Agence Nature. ANT Australasian Nature Transparencies. BCL Bruce Coleman Ltd. DMD David M. Dennis. FL Frank Lane Agency. MF Michael Fogden. NHPA Natural History Photographic Agency. NSP Natural Science Photos. OSF Oxford Scientific Films. RWVD R.W. van Devender. SAL Survival Anglia Ltd.

1 A. Bannister. 2-3 MF. 3*t* RWVD. 8*tl*, 8*b*, 8-9, 10*t* MF. 10-11 Nature Photographers/S. Bisserot. 12*bl* K.T. Nemuras. 12*br* RWVD. 12*tr* NSP/C. Mattison. 12*cr* E. Brodie. 13, 14, 14-15, 15 MF. 16 RWVD. 17 MF. 18-19 DMD. 19*b* OSF/G. Bernard. 20-21, 22*l* DMD. 22*r* Nature Photographers. 23 DMD. 24 NHPA/R.J. Erusin. 25 BCL/J. Dermid. 28-29 K.T. Nemuras. 29*t* RWVD. 31 MF. 34, 35 RWVD. 36 DMD. 36-37 RWVD. 38*t* C.A. Henley. 38-39, 39*t* MF. 40-41 Nature Photographers. 40*b* MF. 41*b* SAL/M. Read. 44*t* M. Crump. 44*b* MF. 45*t* ANT/P. Kraus. 45*bl* ANT/R. & D. Keller. 45*br* ANT/M. Cianelli. 48-49 DMD. 49*b*, 52-53 MF. 56-57 NHPA/S. Dalton. 58-59 MF. 66 A. Bannister. 66-67 Biofotos/K. Holgard. 67 NSP/C. Mattison. 70-71 Premaphotos. 71*c*, 71*b* Dwight R. Kuhn. 73 DMD. 74-75 Biofotos/Heather Angel. 76-77 Dr. H.R. Bustard. 77 SAL/R. & M. Borland. 84-85 A/F. Gohier. 87 Frithfoto. 88 ANT/R. McCann. 89*t* MF. 89*b*

NHPA/H. Switak. 90*l* Biofotos/Heather Angel. 90-91 Frithfoto. 91*r* AN. 92*b* FL. 92-93 J. Gibbons. 96-97 MF. 98-99 A/H. Dossenbach. 98*b* J. Gibbons. 99*b* C.A. Henley. 102*b* NSP/C. Mattison. 102-103 G. Mazza. 103*b* RWVD. 106*l* ANT/J. Weigel. 106-107 A/H. & J. Beste. 107*b* Biofotos/S. Summerhays. 109 Frithfoto. 113 ANT/S. Wilson. 114-115*b* MF. 114-115*t* RWVD. 114-115*c* Frithfoto. 116*t* NSP/C. Banks. 116*b* AN/Lanceau. 117 FL/D. Austin. 120*b* MF. 120-121 FL/T. Allan. 121*b* ANT/O. Rogge. 122-123 A/J.P. Ferrero. 126 NHPA/J. Shaw. 127*t* A. Bannister. 127*b* SAL/Jeff Foott. 127*b*, 130 MF. 130-131 NHPA/S. Dalton. 132-133 G. Mazza. 133*b* RWVD. 134, 134-135 Biofotos/Heather Angel. 137*t* K.A. Vliet. 137*b* John Visser. 138-139 AN/Lanceau. 140*b* ANT/D.B. Carter. 140-141 SAL/A. Root. 141*b* Dr. H.R. Bustard.

Artwork

Abbreviations: DD David Dennis. SD Simon Driver. ML Michael Long. RL Richard Lewington. DO Denys Ovenden.

4, 5*t* ML. 5*b*, 6, 7, 11, 22 SD. 26, 27, 32*b*, 33 DD. 32*t* SD. 34 DO. 42, 43, 46, 47, 50, 51 DD. 58 SD. 60, 61 ML. 62, 63, 64, 65, 68*t* SD. 68*b*, 69 ML. 70, 72 SD. 76 DO. 78, 79, 80, 81 DD. 82, 87 SD. 91, 92 DO. 93 SD. 94, 95, 100, 101, 104, 105 DD. 116 SD. 118, 119, 124, 125 DD. 129, 131, 132 SD. 142, 143 DD. Maps and scale drawings SD.

GLOSSARY

Acrodont teeth Teeth that are attached to the upper edge of the jaw, as opposed to the inside surface (pleurodont) or in sockets (thecodont).

Adaptation a morphological, physiological or behavioral feature that particularly suits an organism (or group of related organisms) to its (or their) way of life.

Adaptive radiation the evolution of several species or groups of SPECIES (eg FAMILIES, ORDERS, etc) from a common ancestral species or group, so that the descendant species or groups show individual adaptations to several different ways of life.

Adult fully grown (or nearly so) and sexually mature.

Advanced of more recent evolutionary origin (cf PRIMITIVE).

Advertisement call sound produced by male frogs during the breeding season that serves to attract females and, in some species, deter other males.

Aestivation a state of inactivity during prolonged periods of drought or high temperature.

Algae primitive plants ranging from microscopic single-celled forms, through thin threads to large forms, such as seaweeds.

Allantois sac-like outgrowth of underside of hind part of gut in EMBRYOs of reptiles, birds and mammals. During development, it grows around the embryo and, with associated blood vessels, functions in RESPIRATION. The embryo's excretory products are stored in the fluid within the allantois.

Ally close taxonomic relative.

Amnion a membrane forming a fluid-filled sac that encloses the EMBRYO of reptiles, birds and mammals.

Amniote any higher vertebrate whose EMBRYOs are enclosed within an AMNION during development; includes reptiles, birds and mammals.

Amphibian a member of the class Amphibia.

Amphibious capable of living both in water and on land.

Amplexus a position adopted during mating in most frogs and many salamanders, in which the male clasps the female with one or both pairs of limbs.

Anapsid a type of skull, found in more primitive reptiles, in which there are no openings in the TEMPORAL region of the skull.

Annelid a member of the phylum Annelida, wormlike animals that include earthworms and leeches.

Anterior toward the forward or head end of an animal.

Aposematic coloration bright coloration serving to warn a potential predator that an animal is distasteful or poisonous.

Aquatic living in water.

Arboreal living in or among trees.

Arthropod animal, including those of several different phyla, usually with a hard, jointed external skeleton: includes crabs, insects, spiders and scorpions.

Atrium (plural atria) a chamber of the heart receiving blood from veins.

Auditory nerve a nerve linking the inner ear and the brain.

Autotomy the self-amputation of part of the body, as of the tail of some lizards when they are attacked.

Axil the angle between the stem of a plant and a leaf or branch.

Axillary of or pertaining to the armpit. Axillary AMPLEXUS is a mating position in which a male frog or salamander clasps a female beneath her armpits.

Barbel a slender, elongated sensory process on the head, usually of aquatic animals.

Basal basic, fundamental. The basal METABOLIC RATE is the rate of energy expenditure by an animal at rest.

Bask to hold the body in a position directly exposed to the sun.

Binocular vision type of vision in which the eyes are so positioned that an image of an object being observed falls on both retinas.

Biped an animal with two feet.

Bisexual species a species containing both male and female individuals.

Body temperature the temperature of the interior of an animal's body, usually measured in the rectum or, by telemetry, in the stomach.

Bridge the segment of a turtle's shell joining the CARAPACE and the PLASTRON.

Brille a transparent covering over the eyes of snakes.

Bromeliad member of a family of plants, many of which live attached to larger plants, eg Spanish moss.

Brood a group of young raised simultaneously by one or both parents.

Brood pouch a space or cavity in which young develop.

Buoyancy the capacity to float, or remain suspended in water without sinking.

Bursa a sac or sac-like cavity.

Calcareous consisting of or containing calcium carbonate.

Calcified CALCAREOUS.

Cannibalistic eating the flesh of one's own species.

Capillary a very narrow, thin-walled tube carrying liquid, eg blood.

Capillary action the tendency of liquids to move, without external pressure being applied, along narrow spaces between objects, such as soil particles or in narrow tubes.

Carapace a hard structure covering all or part of an animal's body; the dorsal part of the shell of turtles and tortoises.

Carnivore an animal that eats the flesh of other animals.

Cartilaginous containing cartilage, a tough elastic skeletal material consisting largely of collagen fibres.

Castration removal of the gonads; usually refers to removal of the testes of males.

Cerebral cortex the outer layer of cells (gray matter) covering the main part of the brain, the CEREBRUM.

Cerebral hemisphere one of the two halves of the CEREBRUM.

Cerebrum that portion of the vertebrate brain which lies above and in front of the brain stem; it contains sensory and motor centers and is involved in learning.

Chemosensation the ability to detect and differentiate substances according to their chemical composition.

Chorion a MEMBRANE that surrounds the EMBRYO and YOLK SAC of reptiles, birds and mammals.

Chromatophore a specialized cell containing PIGMENT, usually located in the outer layers of the skin.

Chromosome a thread-shaped structure, consisting largely of GENETIC material (DNA), found in the nucleus of cells.

Cilium (plural cilia) minute, hairlike process from a cell, capable of beating rhythmically.

Circumtropical encircling the Earth, in an area between 22.5°N and 22.5°S.

Class a taxonomic category ranking below PHYLUM and above ORDER.

Cloaca the common chamber into which the urinary, digestive and reproductive systems discharge their contents, and which opens to the exterior.

Cloud forest moist, high-altitude forest characterized by dense undergrowth, and an abundance of ferns, mosses, orchids and other plants on the trunks and branches of trees.

Clutch the eggs laid by a single female in one breeding attempt.

Cocoon a tough protective covering.

"Cold-blooded" an outmoded term, referring to animals whose body temperature varies with environmental temperature.

Colonize to invade a new area and establish a breeding population.

Compressed of lizard body form, flattened vertically, as opposed to DEPRESSED.

Constriction a method of killing prey, used by some snakes, in which the body is coiled tightly around the prey, inducing suffocation.

Continuous breeder an animal that may breed at any time of year.

Cooperative breeding a breeding system in which parents are assisted in the care of their young by other adult or subadult animals.

Core temperature body temperature of an animal measured at or near the center of its body.

Cornea the front, transparent portion of the eye of a vertebrate.

Courtship behavioral interactions between males and females that preceed and accompany mating.

Cranial of or pertaining to the cranium (skull).

Crest a raised structure running along the back of the head and/or body.

Crustacean a member of the arthropod phylum Crustacea that includes shrimps, crabs, lobsters, barnacles and water fleas.

Crypsis The ability to be hidden or camouflaged.

Cryptic hidden or camouflaged.

Cutaneous of or pertaining to the skin.

Cycle a series of events that occurs repeatedly in the same sequence.

Depressed of lizard body form, flattened laterally (from side to side), as opposed to COMPRESSED.

Dermis the layer of skin immediately below the EPIDERMIS.

Desiccation the process of drying out.

Diapsid a type of skull, found in a variety of reptiles, in which there are two openings in the TEMPORAL region.

Dichromatism the condition in which members of a species show one of two distinct color patterns.

Differentiation the process by which unspecialized structures (eg cells) become modified and specialized for the performance of specific functions.

Diffraction the process by which light, on passing through an aperture or past the edge of an opaque object, forms a pattern of colors.

Dimorphism the existence of two distinct forms within a species. Sexual dimorphism is the existence of marked morphological differences between males and females.

Direct development transition from the egg to the adult form in amphibians without passing through a free-living larval stage.

Display a stereotyped pattern of behavior involved in communication between animals. Any of the senses — vision, hearing, smell, touch — may be involved.

Distress call a vocalization produced by an animal when under physiological or environmental stress. In many cases it attracts assistance or care from another animal, such as a parent.

Dorsal pertaining to the back or upper surface of the body or one of its parts.

Ectoparasite a parasite that lives on the outer surface of an organism, eg a tick, flea or louse.

Ectothermic dependent on external heat sources, such as the sun, for raising body temperature.

Eft the juvenile, terrestrial phase in the life cycle of a NEWT.

Embryo the young of an organism in its early stages of development. In amphibians and reptiles, the young before hatching from the egg.

Endothermic able to sustain a high body temperature by means of heat generated within the body by METABOLISM.

Environment all the factors, forces or conditions which affect or influence the growth, development and life of an organism.

Enzyme a substance produced by living cells which is capable of catalyzing a specific chemical reaction.

Epidermis the surface layer of the skin of a vertebrate.

Epiphysis a portion of a bone which develops from a separate center of ossification and later becomes the terminal portion of the bone.

Epiphytic of a plant, growing on another plant but not parasitic on it.

Erectile capable of being erected or raised, as of a penis or crest.

Esophagus part of the GUT, from the throat to the stomach.

Estuarine living in the lower part of a river where freshwater meets and mixes with sea water.

Explosive breeder a species in which the breeding season is very short.

resulting in large numbers of animals mating at the same time.

External fertilization fusing of eggs and sperm outside the female's body.

Family a taxonomic category ranking below ORDER and above GENUS.

Fauna the animal life of a locality or region or that existing during a particular period of time.

Femoral gland a gland situated on an animal's thigh.

Fertilization the union of an egg and a sperm.

Fetus the unborn young of a VIVIPAROUS animal in the later stages of development.

Flora the plant life of a locality or region or of a particular period of time.

Fossil any remains, impression, cast, or trace of an animal or plant of a past geological period, preserved in rock.

Fossilize to be preserved as a fossil.

Fragile tail a tail that can be shed by AUTOTOMY if the animal is attacked.

Frog any member of the order Anura. Also, an anuran which is smooth-skinned, long-lived and lives in water.

Gamete OVUM or sperm.

Gastralia rib-like bones present in the under part of the body of some reptiles.

Genetic of or pertaining to genetics or heredity.

Genus (plural genera) a taxonomic category ranking below FAMILY and above SPECIES; contains one or more species.

Germ cell GAMETE.

Gestation carrying the developing young within the body.

Gill a respiratory structure in aquatic animals through which gas exchange takes place.

Girdle a group of connected bones that provide support from a pair of limbs; pectoral or shoulder girdle, pelvic or hip girdle.

Gland an organ (sometimes a single cell) that produces one or more specific chemical compounds (secretions) which are passed (secreted) to the outside world.

Glottis the opening of the LARYNX between the vocal cords.

Gregarious tending to congregate into groups.

Gut the alimentary canal, especially the intestine.

Habitat the type of conditions in which an animal lives.

Hatchling a young animal that has just emerged from its egg.

Hemipenis (plural hemipenes) one of two grooved copulatory structures present in the males of some reptiles.

Herbivore an animal that eats plants.

Homeothermic having the ability to maintain a constant, or nearly constant body temperature, irrespective of the temperature of the environment.

Home range an area in which an animal lives except for migrations or rare excursions.

Hormone a substance secreted within the body which is carried by the blood to other parts of the body where it evokes a specific response, such as the growth of a particular type of cell.

Hybrid an individual resulting from a mating of parents which are not genetically identical, eg parents belonging to different species.

Hyoid a U-shaped bone to which the larynx is attached.

Hypophysis the pituitary gland.

Ilium (plural ilia) dorsal part of the pelvic (hip) girdle.

Imbricate scales overlapping scales, like tiles on a roof.

Incubation the act of incubating eggs, ie keeping them warm so that development is possible.

Infrared radiation invisible heat rays beyond the red end of the visible light spectrum.

Inguinal of or pertaining to the groin. Inguinal AMPLEXUS is a mating position in which a male frog or salamander clasps a female around the lower abdomen.

Insectivore an animal that feeds on insects.

Insemination the introduction of sperm into the genital tract of a female.

Internal fertilization fusing of eggs and sperm inside the female's body.

Introduced of a species, brought from lands where it occurs naturally to lands where it has not previously occurred.

Intromission the act of inserting the male copulatory organ into the body of the female.

Intromittent organ a male copulatory organ, eg penis, HEMIPENIS.

Jacobson's organ (or vomeronasal organ) one of a pair of grooves extending from the nasal cavity and opening into the mouth cavity in some mammals and reptiles. Molecules collected on the tongue are sampled by this organ in CHEMOSENSATION.

Juvenile young, not sexually mature.

Juxtaposed scales scales with edges touching, but not overlapping.

Keel a prominent ridge, eg on the back of some turtles and on the dorsal scales of some snakes.

Keratin a tough, fibrous protein present in epidermal structures such as horns, nails, claws and feathers.

Kinesis movement in response to a stimulus.

Labyrinthodont teeth teeth with complex infolding of the enamel.

Larva the early stage in the development of an animal (including amphibians) after hatching from the egg.

Larynx a sound-producing organ located at the upper end of the trachea (the wind-pipe), containing the vocal cords.

Lateral line organ a sense organ embedded in the skin of some aquatic animals which responds to water-borne vibrations.

Life cycle the complete LIFE HISTORY of an organism from one stage (eg the egg) to the recurrence of that stage.

Life history the history of an individual organism, from the fertilization of the egg to its death.

Life-style the general mode of life of an animal, eg nocturnal predator, aquatic herbivore, parasite, etc.

Live-bearing giving birth to young that have developed beyond the egg stage.

Lymph gland organ on the course of a lymphatic vessel, containing lymph (a colorless fluid originating from the spaces between cells) and white blood cells which remove foreign bodies, especially bacteria, from the lymph.

Mammal a member of a CLASS of vertebrates possessing hair and in which females nourish their newborn young on milk.

Mandible the skeleton of the lower jaw.

Mangrove a tropical tree or shrub with numerous exposed roots forming a dense interlacing mass.

Marine living in the sea.

Maxillary pertaining to the skeleton of the upper jaw.

Medial located at or near the middle of the body or of a part of the body.

Melanophore a pigment cell (CHROMATOPHORE) which contains the black or dark brown pigment melanin.

Membrane a thin sheet or layer of soft, pliable tissue which covers an organ, lines a tube or cavity, or connects organs together.

Mesoplastral in the middle of the PLASTRON of turtles.

Metabolic rate the rate of energy expenditure by an animal.

Metabolism the chemical or energy changes which occur within a living organism or a part of it which are involved in various life activities.

Metamorphosis the transformation of an animal from one stage of its life history to another, eg from larva to adult.

Metatarsal a bone in that part of the foot between the tarsus (the ankle) and the toes.

Microclimate the climate in the area immediately around an organism. Can be very different from the overall climate if, for example, the organism lives in a burrow or a cave.

Microenvironment the local conditions which immediately surround an organism.

Migration the movement of animals, often in large numbers, from one place to another.

Mimic an animal that resembles an animal belonging to another species, usually a distasteful one, or some inedible object.

Mollusk a member of the PHYLUM Mollusca, animals characterized by a broad, ventral muscular foot and a dorsal shell; includes slugs, snails, mussels and clams.

Molt to shed and develop anew the outer covering of the body, the skin in amphibians and reptiles.

Montane of or pertaining to mountains.

Morphological pertaining to the form and structure of an organism.

Mucus a viscous, slimy substance present on the surface of mucous membranes which serves to moisten and lubricate.

Musk a substance with a penetrating, persistent odor secreted by special glands in turtles and crocodiles.

Nares the paired openings of the nasal cavity.

Natal of or pertaining to birth.

Neotropics the tropical part of the New World, includes South America, Central America, part of Mexico and the West Indies.

Neural arch the portion of a vertebra which forms the roof and sides of the space through which the spinal cord passes.

Neurotoxin a poisonous substance that effects the nervous system of its victim.

Newt any salamander of the genera Triturus, Taricha and Notophthalmus; characteristically amphibious.

Niche the specific resources a species obtains from its environment, and its means of obtaining those resources that are essential to maintain its population size.

Nocturnal active at night.

Nutrient a substance, taken in as food, which promotes growth or provides energy for physiological processes.

Occipital condyle one of two rounded, bony processes on the back of the skull that provide articulation between the skull and the vertebral column.

Olfactory of or pertaining to the sense of smell.

Omnivore an animal that feeds on both animal and plant material.

Operculum a lid or covering. A flap covering the gills and developing legs in the larvae of frogs and toads.

Opposable of digits, usually the thumb, which may be brought together in a grasping action, thus enabling objects such as twigs to be held.

Order a taxonomic category ranking below CLASS and above FAMILY.

Organ a part of an animal having a definite form and structure which performs one or more specific functions.

Orthopteran an insect of the order Orthoptera, eg grasshoppers, locusts, crickets.

Osmosis the passage of water through a semipermeable membrane as a result of differences in the concentrations of solutions on each side of the membrane. Water tends to move from a concentrated to a less concentrated solution until the two concentrations are equal.

Osmotic gradient the difference in concentration between solutions on each side of a semipermeable membrane.

Ossification the formation of bone.

Osteoderm a very small bone in the skin of some reptiles.

Otic of or pertaining to the ear.

Ovary the female gonad or reproductive organ, produces the OVA.

Oviduct the duct in females which carries the OVA from the OVARY to the CLOACA.

Oviparous reproducing by eggs that hatch outside the female's body.

Ovoviviparous reproducing by eggs which the female retains within her body until they hatch; the developing eggs contain a YOLK SAC but receive no nourishment from the mother through a placenta or similar structure.

Ovum (plural ova) a female germ cell or gamete; an egg cell or egg.

Paedomorphosis   the retention of immature or larval characteristics (eg external gills) by animals that are sexually mature.

Papilla   a small, nipple-like eminence or projection.

Parietal   a paired bone forming part of the roof and sides of the skull.

Parotoid gland   one of a pair of wartlike glands on the shoulder, neck, or behind the eye in toads.

Parthenogenesis   a form of asexual reproduction in which the OVUM develops without being fertilized.

Pectoral girdle   the skeleton supporting the forelimbs of a land vertebrate; also called the shoulder girdle.

Pedicellate teeth   teeth mounted on a slender stalk.

Peristaltic action   progressive wavelike movements occurring in intestines or other tubular structures, in which a wave of contraction moves along the tube preceded by a wave of relaxation.

Permeable   of a structure such as the skin, allowing the passage of a substance (eg water) through it.

Phalanx   one of several bones (phalanxes or phalanges) in the fingers and toes.

Pheromone   a substance produced and discharged by an organism which induces a response in another individual of the same species, such as sexual attraction.

Phragmosis   using a part of the body to close a burrow.

Phylogenetic   of or pertaining to evolutionary history.

Phylum   a taxonomic category ranking above CLASS.

Pigment   a substance that gives color to part or all of an organism's body.

Pineal   a small outgrowth from the dorsal surface of the brain lying just beneath the skull.

Pit receptor   a pit containing sensory cells sensitive to heat located between the eye and the nose or along the edges of the jaws in some snakes.

Placenta   a structure attached to the inner surface of the female's reproductive tract through which the embryo obtains its nourishment.

Plastron   the ventral portion of the shell of a turtle.

Pleurodont teeth   teeth that are attached to the inside surface of the jaw, as opposed to the upper edge (acrodont) or in sockets (thecodont).

Poikilothermic   unable to maintain a constant, or nearly constant body temperature and therefore having a body temperature similar to that of the environment.

Polypeptide   a compound formed by the union of several amino acids.

Population   a more or less separate (discrete) group of animals of the same species.

Posterior   toward the rear or tail end of an animal.

Preadaptation   the possession of a trait or traits which are not necessarily advantageous to an organism in its present environment but would be advantageous in a different environment.

Predation   the act of capturing and killing other animals for food.

Predator   an animal that feeds by hunting and killing other animals.

Prehallux   a rudimentary digit on the hind foot of frogs.

Prehensile   adapted for grasping or clasping, especially by wrapping around, eg the tail of chameleons.

Premaxillary   of or pertaining to the front part of the upper jaw.

Primitive   of ancient evolutionary origin (cf ADVANCED).

Prostaglandin   any of a number of oxygenated unsaturated cyclic fatty acids present in various body fluids. These compounds sometimes perform HORMONE-like actions, such as controlling blood pressure or muscle contractions.

Protein   a type of organic compound making up a large part of all living tissues, containing nitrogen, and yielding amino acids when broken down.

Proto-   (as in protoalligator, protoamphibian, etc) an ancestral form that was the evolutionary precursor of a taxonomic group, eg of a FAMILY, CLASS, etc.

Pubis   (plural pubes) ventral, forward-projecting part of the pelvic or hip girdle.

Pupa   a dormant, inactive stage between the LARVAL and adult stages in the LIFE CYCLE of insects; a chrysalis.

Quadratojugal   a bone in the skull situated at the point where the lower jaw articulates with the skull.

Quadruped   a four-footed animal.

Race   a subdivision of a SPECIES which is distinguishable from the rest of that species; may live in a distinct area: a geographic race.

Rain forest   tropical and subtropical forest with abundant and year-round rainfall.

Receptive   responsive to stimuli; sexually receptive females are responsive to the sexual behavior of a male.

Rectilinear locomotion   a form of movement, used mostly by heavy-bodied snakes in which the body moves slowly forward and is held straight.

Reduced   (anatomically) smaller in size than in ancestral forms.

Reflectance   the capacity of a body or surface to reflect, rather than absorb, light.

Release call   a brief call given by male frogs, and by unreceptive females, when clasped by a male; it causes the clasper to release his grip.

Retina   a layer of light-sensitive cells (rods and cones) within the eye, upon which a visual image is formed.

Riverine   living in rivers.

Salamander   a tailed amphibian.

Satellite male   a male who, in a group of calling frogs, does not call himself but sits near a calling male and intercepts females that are attracted to the calling male.

Savanna   a term loosely used to describe open grasslands with scattered trees and bushes, usually in warm areas.

Scale   a thin, flattened, platelike structure forming part of the surface covering of various vertebrates, especially fishes and reptiles.

Scavenger   an animal which feeds on dead animals or plants that it has not hunted or collected itself.

Scute   any enlarged scale on a reptile.

Seasonal breeder   a species that breeds at a specific time of year.

Semiaquatic   living part of the time in water.

Sinus   a cavity, hollow, recess or space.

Sinusoidal   wavy, tortuous.

Solitary   living by itself.

Species   a group of actually or potentially interbreeding populations that are reproductively isolated from other such groups.

Spermatheca   a pouch or sac in the female in which sperm are stored.

Spermatophore   a structure containing sperm that is passed from the male to the female in some animals, such as in many salamanders.

Splenial   a bone in the lower jaw of some amphibians.

Squamid   scaly. Also (noun) any member of the order Squamata: a lizard, worm lizard or snake.

Sternum   a bone in the ventral part of the pectoral girdle; the breastbone.

Subcaudal   beneath or on the ventral side of the tail.

Substrate   the solid material upon which an organism lives.

Sulcus   a groove or furrow.

Synapsid   a type of skull, found in certain reptiles, in which there is a single opening in the TEMPORAL region of the skull.

Tadpole   the LARVA of a frog or toad.

Tapetum lucidum   a light-reflecting layer in the eye.

Taxonomy   the science of classification; the arrangement of animals and plants into groups based on their natural relationships.

Temporal   of or pertaining to the area of the skull behind the eye (the temple).

Terrapin   any of a number of freshwater turtles, especially semiaquatic species and those that leave the water to bask.

Terrestrial   living on land.

Territorial   defending an area so as to exclude other members of the same species.

Territory   an area that one or more animals defend against other members of the same species.

Thermoregulation   control of body temperature, by behavioral and/or physiological means, such that it maintains a constant or near-constant value.

Thrombosis   The formation of a blood clot within a blood vessel or the heart.

Thyroid gland   a gland lying in the neck that produces the HORMONE THYROXINE.

Thyroxine   a HORMONE containing iodine that is involved in a variety of physiological processes, including metamorphosis in amphibians.

Toad   any stout-bodied, warty-skinned frog, especially one living away from water.

Torpor   a state of sluggishness or inactivity.

Tortoise   any terrestrial shelled reptile apart from box turtles; or (in British usage), any shelled reptile apart from sea turtles.

Transversely   crosswise; at right angles to the long axis of the body.

Tubercle   a small, knoblike projection.

Turtle   any shelled reptile; or (in British usage), a shelled sea reptile.

Tympanic membrane   the eardrum.

Unisexual species   a species consisting only of females.

Unken reflex   a defensive posture, shown by some amphibians when attacked, in which the body is arched inward with the head and tail lifted upward.

Urea   a compound containing nitrogen formed by the breakdown of proteins; a major constituent of urine in many animals.

Uric acid   a compound containing nitrogen found in the urine of certain animals, including many reptiles.

Urostyle   a rodlike bone composed of fused tail vertebrae, present in frogs and toads.

Uterine milk   a MUCOPROTEIN uterine secretion which bathes developing embryos.

Vent   an outlet, the anal or CLOACAL opening from the body.

Ventral   pertaining to the lower surface of the body or one of its parts.

Ventricle   a cavity within an organ; a chamber in the heart which discharges blood into the arteries.

Vertebral column   the spinal skeleton, consisting of a series of vertebrae extending from the skull to the tip of the tail; the backbone.

Vertebrate   any member of the subphylum Vertebrata, comprising all animals with a vertebral column, including fishes, amphibians, reptiles, birds and mammals.

Vestigial   smaller and of more simple structure than in an evolutionary ancestor.

Viscera   any of the organs contained within the body cavities, especially the abdominal cavity.

Viviparous   giving birth to living young which develop within and are nourished by the mother.

Vomeronasal organ   JACOBSON'S ORGAN.

"Warm-blooded"   an outmoded term, referring to animals whose body remains constant, or nearly so, and higher than that of the ENVIRONMENT.

Yolk sac   a large sac containing stored nutrients, present in the EMBRYOs of fishes, amphibians, reptiles and birds.

Zygodactyl   having toes and/or fingers arranged in such a way that two point forward and two point backward.

INDEX

A **bold number** indicates a major section of the main text, following a heading: a ***bold italic*** number indicates a fact box on a group of species: a single number in (parentheses) indicates that the animal name or subjects are to be found in a boxed feature and a double number in (parentheses) indicates that the animal name or subject are to be found in a spread special feature. *Italic* numbers refer to illustrations.

FOR REFERENCE
Do Not Take From This Room